State, Finance and
Industry

State, Finance and Industry

A Comparative Analysis of Post-War Trends in Six Advanced Industrial Economies

Edited by

Andrew Cox
Senior Lecturer in Politics
University of Hull

St. Martin's Press   New York

All rights reserved. For information, write:
Scholarly & Reference Division,
St. Martin's Press, Inc., 175 Fifth Avenue, New York, NY 10010

First published in the United States of America in 1986

Printed in Great Britain

ISBN 0–312–75618–6

Library of Congress Cataloging-in-Publication Data
Main entry under title:

State, finance, and industry.

   1. Industry and state—Case studies. 2. Industrial
promotion—Case studies. I. Cox, Andrew W.
HD3611.S758   1986   338.9   86–1741
ISBN 0–312–75618–6

Contents

The Contributors

Andrew Cox is a Senior Lecturer in Politics at the University of Hull. His research interests concentrate on problems of political economy and urban change in capitalist economies. Recent publications include: *Adversary Politics and Land* (Cambridge UP); ed. *Politics, Policy and the European Recession* (Macmillian) with D.H. McKay, *The Politics of Urban Change* (Croom Helm); with P. Furlong, E. Page, *Power in Capitalist Society* (Wheatsheaf) and with S. Kirby, *Congress, Parliament and Defence* (Macmillan). He is currently working on a book entitled 'The Political Economy of Modern Capitalism'.

Bernard Eccleston is a political economist and Staff Tutor in Social Science with the Open University (Yorkshire Region). He is currently preparing a book entitled *State and Society in Contemporary Japan*, to be published by Polity Press in 1986. Recent publications include 'Malthus and Trends in Wages in the 18th and 19th Centuries' in M. Turner (ed), *Malthus and his Times* (Macmillan) and 'Modernisation and the formation of the Japanese State' in J. Anderson (ed) *The Rise of the Modern State* (Wheatsheaf).

Diana Green is a political economist and is currently Head of the Department of Government and Economics at the City of Birmingham Polytechnic. She acted as a Consultant to the Department of Industry from 1976 to 1981 and was a Hallsworth Fellow of Political Economy at the University of Manchester during 1980-81. She has written extensively on the French economy and the problems of industrial adjustment. Her research interests have now been extended to include labour market problems in Western Europe.

Kenneth Dyson is Professor of European Studies and Chairman of the Postgraduate School of Languages and European Studies at the University of Bradford. He was a founding member of the Association for the Study of German Politics, of which he has been, for several years, an officer. His major publications include *Party, State and Bureaucracy in West Germany* (Sage); *The State Tradition in Western Europe* (Martin Robertson); with S. Wilks, *Industrial Crisis*, (Basil Blackwell); and *European Detente* (Frances Pinter). At present, Professor Dyson is working on the policy and politics of the communications revolution in Western Europe.

Paul Furlong is Lecturer in Politics at the University of Hull. A specialist in Italian Politics, he has published a wide range of topics including voting patterns, Catholicism and Christian Democracy, and terrorism. Recently he has been researching in the area of political economy and the policy process, and is undertaking a research project on the legislative process in the Italian Parliament financed by the Nuffield Foundation. He has also published, with Andrew Cox and Edward Page, *Power in Capitalist Society*.

John E. Owens holds a Ph.D. in government from the University of Essex and teaches United States and British Politics at the Polytechnic of Central London. He has undertaken research on US financial 'institutions' policy and Congress, and contributed articles to the *British Journal of Political Science* and *Political Studies*. He was a visiting Fellow at the Economic and Social Research Council Data Archive at Essex for 1984-5, conducting research on congressional partisanship. He is joint author of *After Full Employment*, to be published by Hutchinson in 1986.

Michael Lisle-Williams is a Lecturer in Social Science in the School of Humanities, Griffith University, Brisbane, Australia. Prior to this he was a Prize Research Fellow of Nuffield College, Oxford University, where he completed a doctorate on the economic sociology of the British Merchant banks. He is currently investigating the relationship between financial system organisation, capitalist class formation and state economic policies in Britain, France and Germany.

Preface

This volume had a strange beginning. It arose from a sense of dissatis-faction by the author having completed an edited volume on the manner in which European States had responded to the problems posed by the 1970s recession. While this volume—*Politics, Policy and the European Recession* (Macmillan, 1982)—indicated that the major European economies had responded with varying degrees of success to the crisis, it was also apparent that a number of these economies did not require the active state role in crisis-management which was evident in some others. It was clear—although not well developed in that volume—that some economies had much more involved and active financial institutions in industrial crisis-management and industrial investment. At the same time Wyn Grant had an indirect effect. In reviewing his otherwise excellent book, *The Political Economy of Industrial Policy* (London: Butterworth, 1981), it became apparent that the analysis of the failure of British industrial policy failed to take account of the continuity of state financial policy in Britain. It was felt that far too much emphasis was placed on the deleterious consequences of adversarial politics and organisational constraints.

It is out of this perception that the decision to compile this volume arose. The volume seeks to illuminate the dilemma for the state of failing to understand the crucial link between financial and industrial policies. This is taken to be crucial in Britain due to the historic problem of financing domestic industry and the well-documented failures of industrial policy. In order to assist in the formulation of more effective state policies it was felt that an understanding of the relationships between the state, finance and industry in other major capitalist economies would prove useful in encouraging informed debate on this crucial issue. If the volume goes some way to achieving this, it will have served its purpose.

ANDREW COX,
North Humberside, October 1985

1 The State, Finance and Industry Relationship in Comparative Perspective
Andrew Cox

This volume seeks to illuminate the way in which the state has been involved in managing industrial investment through its relationship with the financial sector of the economy. Individual chapters deal with the experiences in six major advanced industrial societies — France, Japan, West Germany, Italy, the United States and Britain, respectively. In this introductory chapter an attempt is made to set these individual country studies in a broader comparative perspective. This is achieved by first, outlining what the basic function and role of the financial system is in a modern economy and, then, comparing the various types of state—industry and state—finance relationship which are theoretically possible in modern capitalist economies. Each country studied here is then located historically in relation to the success of its financial system in underwriting industrial investment and the type of state role which has predominated.

THE ROLE AND FUNCTION OF FINANCIAL SYSTEMS

It is perhaps most appropriate to begin our discussion by first asking what the function of a financial system is, and how the state comes to be involved in its affairs. As Hu has argued, at its simplest the financial system is a mechanism by which the savings of households and individuals are channelled into the hands of those needing investment for industry and wealth creation.[1] In the theory of economic textbooks, this role is self-evident and uncomplicated. The financial system — in particular the banking sector — aggregates individual savings into larger amounts which can then be lent to those firms of entrepreneurs requiring large amounts of funding to invest in new productive infrastructure and services. The primary role of the banks and other lending and investment institutions (merchant banks, pension funds, insurance companies, equity markets) is then to assess the risk of their loans or investments being repaid with interest. For the system to work satisfactorily, these institutions must lend only to those entrepreneurs and firms capable of repaying their loans and interest charges.

The risk factor is a crucial element in the financial system because the trick of successful and highly profitable lending for the banking system is the ability to lend most of its deposited assets to borrowers at interest rates which cover costs and make for handsome profits. The banks are able to do this because, although at any one time they are illiquid and could not hope to repay on demand all of the money which depositors have placed with them, if all depositors asked for their money at the same time, under normal conditions the general public has confidence in the banking system. The general public believe that the banks are solvent, and that if they want their money from the banks they will be able to obtain it. Thus, only in financial panics do depositors storm the doors of banks and demand their money. When this happens there is the possibility of a run of bank failures as all banks could not hope to repay their depositors on demand because their funds are loaned to individual and corporate borrowers.[2] So long as depositors are prepared to retain confidence in the financial system, the banks are able to aggregate savings and lend the major proportion of these savings to the innumerable individuals and firms who are prepared to pay handsome interest rates to their bankers for the privilege. In this way banks use their depositors' money to earn profits for themselves and, depending on the type of account a depositor holds, for savers.

But there is a problem inherent to this structure. For the system to work ideally, bankers should be perfectly rational and all-seeing human beings who possess perfect knowledge and foresight of the areas of economic and social life capable of generating wealth and profit. Unfortunately bankers—like everyone else—are fallible and make mistakes. In order to overcome this propensity to human error in the assessment of risk, bankers have tended to develop standard operating procedures. The most important of these has traditionally been that sound banking is based on short-term lending and long-term deposits. In other words, loans should only be made to very safe projects with an assured capacity to make profits to enable the repayment of the initial capital and interest charges. At all times these loans should be made on as short a term as possible to avoid the highly risky possibility of being caught with long- to medium-term loans and a high short-term demand by depositors for the refunding of their savings. In simple terms, banks should not lend long when they are borrowing from savers on a short-term basis — to do so is a recipe for bankruptcy and insolvency. Relatedly, bankers of this ilk are normally concerned that any loans given should be self-liquidating. This means simply that bankers require some form of collateral against a loan (property or share certificates etc.) to ensure that if profits do not ensue the bank will be able to retain its original capital outlay and interest charges.

From this somewhat brief account of the nature of banking practice it should be apparent that a host of problems arises from the clash between banking practice and the optimal functioning of the financial system. In theory, the financial system ought to aggregate savings and pass these on to those entrepreneurs and firms which have the greatest potential for making profits and financing loans. In practice there are clearly obvious difficulties in this being achieved. What will be most profitable in the long term is something most people − whether entrepreneurs or bankers − can only know with hindsight. Like generals who prepare for war by studying the lessons of previous battles, bankers must use past practices and procedures as guides to their future risk-assessment and loan decisions. This may be a wholly sensible practice and one which creates few problems for entrepreneurs in an era of relatively slow technological change and stable markets. In an era of rapid technological change and unstable and volatile markets however, the role of the banker becomes much more difficult, and the certainty that the financial system is always optimising the allocation of loans for maximum economic utility is more doubtful. The chance that bankers (who fear a loss of confidence from making risky investments and loans) will play safe and fail to optimise their function of facilitating national economic growth is certainly higher in such an environment. Furthermore, the size of the borrowing requirement for those operating at the frontiers of technological change is now so large that the reliance by firms on borrowing and debt to maintain costly research and development programmes for new products and processes is far higher than it was in the early years of industrialisation, when retained profits could be used to finance industrial investment. This places an added burden on the capacity of the financial system to choose wisely in its lending decisions; it must become enmeshed in the intricacies of business and industry itself in order to assess market potential and the nature of risk in any loan application. The problem for the banks is compounded, however, by the problem that loans of this size can hardly be self-liquidating or secured as small loans can be.

Given the inherent conservatism of bankers' operating procedures not to take risks, it is clear than an obvious gap may exist in many financial systems as sound banking practice militates against entrepreneurial risk-taking and the optimisation of lending to the most profitable sectors of the economy. Faced with the problem of an unknown future and an increasingly risky lending environment, financial institutions would appear to be able to take one of three potential roads in their relationship to industrial investment.

The first of these might be termed a *laissez-faire* internationalist role. Under this approach the financial institutions can eschew any responsibility for industrial risk-taking and decide that the defence of their institutional shareholders' and policyholders' dividends and profits in the short term is their primary function. Institutions and banks which adopt this approach will tend to favour short-term, self-liquidating loans to medium- and long-term loans. They will also tend to place their funds in areas where, historically, a safe return has been guaranteed. Relatedly, because institutional and organisational interest take precedence over the performance of the national economy, such actors would tend to support open access to international financial markets in order to ensure that – in the absence of safe and high-performing investment opportunities at home – overseas projects can be utilised to maintain corporate profit performance. It might be argued that such institutions would display a low propensity for detailed technical or managerial involvement with industry itself; preferring instead to deal in paper transactions (government debts and share certificates) which can be easily traded for quick, short-term profits. It can be argued that the British and American financial systems have tended to approximate this model most closely historically.

The second approach which institutions might take to the problem of assisting productive industry is for bankers and institutional fund managers to recognise their own inadequacies and, instead of playing safe, decide to try to overcome their inherent ignorance of industrial problems and technological change. Such actors would seek to become heavily involved in industry and develop close working relationships with management in firms, the better to assess the long-term growth potential of particular industrial borrowers. This variant – known as industrial banking – is clearly a rejection of the inherent conservatism of 'sound' banking practice because it requires banks and financial institutions to take greater risks and lend for the medium and long term on the basis of their judgement of the long-term viability of particular industries. Such an approach by a financial system would hardly be possible without a less internationalist and more nationalistic approach to economic performance. It clearly requires a perspective on the part of bankers that their own future viability depends upon the long-term performance of the productive sectors of the economy which they must facilitate and defend in their own self-interest. This approach is clearly discernible in the financial systems of Japan, France and Germany historically.

A third approach might be somewhere between these two extremes. In this cooperative variant, banks may well continue to be concerned about taking risks and adopting unsafe long-term lending practices, but recognise that there is a fundamental problem for the performance of the national economy if they do not provide funds for the medium to long term for industrial change. In this way the financial institutions might seek − or welcome − assistance from the state to provide extra guarantees if they make loans and take long-term risks in the national interest. In these circumstances, compromise cooperative solutions can be worked out between the state and the financial sector. Once the financial sector has accepted the desirability of lending long and allowing some state interference in their markets, the state is then in a position to provide support and credit for the financial sector in the running of special credit institutions for long-term lending. Such institutions are normally supported by active state industrial policies and state loan guarantees, preferential interest rates and export and exchange rate protections. Such structures normally operate in systems where a nationalistic and less internationalist perspective to that of the *laissez-faire* variant exists. It also presupposes a degree of national consensus amongst political, financial and business elites about the future direction of the national economy.

Most advanced industrial economies have experimented with, or have continued to retain, such special credit and state-supported lending arrangements to facilitate industrial investment since the Second World War. Nevertheless, the acceptance of any of these three potential approaches to the problem of financing industrial investment is a highly contested and political issue. It should be clear that, since bankers and fund managers in financial institutions have a choice of options about how to manage their assets and how to approach industrial investment, then that strategic decision will not be dictated solely by economically rational considerations but also by social, ideological and organisational factors as well. Furthermore, when financial institutions can choose between ignoring or taking a directive or a cooperative relationship with the industrial sector, any choice they make will be profoundly political. This is particularly apparent when a financial system chooses to ignore its own industrial base and does little to assist in the regeneration of the competitiveness and performance of the national economy. When such a choice is made in favour of the pursuit of corporate self-interest it is

hardly surprising that this leads to political demands for a fourth variant
to be developed. This variant — nationalisation or the creation of state
investment banks with punitive tax laws against overseas investment —
flows logically from an unwillingness or incapacity of the financial system
to provide domestic entrepreneurs and firms with the necessary long and
medium-term investment finance. While entrepreneurs and firms in a
capitalist economy may reject the nationalisation of financial institutions,
if they cannot find funds within the financial system, it is logical that
they may have to turn to the state to provide it for them in the form of
a state investment bank. The demand for nationalisation and total state
planning of investment is normally associated with left-wing parties in
countries — like Britain — where there has been no historically high
propensity for overseas investment and a lack of industrial or co-operative
banking.[3]

From the foregoing it should now be clear why it is difficult for the
state not to be involved in the relationship between the financial and
industrial sectors under modern conditions. The maximisation of the
allocative function within financial decisions about industrial investment
is crucial to the performance of the national economy in the long term.
Since representative governments must face their electors at regular
elections, when economic performance is one of the most significant
yardsticks by which they are judged, it is hardly surprising that
governments cannot help but be involved in overseeing the relationship
between the financial system and industrial investment. When the system
works well, the state does not have to intervene; when the system fails
to perform adequately, it is hardly surprising that the state faces political
and economic pressures to resolve the difficulties. The problem that faces
government, however, is that while the financial system may not be
adequately allocating funds for long-term industrial competitiveness
domestically, the financial institutions may very well be making very high
profits from the adoption of their standard operating procedures without
fully realising the damage these actions are causing to the national
economy as a whole. Under these conditions it is hardly surprising that
a major political confrontation may occur. The financial institutions will
point to the success of their standard operating procedures and blame
industry for lacking adequate opportunities for profitable lending. The
state and industry will, on the other hand, appeal to national rather than
organisational interests and blame the financial institutions for failing to
take a long-term view of industrial performance. Under these
circumstances the scene is set for continuous adversarial political conflict

over whether the state should intervene in the financial system and in what ways.

This politically contested nature of the state, finance and industry relationship is one which is often overlooked in economic treatments of the role of the financial system. All too often such accounts tend to assume either that the financial system behaves in an economically rational and apolitical way, or that the structure of a country's markets is inviolable, predetermined and incapable of profound political change.[4] This type of approach tends to idealise the structure of a particular country's financial system and fails to take account of the continuous political struggle which takes place over the proper role of the state in financing industrial investment as economic and political circumstances change.

One intention of this volume is that it should go some way to filling this gap in the literature by throwing some light on the politically contested nature of state, finance and industry relationships in six major capitalist economies since 1945. Before turning to these country studies it is, however, necessary to locate each of these countries in a broad comparative perspective. This will be achieved by, first, describing the potential roles which the state might perform in assisting industrial change, and relating this to the hypothetical relationships which the state might have with the financial system in managing industrial investment. Each of the six countries to be analysed will be located in relation to these idealised types historically with a summary of the efficacy of these relationships in practice.

THE STATE AND INDUSTRIAL POLICY

The performance of industry in terms of profits, competitiveness and market share is of crucial importance for the modern state. It is also of particular significance for the privately-owned financial system because it shapes its willingness to invest funds in companies and entrepreneurs. If profits are low, competitiveness weak, and market share in decline, financial institutions are unlikely to be willing to act on their own to provide funds for industry. When this occurs the state must act and try to stimulate investment to ensure the long-term profitability and future of industry. In these circumstances the state, like the financial system, has a range of alternative approaches from which it can choose to assist and support the financing of industrial investment.

The state could nationalise the financial institutions and private companies and direct savings into industry on the basis of a state-controlled imperative (physical) planning system. In reality this is not an option which has been seriously considered within many capitalist economies, although the French banking system has been gradually nationalised since 1945. Nevertheless, even in France, where the state plays a significant ownership role in the financial system, the majority of private companies and most non-banking financial institutions are privately owned. Given that outright nationalisation and physical planning would be a rejection of capitalism in favour of state planning, ownership and control, this option is one only those on the far left of the political spectrum countenance as a serious practical alternative for modern capitalist economies. There are, however, a number of alternative solutions − of which the French model would be one − which allow the state something of a controlling or directive role over industrial change and investment decision-making while falling somewhat short of a totally planned economy.[5]

The first broad approach − which can operate with a partially nationalised financial system (as in France) or *ad hoc* special state credit institutions for industrial investment, coexisting with a largely privately-owned financial system (as in Germany and Japan) − is often referred to as indicative planning. Under an indicative planning system the state does not own private industry but works to bring industry, financial institutions and labour together to discuss national economic priorities under the aegis of a flexible central government planning structure. The aim of the state is to seek cooperation by all sides necessary to sectoral, structural, manpower and financial policies to facilitate industrial change. The emphasis is on a bargained or negotiated relationship in which the state outlines its own planning, public expenditure and spending priorities within the framework of a national target for future economic growth performance. Beneath these global totals the state seeks − after bargaining and negotiation amongst the social partners − to arrive at agreed policies for particular sectors of the economy. This may involve contraction of labour-intensive, uncompetitive sectors in favour of special assistance for high-technology, capital-intensive sectors. It would certainly involve active manpower and education policies aimed at retraining and fitting the workforce to the needs of modern industry. It might also involve welfare-related and pay and price policies in order to win popular support and consensus nationally over the burdens and benefits any industrial restructuring would necessitate in an era of rapid technological change.[6]

This type of approach has been associated with the development of 'bargained corporatism' in advanced industrial societies.[7] By this is meant a society in which state control and influence over private investment decisions is expanded, but in the absence of any major increase in state ownership or direct physical planning. In return, the state expects to negotiate with, and incorporate in state decision-making, the key social and economic interest in society in order to arrive at a consensus over national economic goals. If consensus is agreed between social partners then the state − as we shall see, West Germany has been a case in point − may well be able to leave the implementation of bargained policies to the private industrial and financial sectors. Whether this will work in practice obviously depends a great deal on the attitude of industry and financial institutions. If industry is prepared to involve itself in the planning process and reveal confidential information to the state and the financial institutions then the system may work reasonably well. It also requires that the financial institutions have a capacity to indulge in industrial banking and be prepared in take some risks in long-term lending to industry. If the financial or industrial systems are reticent then the state is faced with little alternative − short of outright nationalisation − but to ensure compliance through the power of financial control. This may take the form of some nationalisation of the financial system or the creation of special credit institutions to direct investment funds into those industrial sectors which are seen as crucial to the future of the national economy.

There are immense difficulties with the successful implementation of this approach in practice.[8] Only small countries with historic traditions of cultural homogenity and consensus (Austria, Sweden and the Netherlands) have come close to the successful adoption of a 'bargained corporatist' approach;[9] although all of the countries studied in this volume have, with varying degrees of success and enthusiasm experimented with such policies. Indeed, one can go further and argue that none of the six major western nations analysed here is fully corporatist. This is so because a bargained corporatist regime would be one in which all social partners (labour, business, finance and government) would have a relatively equal and effective voice in state decision-making. None of the countries discussed in this volume has ever possessed such a state − society relationship; yet some have seen the development historically of a more limited form of consensus between government, industrial and financial elites over national economic goals. Under such arrangements a looser form of indicative planning becomes possible, with scope for more *ad − hoc* special interventions by the state to rationalise, support and favour particular sectors of the economy on a highly selective basis.

This approach — sometimes termed *'dirigisme'* — has been witnessed in many of the countries to be discussed here, but particularly in France and Japan. In these countries the state may have a formal indicative planning structure but this is not directed to the creation of a bargained national consensus because labour and small business is politically weak and largely excluded from effective influence over national economic decision-making. On the contrary the planning system is used much more selectively by the state in conjunction with industry and finance to pick industrial growth sectors and winners. The state's role then becomes one of single-mindedly making sure that sufficient investment funds are available at the right price to those sectors of industry singled out for special treatment. The mechanisms utilised will depend very much on whether the financial system possesses the expertise to handle this crucial industrial banking role. In any case it would be normal for the state to create special credit institutions and provide preferential loans and interest rates and export guarantees whether it dominated the system or left it to the private sector to implement the policies agreed under this approach. This policy scenario is clearly similar to the 'bargained corporatist' approach outlined above. It is sufficiently different however in that a 'bargained corporatist' approach normally seeks to involve all social partners and necessitates more complex policy bargains extending to social areas of society. *Dirigiste* solutions are normally shaped by government, business and financial actors alone and can, therefore, be much more selectivist and primarily economic in orientation.

While Japan and France — and to a lesser extent West Germany — are the best examples of this approach; it is clear that most advance industrial societies have adopted this type of solution with varying degrees of success and commitment over time. An alternative to this active state role in the supply side of the economy is for governments to reject totally any direct involvement in the enforcement of policies to overcome problems with the production and sale of commodities. The state leaves the financing of industry to the private sector alone and the process of managing industrial firms to private firms and entrepreneurs. The state's role is then confined primarily to the stimulation of effective demand to ensure that consumers can afford to purchase goods and maintain confidence amongst investors that demand will be high. This Keynesian approach would also normally involve a regulatory role for the state. Under this the state provides arm's length agencies — like the Securities and Exchange Commission in America or the Bank of England and Bundesbank, to regulate the activities of private financial institutions to ensure the viability of the currency and the sanctity of financial transactions. Other special regulatory agencies for wages and prices and the competitiveness of markets (Monopolies and Merger Commissions) might also be created. The basic function of these agencies is not to resolve bottlenecks in the supply of industrial investment finance but to protect the individual from the potential concentration of market power in the hands of cartels and monopolies − whether company or trade union - dominated. The state's role under this approach is primarily one of regulating competition, defending consumer interests against imperfect markets and stimulating effective demand. If the financial system fails to provide adequate finance for industry it is not the state's job to rectify this problem. This is a job for markets and privately constituted industrial and financial actors.

A final alternative − *laissez-fairism* or neo-liberalism − is possible. Under this approach the state does not seek to resolve the problem of financing industrial investment or the stimulation of effective demand. On the contrary the state tries to disengage itself as much as possible from the demand and supply sides of the economy. This would involve the state leaving the allocation of financial resources to private markets with, perhaps, some limited regulation of financial transactions and market conditions to ensure the stability of the currency and the operation of perfect market conditions. While this variant is much vaunted by right-wing and conservative political parties in the early 1980s, and has lineages going back to Adam Smith and the eighteenth century, in practice few countries historically have ever fully adopted such an approach to economic affairs. Britain and the United States probably came closest to approximating to this model in the late eighteenth and early nineteenth centuries, but even these countries had a high degree of social intervention and trade protection by the 1880s.[10] While the Reagan and Thatcher administrations would ideologically support moves in this direction in reality most advance countries have adopted industrial investment policies somewhere between Keynesian - *dirigiste* - indicative planning since 1945. The reason for this is self-evident. In an age of regular elections governments must at least attempt to make a show of doing something about protecting industry and overcoming financial bottlenecks. To wash one's hands of any responsibility and rely on private markets can only keep a government in office if there is no problem with the financing of industrial investment. Given our earlier discussion of the inherent problems about a perfectly operating system being generated in the private sector, it is not surprising that most governments have been forced to intervene in the industry - finance relationship.

We can see, therefore, that just as the financial and industrial sectors have choices about the strategies they might adopt to assist industrial investment and change, the state itself has a range of options available to it when it is asked, or decides, to intervene in the process. It is hardly surprising then that there will be tremendous scope for ideological controversy and party political debate over the most desirable relationship between the state, finance and industry in modern capitalism. This implies that the state's role will be constantly prey to political struggle and change depending on the balance of political forces which control the state's activities at any particular historical moment. As the political coalitions around the state in any one country change then it is probable that the desirability of particular state, finance and industry relationships will change with it. But there is a further problem for the state and for the creation of a viable relationship which ensures the maximisation of investment allocation for future economic growth. While the state has the power politically to formulate policies which modify its relationship with the financial and industrial systems, as Zysman has argued, the structure of the financial system within which any of these alternative approaches must be enacted may very well be inimical to successful policy implementation.[11]

THE STATE AND THE STRUCTURE OF THE FINANCIAL SYSTEM

Since the financial institutions always have a choice of alternative approaches when they face difficulties in financing risky industrial investment, it is plain that they are equally political actors with the industrialists and politicians who seek reforms to facilitate successful industrial change. It is inevitable then that, when a government chooses a particular industrial and financial strategy, it will confront the political defence of existing institutional practices and procedures by established financial actors and institutions in the market. The problem, then, may be, as Zysman has shown, that the government may well be pushing against a locked rather than an open door.[12] It is not sufficient for governments to want to resolve the problems of financing investment: if governments are to be successful they must fashion policies which take account of the historical traditions and relationships which exist in their domestic financial markets. Rather than attempting to introduce policies which will generate intense political controversy and effective opposition from finance and industry, it would seem logical for governments to try to create policies which have a change of successful implementation. Such policies would normally work with existing financial institutions rather than against them.

Thus, according to Zysman, what any state can do will be determined by the historical structure of its financial system. The political representatives of the state cannot do just as they please. While they may desire to nationalise or control their financial system, whether they will be able to do so effectively will depend on whether or not the underlying structure of the financial system allows such a role to be implemented effectively. If a government does not choose wisely in its financial and industrial policies, then political conflict will ensue which will be inimical to industrial investment and growth.

Accordingly, Zysman argues there are three basic types of financial system in capitalist economies.[13] First of all there are *Capital Market Systems*. These systems are characterised by resource allocation through competitively established prices by private institutions financially and industrially. Investment and production decisions are company-led with the government's role indirect and at arm's length. Government policies may influence markets but are not consciously directive (e.g. USA and UK). A second type is the *Negotiated Credit System*. Under this structure the financial institutions dominate a credit-based system and their market power shapes industrial choices over investment and production. In order to assist industry and the financial system, the government is however allowed to participate, and a negotiated relationship between the major social partners exists which is aimed at resolving financial and industrial bottlenecks. The government does not, however, control the financial system directly; it may provide ad hoc special assistance (e.g. West Germany and Sweden). The final type is termed a *Credit-Based System*. Under this structure the government administers prices and the quantity of credit available to most sectors of the economy. The government is a major actor in industrial affairs either through nationalisation or the control of the flow and quantity and price of privately administered credit (e.g. France and Japan).

Zysman, however, contends that each of these structures will delimit the scope for government political action in industrial and financial affairs.[14] Governments may choose any of three roles. They can be economic actors, economic administrators or economic regulators. For any of these roles to work effectively, according to Zysman, they must be implemented within the financial structure which is appropriate for them. Thus, the state cannot be an economic actor shaping industrial and financial affairs if it does not function in a credit-based system in which the state controls prices and the quantity of credit. Similarly, the bargained and negotiated credit system requires the state to play a largely economic administrative role in which the government assists the financial and industrial structures by operating clearly-defined and agreed policy goals. Finally, an economic regulatory role (defending the value of the currency and policing monopolies and corruption) is best facilitated within a capital market system in which the government's role is minimal.

The message here is crystal clear. Governments may choose to act in a variety of ways to shape their respective financial and industrial structures. They can only operate successfully, however, if they first recognise that the structure of the financial system delimits – as a constraining invariable – their capacity for successful policy implementation. Thus as Zysman argues, a government which tries to shape industrial policy and investment decisions through exhortation and regulation in a credit-based system based on the private sector is unlikely to be successful. Furthermore, if a government in such a system tries to direct and earmark funds for industry it will run into opposition from private firms and financial institutions. Zysman's message is therefore self-evident. The structure of the financial system is such a constraint on government policies that it behoves governments to eschew radical tinkering with the structure which confronts them, and attempt instead to fashion policies which will work within the existing structure of the financial system. The alternative is unlikely to be disfunctional political conflict and a failure of industrial and economic policy.

There is much truth in this argument and it does allow one to understand the relative successes of Japan, France and West Germany in achieving economic success since 1945. These countries have fashioned policies which have not challenged the structure of the financial system. Other countries – Britain in particular – have attempted to implement industrial policies without the requisite financial structure of controls to facilitate a positive state role, and this has led to disfunctional and economically wasteful political conflict. There are, however, two major problems with this argument which this study hopes to illuminate. It is one thing to argue that the structure of the financial system must confine the state to only those policies which can work successfully; but this can become a counsel for doing nothing. If the state and/or the financial system are functioning optimally and earmarking funds for industrial growth effectively, then arguably, it does not matter very much that change does not occur. But when the relationship is one that is inimical to effective financial investment, the existing structure of the financial system may well require radical change. Unfortunately, the underlying logic of Zysman's thesis might well lead one to the conclusion that, since radical restructuring of the existing financial system will only generate political conflict, it is better to do nothing at all. This is a recipe for financial and political immobilism. It may also lead one into tautological reasoning. Zysman has argued that France and Japan are state-led economies because they have credit-based, price-administered financial systems.[15] This is surely to put the argument the wrong way round. Both these countries have credit-based, price-administered financial systems because they choose to have state-led economic structures. Britain and the USA have capital market systems because they choose not to be state-led economies.

This may seem a minor point but it is not. Zysman's analysis of the state - finance - industry relationship is a seminal work which describes in detail the post-war relationship between state, industry and finance. Yet is suffers from a tendency to underplay the necessity for fundamental conflict and political struggle when it is clear that the domestic financial system is clearly failing to meet the requirements of the domestic economy. Secondly, Zysman's approach has a tendency to view the financial system as immutable and a constraining invariable. This is clearly an over-simplification which tends to underplay the continuous political conflict which occurs between political parties, pressure groups, industrialists, bureaucrats and financial institutions over the proper role for the state in the financial system. To say in an idealised and simplified way that certain countries have credit-based systems while others have negotiated or capital market structures is to ignore this continuing political battle. Furthermore, it tends to underplay the degree to which even in countries with apparently agreed and successful financial systems, there is still tremendous scope for political debate. This is particularly true in countries like West Germany which are normally depicted as consensual. But as our study will attempt to show, there has been continuous political conflict within all the six countries analysed. So much so that, although we might be able to agree with Zysman that each can be characterised in terms of his threefold categories, such an analysis does scant justice to the highly political role of the state and the financial institutions over the proper role of government in the financing of industry. Even if countries historically have favoured one particular financial structure, this does not imply that this structure has not been subject to continuous political struggle.

Indeed, the issue may not be whether or not the state's policies are functionally related to the existing financial structure but whether or not the financial system itself — whatever type it is — is capable of providing the financial resources to sustain industrial investment consistently and for those sectors of the economy which play a crucial role in national economic performance. Thus it may be that Britain's relatively poor record in financing industrial investment is not due to inherent conflict between an interventionist state lacking the requisite controls over the financial system, but more fundamentally due to the operating procedures of the privately constituted financial markets and their ability to ignore the needs of the industrial base of the domestic economy. If this interpretation is adopted the solution that one might arrive at is very different from that implicit in Zysman's analysis. Instead of arguing for a recognition on the part of government of its limited role, the only effective solution might well be a sustained and highly contentious political struggle to provide the state with those instruments necessary for it to direct investment into areas of crucial importance to the economy. As we shall see in this study, even those nations with state - finance relationships which are seen as being successfully geared to the needs of industry — Japan, France and West Germany in particular — the role of the state has been, and continues to be a subject of intense political debate and change.

THE POLITICS OF THE STATE—FINANCE—INDUSTRY RELATIONSHIP

In this brief overview of the material to be presented in the analysis of the six countries discussed here, it is intended that the continuing nature of political conflict between government, industrial and financial actors will be indicated. This is seen to be true even in those countries which have had a history of fairly close and detailed state control over financial markets. The conclusion that is drawn from this is that the debate over the proper and most effective role for the state is likely to be a continuous one and not capable of simplistic categorisation in terms of the need for the state to limit its activities to only those which fit the needs of the financial structure currently in existence. It may well be necessary, as international economic circumstances change, for the state to act positively to restructure the current financial system to facilitate domestic economic performance. As we shall see, some countries are well aware of this need, others are not.

Japan is normally seen as the most successful post-war economy in the West, and there is little doubt that the Japanese state historically has recognised the need to direct the financial system towards the needs of domestic industry. This tradition has a long lineage dating back to the appearance of Admiral Perry's American warships in the nineteenth century, which threatened the possible colonisation of Japan due to its industrial and military backwardness. As a result, it has been a common assumption that political elites in Japan consistently adopted a positive approach to the financing of industry to protect Japanese culture and sovereignty. Evidence for this is seen in the history of state-supported industrial banking and the creation of special long-term credit institutions. The creation of the Industrial Bank of Japan in 1902, modelled on the French Crédit Mobilier of the nineteenth century, is just one example of the recognition by the state of the need to provide continuous long-term credit for industry. Other evidence is derived from the fact that the Japanese commercial banking system has historically eschewed lending to individuals in favour of loans to firms. Indeed, the commercial banking system has a tradition of industrially relevant specialisation. Large City banks normally have provided loans only to large oligopolistic firms on a long-term or renewable short-term basis. Local banks normally provided similar loans to small and medium-sized firms; while special credit banks and life assurance companies provided the bulk of their assets to the equipment funds of companies.[16]

Given the detailed state control over credit formation and price, which Eccleston demonstrates has taken place in Japan since the Second World War, one might be excused for believing that the Japanese state and its bureaucracy has played a continuous and consistent role in financing industrial investment. The reality is of course far more complicated than this. While it is true that the Japanese economy has experienced a history of industrial banking, the role of the state in controlling and directing investment for industry has only been a blanket kind since the 1950s in the aftermath of the American occupation of the country. Prior to that date, while the state might have facilitated banking specialisation and underwritten special credit institutions for industry − the 1936 Shoko Chukin Bank (Central Cooperative Bank for Commerce and Industry) being but one example − the engine of Japanese economic growth and trade policy was the privately-owned *zaibatsu*. These industrial and financial holding companies fused the industrial and financial sectors of the economy. As a consequence it has been argued that they, rather than the state bureaucrats, were the key actors in the transformation and modernisation of the Japanese economy from a backward and largely agricultural base to the thrusting, and increasingly militarised, structure which became involved in the colonisation of Manchuria and, ultimately, the Second World War.[17]

Since the Second World War the role of the state and its bureaucracy has changed, indicating clearly that whatever the structure of the financial system, historically profound and fundamental change is possible in the role of the state. As Eccleston shows, the dismantling of the *zaibatsu* and the discrediting of the military in the aftermath of the war left a yawning gap in the relationship between finance and industry. Into this gap the state bureaucrats stepped with the goal of rebuilding the Japanese economy and making it a major international political actor once more. This implied a more directive role for the state than had been the case before. Yet it would be wrong to see the Japanese state as monolithic. Eccleston shows clearly that the new engine of economic growth and industrial expansion − the Ministry of International Trade and Industry (MITI) − was very much an innovative creation of the post-war period by politically and economically aware civil servants. These actors had to fight ceaseless political battles with the old Ministry of Finance and the Bank of Japan to ensure that sufficient funds were available for industry in the face of the inherent financial conservatism for balanced budgets residing in these institutions. Similarly, MITI had to use indirect means cleverly to manipulate the privately-owned commercial banks to provide long-term loans to those large firms and industrial sectors − initially in capital-intensive production − which it had earmarked as the future driving force of the Japanese economy. The mechanism adopted was through the strengthening of the state's control over the provision and price of credit. MITI did not nationalise the financial institutions but created a situation in which it could act as a financial intermediary between savers, banks and industry. Eccleston shows how, in the liquidity crisis after the war, the large commercial banks were forced to rely increasingly on the Bank of Japan. At the same time MITI encouraged these banks to lend to companies but restricted their ability to retain deposits. This ensured continuous liquidity problems for banks and their subservience to the state: a subservience reinforced by the state's control of credit through direct rationing of funds to industrial sectors earmarked by MITI.

At the same time the state moved to control savings funds by restricting bank branching and directing individual Post Office savings through special credit institutions − the Export - Import Bank and the Japanese Development Bank − into those oligopolistic firms designated as crucial to the performance of the economy. These indirect mechanisms of control have ensured − along with import restriction, preferential loans to large firms, export guarantees, trade licensing, government-sponsored cartels and dualistic productive processes – that MITI has been able to exert a continuous indirect control over the financing of industrial investment since the 1950s. This is clearly a much more involved role for the state than was the case before 1945 and indicates that there is scope for positive political action to restructure traditional market relationships. Furthermore, this discussion also indicates that the role of the state is likely to remain prone to intense political debate. MITI has continuously had to fight political battles with more conservatively-minded bureaucratic institutions (the Ministry of Finance and Bank of Japan) concerned with sound money and balanced budgets. Having indirect means of control MITI, until recently, was normally able to circumvent these demands. In recent years, however, as Eccleston shows, these actors and the commercial banks have been more successful in demanding a more liberalised financial structure. Indeed, it could be argued that MITI has suffered the consequences of its own financial success. The massive growth in Japanese exports and restrictions on imports have created assertive and highly profitable oligopoly companies demanding greater autonomy in their investing and trading policies. At the same time the very trading success of Japan has generated demands from its competitors – particularly the United States – for a liberalisation of the Japanese domestic economy to imports and greater access to Japanese financial markets by international investors. Eccleston indicates that these combined pressures have created new problems for MITI which have resulted in some halting moves towards liberalisation since the 1970s. Despite a willingness to allow some freeing of capital markets and rely more on interest rates to allocate credit rather than indirect quantitative controls. Eccleston argues that MITI has retained sufficient caveats to ensure that free competition does not undermine its own conception of what is in the national interest.

Notwithstanding this conclusion, it can be seen that the post-war relationship between the state and the financing of industry has been subject to change and continuous political conflict. From what Zysman might term a negotiated market relationship prior to the Second World War, in which the state's role was as *dirigiste*, the Japanese system has more closely approximated a state-controlled, credit-based system in which the state is a clear economic actor. This role has involved an acceptance of dirigisme, indicative five year planning, and a form of bargained corporatism (without labour), structured round extensive indirect forms of credit control. In recent years, however, the success of this approach internationally has given opponents of MITI ammunition to force moves towards greater liberalisation of the state - finance - industry relationship. While there is little doubt at the moment that these moves are unlikely to emasculate the role of MITI, it does seem that, in an era of threatened trade protectionism, MITI may well be forced to loosen its hold on the financial and industrial system in the face of international and domestic pressure. While this is unlikely to mean MITI giving up its extensive indirect control over the economy, it may well mean that the future relationship between the state, finance and industry in Japan may be one that is more like the period before 1945, when the state's role was largely *dirigiste* then the all-encompassing relationship which has normally characterised the period since the 1950s. This may not be an indication of impending impoverishment and economic failure in the Japanese economy. Rather it may well be a reflection of the fact that private actors in the Japanese economy − whether banks or firms − are now in a stronger position to deal with their financial and industrial needs than was the case in the immediate aftermath of the war when state control and coordination was imperative for national recovery. In this way, whatever the underlying structure of the post-war financial system, it is highly unlikely that it will, or should, remain static.

If the Japanese case indicates the possibility of fundamental change in the relationship between the state, finance and industry and the continuing political struggles which takes place even in highly successful economies, the French case reinforces this finding. Prior to the Second World War the French state did not play a major role in the financing of industry. The French financial system did have a tradition of industrial banking: in fact Credit Mobilier (established 1852) was one of the first examples of special banking for industry. It used household savings and picked industrial winners for Europe as a whole. This tradition was maintained in the inter-war period with the creation of the Credit National (1919), the Caisse Centrale de Credit Hotelier, Commercial and Industriel (1923) and the Caisse National des Marches de L'Etat (1936). Despite these state-sponsored special credit institutions the financial system was still largely dominated by commercial deposit banks (like Credit Lyonnais) and the Bourse which were not interested in long-term industrial risk, and preferred overseas investment to domestic industry.[18] After 1945, however, with the recognition of France's relative economic backwardness and liquidity problems which could only be met by state-administered Marshall Aid, the role of the state in the financial system has been transformed. The experience has parallels with the Japanese case.

As in Japan a negotiated financial system has, since 1945, been transformed into a credit system with the state playing a major role in directing economic investment to sectors of industry. The *dirigiste* activities of pre-war special credit institutions have been supplemented and enhanced. This was achieved initially by the nationalisation of four major deposit banks and some insurance companies. Relatedly an indicative planning system administered by a Commissariat du Plan was created to guide industrial growth and sectoral decision-making — particularly for Marshal Aid, which was used to finance a quarter of French public investment.[19] At the same time, a plethora of special credit institutions for particular activities and sectors was created to ensure that savings were channelled into industrial investment — the most important of these being, perhaps, the Caisse des Depots et des Consignations, which channels Post Office savings, social security funds and pension funds into industry, local authorities and housing. This institution also provides loans to the Credit National, which provides long-term loans for industry (public and private). Credit National is in mixed ownership: of nationalised banks and private insurance companies, pension funds and investment companies. The state maintains close links strategically, and sometimes operationally, in this institution's activities.

A more active role for the state was essential in the immediate post-war environment due to the unwillingness of the commercial banks to countenance long-term lending. Yet ironically, there is evidence that even the nationalised banks were themselves unwilling to operate as industrial bankers and maintained their penchant for the short-term lending which had been the hallmark of pre-war French commercial banking. Out of this realisation — and mirroring the similar post-war developments in Japan — the French state was forced to adopt more effective indirect forms of control and influence. These were made possible by the state's quantitative control of credit formation and prices. The kernel of the French indirect approach, which involved forcing nationalised as well as privately-owned banks to finance industry, has been through the creation of mobilisable medium-term credit. This form of credit (for up to seven years) brought the commercial banks into close relationship with public and semi-public bodies, like the Commissarat du Plan, Banque de France and Credit National. These bodies were able to encourage the commercial banks to provide designated firms and industrial sectors with state-guaranteed loans. This allowed banks to make loans to firms, knowing that Credit National and the Banque de France would refinance the loans and underwrite the risks involved. In this way the Planning Commission and the state were able to encourage investment in industrial equipment, housing construction and export industries. It is probable that these instruments — which are supplemented by state guarantees for overseas borrowing, direct industrial subsidies and indemnities against exchange rate fluctuations caused by the French Treasury — rather than the direct nationalisation of the banks, or state indicative planning were the main reasons for the rapid industrial growth experienced in the 1950s and early 1960s.[20]

Like Japan, then, France developed a credit-based system after 1945 in which the state came to take on a far more active role than hitherto. The French system was also assisted by a relatively weak parliamentary system and a well-developed and elitist civil service tradition, based upon the Grandes Ecoles. Similarly, while indicative planning was created, the French also faced a relatively weak labour movement which has been unable to question the financial, bureaucratic and industrial imperatives built into the financing of industry.[21] Like the Japanese, therefore, the French case indicates that it is possible for the state to intervene and take a much more active role and fundamentally restructure the financial system. Green's paper indicates clearly, however, that such a change does not necessarily end traditional banking operation practices; nor does it terminate the constant political in-fighting between bureaucratic institutions, industry and political groups over the proper role of the state. While it is true that the state shapes the financial system now far more than it ever did, this influence is not inviolable and the state's role in France has been subject to modification and radical change since 1945.

Green argues, in fact, that the state's directive role for industry was at its highest during the administration of Marshal Aid, when planning assumptions became strategies for development. Nevertheless, many of these targets were not met effectively and the role of the Treasury and traditional spending Departments were always of crucial importance in the allocation of investment. Clearly such spending decisions are always likely to be prone to political in-fighting between political groups and well-connected industrialists and financial actors. This implies that the assumption of a monolithic and benevolent state directing investment to industry in the national interest is at best a gross over-simplification of the process in France, just as it is in Japan. Indeed, given the political importance of the agricultural lobby in France, particularly in the context of the 1960s Gaullist coalition, it is hardly surprising that this sector has benefited remarkably from high state subsidy and investment — often at the expense of industrial investment and consumption. Similarly, it is clear that throughout the 1960s the planning system was continually undermined by short-term political expediency and, in the 1970s, a growing penchant under Giscard d'Estaing and his Prime Minister, Raymond Barre, for a more liberalised financial system. This took the form of a greater reliance on variable interest rate and monetary policy and a significant downgrading of the role of the planning process.[22]

Despite this it would be fallacious to argue that French governments after de Gaulle attempted to dismantle the state's indirect and dirigiste quantitative controls over the financial system. Clearly, special credit institutions for industry, housing and agricultural investment were mobilised throughout the period to provide preferential loans and subsidies for particular sectors, even at a time when the Treasury and Banque de France were operating tight monetary policies.[23] This is indicative of two things: the similarity of the French indirect approach to the Japanese industrial investment process; and, at the same time, its more political clientelist flavour. The protection of agriculture has clearly been of much more importance to the French state than its Japanese counterpart; and lacking the dualist productive system of Japan, the French have been unable to force the burden of industrial and technological restructuring on politically and economically weak industrial actors. Instead, as Giscard and Mitterrand discovered, restructuring has often forced the state to become involved in bailing out 'lame duck' enterprises with finance which ought perhaps to have been earmarked for growth sectors of the economy.

There are, perhaps, two major reasons for these different records despite similar state, finance and industry relationships. The French state has legitimised its activities in terms of economic performance and social welfarism. This has led the state into the nationalisation of major industrial enterprises. The Japanese have not accepted the need for extensive welfarism, and consequently they have not found it necessary to bail out ailing industries. On the contrary, they have been able to protect their industrial giants and encourage them to rationalise while forcing the costs of change on the unprotected small and medium-sized firms in the economy. The second major reason relates to the continuity of a conservative Liberal Democratic coalition in the Japanese legislature. White the French National Assembly was not an effective participant in the state - finance - industry relationship for much of the Fourth Republic and the Gaullist interregnum, in recent years electoral politics have become more important with the breaking of the Gaullist coalition and the rise to prominence of the Socialist Party. This resurgence of popular, anti-conservative opinion in the activities of the state has not been experienced as effectively in Japan and has allowed MITI to continue to dominate the process. In France the coming to power of Mitterrand and the Socialists in 1981 has introduced a further problematic into the relationship between the state, finance and industry.

At a time when, due to the need to restructure the French economy in a period of declining economic performance and intensifying international competition, Giscard was moving towards a loosening of the state's role and responsibilities, along lines similar to those being developed in the 1970s in Japan, the election of a Socialist government committed to high public expenditure and further nationalisation of the banking and industrial sectors fundamentally questioned the relationship which has existed between key industrial, financial and bureaucratic actors in France. Instead of the populace as a whole shouldering the burdens of economic transformation through reduced living standards, the people voted into office a government committed to extending the state's control over the financial and industrial sectors: a government, furthermore, which had promised that in so doing it would be able to rebuild the French economy and still maintain high welfarism and state services. This indicates, clearly, that the French state - finance - industry relationship is at once more prone to political change than the Japanese. Yet it is debateable whether this is a strength or a weakness in the French economy.

Zysman has argued that a state cannot be an effective economic actor without the controls which a credit-based system affords. Presumably, this implies that states can be economic actors and direct their own economies once they have these instruments and controls over credit formation and price. Undoubtedly, this view of the world is one shared by left-wingers everywhere who believe that if they nationalise all of the banks and major firms then they will be able to shape their own national economic destinies. Clearly there was something of this thinking in the approach of Mitterrand's administration when it came into office. Subsequent events have fundamentally questioned this assumption and revealed that even when states give themselves powers to control the financial and industrial system they are not always able to implement these effectively.

As Green shows, in some detail, by 1982 Mitterrand had nationalised a further 36 private French banks and two major investment groups, as well as nationalising key industrial sectors of the economy. The Ninth Plan was given a far more prominent role in earmarking sectors for future industrial growth and investment than had been the case under Giscard's Eighth Plan. Pressure was exerted on the banks to be more liberal in providing funds for ailing industries, and long-term fixed interest rates (as opposed in Giscard's variable rates) were reintroduced. The new government also placed far greater reliance on special credit institutions than Giscard, and provided the Ministry of Industrial Development with funds to circumvent the controls exerted through the Treasury on direct investment funds. The clear logic of this approach was to give the state, potentially even more directive controls over industrial and financial policy and actors than had been the case since 1945. This leads to two major conclusions. It is perfectly possible for a coalition of political interests to seize the power of the state in capitalist societies and use this to refashion the financial system fundamentally. It is not, however, always possible for such a political coalition to ensure that its policies will be successful in achieving their intended effect. The French case reveals clearly that, after 1982 and the effects of a crippling run on the franc, Mitterrand was forced to make a U-turn from this directive state role.

Since then, Green argues, Mitterrand has had to limit the state's interventions into banking practices in order not to undermine the credibility of these institutions abroad in defence of the franc. At the same time the government has moved towards encouraging increased trading on the Bourse in order to raise finance for industry. By turning to the capital markets it is clear that the government is now aware of the inflationary consequences of relying on taxation or borrowing in order to finance the increases in public spending which its initial Keynesian and nationalisation approach occasioned. Despite this one must be cautious about arguing that there is any inevitability about this fundamental change in policy. Nor should one make too much of these shifts in policy. It is clear that the Socialist government is far more interventionist in intent and practice than its predecessors and it has certainly increased the scope and range of instruments at the state's disposal for shaping industrial and financial policy. This is clear evidence that there is scope for political change in state, finance and industry relationships; and further evidence of the continuing political conflict which these relationships have engendered in France. The interesting conclusion is that while there are similarities between Japan and France in the financing of industry, the evidence presented here seems to indicate that the French process is at once more prey to political conflict and the clientelism which derives from the lack of a clear national consensus over economic policy goals. While this is not to argue that Japan lacks political conflict, it is another way of saying that while France has many similar instruments and powers over finance and industry it has never created the hegemonic and politically insulated bureaucratic agency (MITI) which has been able to use the instruments available in a relatively politically unconstrained manner.

Lest this be seen as a covert apologia for the Japanese system it is apposite at this time to dwell on the case of West Germany. This is necessary because the French and Japanese cases demonstrate that having a similar financial structure does not necessarily mean that the instruments available will always be used in ways which maximise economic performance. We have seen that the Japanese case is one in which political self-interest is not allowed to overturn the search by MITI for a successful industrial and trading policy. The Japanese appear ready to adapt their financial system and liberalise somewhat in the face of international pressure. On the other hand, the French state has recently found itself responding to political, ideological and welfarist demands which have at once extended the state's physical powers in the process domestically without providing for the successful utilisation of these new instruments in the context of the international economy.

What can one learn from this very different experience? One argument might be that the French ought to create a super-Ministry similar to MITI to ensure that the state's imperatives are always fulfilled. But one might argue that the real problem for France is not the absence of a MITI but the relatively exposed position it finds itself in when one compares relative international competitiveness and productivity. If this is the case then no amount of domestic institutional tinkering will solve the state's problems. It is whether or not the state and the financial and industrial systems are able to agree on policies to make industry competitive which is ultimately crucial. The French case reveals that the Socialist government was somewhat naive in this respect when it first came in to office, it opted for greater state control without thinking about the policies which the state would have to adopt with the new instruments available. The strength of the Japanese system, it can be argued, lies less in its direct and indirect instruments of control over the financial and industrial systems and more in the way in which MITI is able to arrive at policies which ensure that the Japanese economy is competitive internationally.

This implies that having a state-led, credit-based financial system is not necessarily the panacea for the ills of capitalism. The Japanese approach may well be one model which could be adopted but, as the French case reveals, if the state is a site of conflicting political struggle and clientelism then simply possessing instruments of control will not necessarily ensure that they will be used to maximise economic performance.

This is why the West German case is worthy of close scrutiny. There is little doubt that the West German economy has had one of the best records in the post-war world. Yet its state - finance - industry relationship is very different from the Japanese model. This indicates that there may be a variety of models which may be utilised by countries to maximise their economic performance and competitiveness. As the West German case reveals, the trick of successful economic management is to adopt an approach which does not create opportunities for disfunctional ideological, social and political conflicts to overturn the search for industrially and financially rational policies. This is not to argue that either the West Germans or the Japanese have eradicated political conflicts. Rather it is to argue that they have fashioned state, finance and industry relationships which minimise their disruptive effects. As we shall see the systems are very different, yet they do appear to provide an environment in which the role of the state in industrial and financial policy-making is rarely the political football it has become in France.

While the West German system does not have the state-led, credit-based relationship evident in France and Japan, it is true that, of all the countries to be studied in this volume, Germany historically has had the longest tradition of sustained industrial banking. Before the formation of the modern German state in the latter half of the nineteenth century, Prussian economists, such as Friedrich List as early as 1841, had attacked *laissez-faire* policy and argued for a national, directed approach to economic modernisation.[24] Not surprisingly, given this tradition, Prussian bankers recognised the need for their domestic financial system to be a servant of industrialisation. German bankers were, therefore, heavily involved in the creation of Credit Mobilier in France and, following the collapse of this institution, were instrumental in the creation of the first German industrial bank − the Darmstader − in 1852.[25] Following from this, and in recognition of the new German state's relatively undeveloped industrial system *vis-à-vis* Britain, the 1870s saw the creation of the three major German banks − the Deutsche, Commerz and Dresdner. These banks were set up with the explicit intention of assisting industrial development in coalmining and heavy capital goods. As a result they became pre-eminent industrial banks which created and promoted individual firms, encouraged mergers and joint stock capitalisation, and even took direct equity shares in these companies and sold their shares to the public through their own branching networks. Not surprisingly these banks developed as universal (commercial and industrial) banks; they took risks, were heavily involved in management details and often made mistakes in assessing risks.[26]

There is little doubt that these banks were the primary engine of Germany's rapid industrialisation in the late nineteenth and early twentieth centuries. The state did provide a conducive environment and even created special credit institutions — like the Bank für Deutsche Industrie-Obligation in 1924 — to assist the role of the three main privately-owned banks. Nevertheless the state's role was not extensive and in the Weimar period, as Dyson argues (Chapter 4), the lax financial policies of the state in fact undermined the role of these banks in financing industry. Fearing inflation and the politics of the Social Democratic government, the banks clung to conservatism and refused to invest in industry. Since the collapse of the financial system in the aftermath of the Second World War, a more consensual approach to state, finance and industry relationships has developed. This has followed the lineages of the past in the sense that the German system is what Zysman has called a negotiated system. Under such a system the state may have powers to control the credit system but the policies it implements are normally negotiated with the full cooperation of major financial and industrial actors. These actors are normally privately owned and, as in the past, while the state may have developed further the range of special credit institutions to finance industry, the major role is left very much to the private banking system.

As Dyson argues, however, it is an over-simplification to argue that the German economic miracle has been solely due to the positive role of the major universal industrial banks. For one thing, the banks are political and economic animals in their own right and, in recent years, have shown a desire to place their own commercial considerations above those of the national interest when there has been pressure on them to bail out ailing companies. They are certainly not the puppets of the government and the state's regulation of the banking -industry relationship has normally been fairly lax. While the Bundesbank is one of the strongest central banks in the world and has the power to vary bank reserve requirements and direct public sector deposits, Dyson contends that in most respects it has been the spokesman for the banks in Bonn rather than the other way around. This does not imply, however, that the major universal banks dominate industry. While the top three banks dominate commercial banking there is a very liberal structure beneath these. There has developed a plethora of state savings banks, local universal banks and a national giro bank. All of these institutions are involved in non-commercial banking and provide loans to local and medium-sized firms basing their lending decisions on their own criteria of commercial risk.

Furthermore, the state's post-war role in directing investment in a *dirigiste* way has been far more marked than had been the case before. While the German state has adopted a social market approach which eschews a planning or centrally directive role for the state in financing industry, there is little doubt that, in the aftermath of the war, the state has had to work more closely with the major banks than it had before. As a result, in 1948, the state created the Kreditanstalt für Wiederaufau (KfW) to co-finance German export industry with the banks. Other agencies, like Hermes, to provide export loan guarantees to allow German firms to compete internationally, were also created. In the immediate post-war period, then, the state, through KfW, found itself playing an extensive role in allocating Marshal Aid funds to rebuild the economy in a *dirigiste* manner. Most funds were consciously earmarked for industrial fixed investment in the private sector. Some assistance was, however, also provided for agriculture, housing, refugee settlement, the promotion of exports and regional development. The banks also played a crucial role. Given that there was no significant domestic saving in this period, the banks consciously accepted with the government the need to rebuild the industrial base of the economy. The banks therefore took commercial risks and provided extensive funds for German industry. This recognition of the need to ensure West Germany's industrial future did not abate in the 1950s and 1960s as personal savings revived the capital markets. The traditional top three, and the newer banks created in this period (Landesbanken and Sparkassen), continued to purchase equity in companies and became involved in the day-to-day operations of individual firms.[27]

This tradition of recognising the crucial link between the performance of industry and the long-term health of the banking system has persisted from the nineteenth century, and explains much in the state - finance - industry relationship in West Germany. Since the major banks as well as the newer state banks recognise this fact, it absolves the government from having to act to bail out inefficient firms or ensure that savings are channelled effectively into industry. In Japan MITI has to fulfil this role. In France the state's nationalisations and special credit institutions have attempted to do this. In West Germany the state may assist through the KfW; it does not, however, have to take a dominant role because the equity shares owned by the banks in the major companies ensure that the banks are closely in touch with the needs and problems of domestic industry. This, as Dyson shows, has not always obviated the need for the state to become involved in bailing out industries (steel, for example); it has, however, ensured that the state's role is a relatively limited one compared with other countries. Only when the banks perceive the long-term commercial viability of an industry to be fundamentally unviable are they likely to refuse to assist in restructuring. If the state chooses to act after this for electoral, ideological or social welfare reasons, this is seen as part of the state's role. The banks confine themselves to assisting industry on economically rational and commercially defineable criteria. Clearly, this approach minimises the problem which are witnessed in France of political, ideological and social considerations intruding to distort decision-making for the financing of industry.

In this sense the West German system, which sees close interpersonal contact at all levels between top industrialists, bankers and government representatives, is one which seems to work in ensuring that the primary function of the financial system − providing capital for those sectors and firms best able to support the national economy − is fulfilled. As we saw, it is a very different system from that of Japan or France, and yet one might argue that it has had similar success to that in Japan. An interventionist body like MITI has not been necessary because there has been a consensus between the historically stronger German banks and the state and industry over the need to direct German industry towards exports and competitive and productive efficiency. Further, the banks in Germany have always had a tradition of close involvement with firms and have been prepared to take risks and make decisions based on long-term growth rather than short-term profit criteria. Since Japanese and French banks and financial institutions have not traditionally favoured such an industrial banking role the need for the state to intervene − with varying degrees of success in each country − has been obvious.

One might argue, then that despite political conflict electorally and changes in the ideological disposition of governments since the war, the major West German political parties have agreed on the need to mobilise capital for investment and credit for trade. This has ensured that the financing of industry can continue without adversarial conflict over the proper role for the state - a consensual approach which is assisted by the fact that the banking system acts as as early warning system for industrial problems obviating the need for the state to act publicly. This, together with the coincidence of interest in this minimalist state role by industrialists and bankers alike, ensures that − as in Japan − the financing of industry does not become an acute political problem. This does not mean that there is no disagreement between the state and financial and industrial interests. Rather it implies that conflict is confined within a framework the boundaries of which all the players are in fundamental agreement with. In this way it is clear that the West German system can be seen as one which accommodates key economic and political interests and ensures − like the Japanese − that the political game does not undermine economically rational investment decision-making.

This conclusion cannot be drawn for the one country analysed in this volume which comes closest to approximating the negotiated West German system. Just as the Japanese and French cases are examples of broadly similar structures having different utility for the performance of the economy the West German and Italian cases demonstrate a similar disjuncture. The Italian state - finance - industry relationship is extremely enigmatic. The Italian economy has for much of the post-war period been characterised by a relatively high-growth performance and yet this has been achieved with endemic financial and currency instability and inflation. This paradox is difficult to comprehend without a detailed knowledge of the Italian political and economic system yet it is possible to point − as Furlong does here − to the major features of the Italian system which seem to explain why sectors of industry are able to remain competitive internationally despite the inherently political and clientelist nature of the state - finance - industry relationship.

The first point to make about the Italian system is that it is negotiated, but in a very different sense from the West German model. Whereas the West German state, banking and industrial structures recognise the need to pursue economically rational goals, no such common consensus about the objectives of the state - finance - industry relationship exists in Italy. Rather than there being a positive negotiation over means and ends, within a system in which the main protagonists recognise that the imperatives of a capitalist trading relationship are the ultimate constraints on choice, negotiation in the Italian system is between protaganists who sometimes recognise these constraints (the Bank of Italy, Confindustria and to a much lesser extent state-funded special credit institutions); those who see the system as a means of corporate, family or individual enrichment and political preferment (the Christian Democratic coalition and the privately-owned firms and families attached to it); and those who desire to use the state for their own ideological perception of the national interest (Socialists and Communists in government, the public sector and the special credit institutions).

A negotiation takes place between all of these actors, especially as the state has the ability to control domestic credit through the Bank of Italy and special credit institutions, but it is not a negotiation in which all of the actors operate in terms of the same ground-rules. The Bank of Italy may well operate like other Central Banks and apply sound money policies consistent with international monetary relationships and a desire to defend the sanctity of the currency; Confindustria and some of the special credit institutions may wish to see finance channelled into industry for modernisation and trade competitiveness. Unfortunately, in the Italian system, this economically rational goal is baulked by the fact that the private capital market has remained historically weak and underdeveloped. This has meant that the goals of these actors have been undermined by the ability of private firms to fund investment for themselves from overseas investors and, thereby, circumvent state planning and *dirigiste* investment policies. At the same time the corrupt and clientelist nature of the unstable coalitions which have dominated Italian government for most of the post-war period has ensured that the political system is highly fragmented and incapable of consistent and coherent policy-making. When political office is regarded as a means of self-enrichment and the paying of political favours through a modern sinecure system, the chance of a directive state role or a negotiated relationship of the West German kind is improbable. As Furlong concludes, in Italy neither the state nor the privately-owned financial and industrial sectors are able to give a clear lead for industrial development because all of the actors involved possess veto powers over everyone else involved when they attempt to give some direction to the financing of industrial investment.

In this context it may be surprising that the Italian economy ever modernised at all or experienced fairly rapid growth in the 1950s and 1960s. The main reasons for this, as Furlong shows, reside largely in the activities of the Bank of Italy, the special credit institutions, and the ability of very large and concentrated industrial firms to raise finance overseas. This has been a gradual and halting historical process which indicates once again that even in highly politicised systems there is scope for a fundamental restructuring of the financial system. Despite attempts to transform the state's role and provide some lead for industrial development, success has been patchy and prey to continuous political interference and amendment in the service of clientelism and corruption - further testament to the highly political nature of the state, finance and industry relationship in all countries.

The creation of the post-war Italian system can only be understood in terms of the late development of the Italian state within a primarily agrarian economy. Industry was underdeveloped and the state's role was non-existent. Foreign capital was the major source of industrial investment because the loans from the three major Italian banks − Comit, Credito

Italiano and the Banco di Roma — were underwritten by foreign credit. After the 1929 Depression and the coming to power of the Fascists, moves were made to give a *dirigiste* lead to the further industrialisation of the economy through domestic means. In this period the three major banks were replaced by a more state-controlled credit-based system. IMI was set up to provide long-term finance for industry; while IRI was given the task of giving some direction to the company holdings it acquired from the three major banks. The Bank of Italy was also given extended powers to defend the value of the currency and control monetary policy. Perhaps the most important role given to the Bank, however, was that of keeping finance and industry separate through policies which ensured that commercial banks operated only as sort-term deposit-takers and lenders: long-term lending was to be provided mainly through IMI because the Stock Market was, and has remained, weak.

Although the Fascist regime was discredited after the war many of the *dirigiste* instruments and the essentially negotitated system created by it have been maintained. Indeed, since 1945, Furlong shows that the state has intervened even more through the creation of additional special credit institutions and public enterprises to provide some lead for industrial development. Despite this attempt to construct a state-led, credit-based system along lines similar to France and Japan — indeed, after 1968 the three major special credit institutions (IMI, Mediobanca and Italcasse) were encouraged to operate a refinancing system of mobilisable credit like the French — the Italian system has remained an obstinately negotiated structure due to the clientelism and corruption embedded in the political process. Furlong indicates that attempts at refinancing have failed due to an inability to coordinate the decisions of the various Ministries involved in the process, and due to a lack of clear criteria by which loan applications might be judged. This failing is compunded because the special credit institutions are themselves often corrupt and function within the traditional clientelist pattern of Italian politics. IMI, for instance, is dominated by the Christian Democratic coalition; while Mediobanca is controlled by large private firms and competes with IMI. The result has been a lack of coherent direction and a tendency for the proliferation of small regional credit institutions to meet the needs of local industry which is largely ignored by the major credit insititions. This fragmentation militates against any coherent approach to the financing of industry. As a result, the availability of loan finance is likely to have more to do with political affiliations than with the underlying long-term viability of the industrial process involved.

The problems with this politicised and fragmented system are legion and indicate that simply having a negotiated system will not necessarily solve a nation's problems of financing industry. While the system may work extremely effectively in West Germany, where industrial banking has a long history and there is a national consensus amongst most of the key actors involved over the goals of industrial investment, Italy simply does not possess these prerequisites of a successful negotiated system. There is no national consensus over policy goals and the commercial banking system is weak and has had no history of industrial banking. Relatedly, even those institutions which have been created to overcome these shortcomings have become enmeshed in the corrupt and clientelist political system, militating against their being able to provide any coherent lead in the manner of the KfW in West Germany or MITI in Japan. The Italian system is best characterised, then as in ineffective, negotiated financial system in which, since the Fascist period, some actors have continuously attempted to shift the balance in favour of a more state-led, credit-based system. While some success has been recorded in creating the instruments to provide the state with a directive role since 1945, it has been more difficult to ensure that the personnel heading these state agencies would use their powers to pursue economically rational, as opposed to politically and personally convenient, policy goals. In this sense the state - finance - industry relationship in Italy demonstrates once again that fundamental change is possible in the structure of the financial system. Unfortunately, the Italian case also indicates the disfunctional and deleterious consequences of continuous political conflict. Indeed, as Furlong concludes, this problem is likely to grow in the future as, in present circumstances, the private sector is having to rely increasingly on state finance rather than overseas borrowing to deal with the restructuring problems posed by the current recession. The future for the long-term performance of the Italian economy is hardly likely to be bright if neither the state and its institutions, nor the private banking system, is able to arrive through negotiation at a viable approach to the financing of industry.

Having discussed the failures which can arise from operating both state-led and negotiated credit-based financial systems it is as well to realise that this does not provide central support for those who would advocate a more *laissez-faire* approach to the financing of industry. As the British and American cases reveal, the adoption of a capital market approach, in which the state does not play a major role in controlling or directing industrial investment, is also prone to numerous problems and weaknesses. As the evidence presented here reveals, under some circumstances – particularly if the commercial banks and financial institutions which dominate the system are the paragons of economic rationality – the system may well assure a virtuous circle of highly profitable investment and high economic growth. On the other hand, if the financial institutions do not possess the ability to square the circle of the pursuit of their own independent commercial rationality with that of the defence of the national economy within which they are based, then it is likely that the system will generate intense opposition and continuous political controversy. The end-result of such controversy is likely to be adversarial conflict between the major economic, financial and political actors and no consistent direction from either the financial sector or the state for the financing of industry.

As we shall see, since 1945 the United States has come closest to achieving success in administering a capital market system due to the strength and size of its economy. In recent years, however, there have been growing fears about the effectiveness of this approach and demands in some quarters for a move to greater state direction of credit for industry to ensure the future competitiveness of the American economy. The British case is different altogether. Having had a glorious past based on *laissez-fairism* the British economy has moved inexorably towards economic impoverishment in both absolute and relative terms this century. Despite this, the British have persisted with a largely capital market approach, while at the same time creating institutions to direct investment into industry without providing these agencies with either the finance or tools to ensure that they were capable of achieving their intended roles. The resulting attempt to intervene in the financing of industry without the ability to control the process directly or indirectly has left Britain in the worst of all worlds: it has a financial system geared more to overseas investment with no tradition of industrial banking; an underfunded and uncompetitive industrial base; and an adversarial political system which is incapable of arriving at a national consensus over economic policy. Like the Italian negotiated system, the British approach appears to be capable of enriching a minority, but only at the expense of the performance of the national economy and the majority of its people.

The American system has had fewer immediate problems and this arose because, since 1945, the American economy has been the engine of post-war recovery and boom. In 1945 its industry was unscathed; its currency was the medium of international exchange; its technology was superior; and it experienced burgeoning pent-up domestic and international demand.

Under these circumstances it was hardly surprising that there should have
been little post-war pressure in the United States for any extension of
the powers and role of the regulatory agencies of the state which were
set up in the 1930s Depression to ensure financial solvency and underwrite
the stability of industrial investment. Indeed, as Hu has argued, after 1945
New York increasingly competed to become an international financial
centre, and its major commercial banks turned to long-term lending.[28]
With the major banks taking this role and the plethora of state and local
banks providing sort-term loans to firms inundated with orders, it is hardly
surprising that the role of the Federal government should be confined
to a minimalist Keynesian and regulatory role, similar to that being
adopted in Britain as well in the late 1940s and 1950s.

As Owens shows (Chapter 6), the major battle has not been whether
the state should intervene in industry or the financial sector; rather it
has been whether the financial and industrial sectors should or should
not be regulated. From 1791 until the 1860s the state attempted —
unsuccessfully — to regulate the growth of banks and financial institutions.
The result was an explosion of state banks and the gradual development
of national banks. Many of these banks were unsound and there was little
effective regulation. After the Civil War until the 1930s there was an
extension of the state's role with the creation of an Office of the
Comptroller of the Currency (Treasury Department) and the Federal
Reserve Board (1913), but this was still inadequate. The piecemeal
regulatory system failed to end the dominance of New York which denuded
the South and the frontier of the West of investment funds, and could
not control the insane speculation in stocks on Wall Street which resulted
in the Great Crash.[29]

It was out of this collapse and ensuing depression that the basis of the
new regulatory system was born. While there were those around the
President who desired a more interventionist—corporatist role for the state,
in which the private capital markets would come under the indirect or
direct tutelage of a state planning machinery, by 1936 the inherent
pluralistic pro-*laissez-faire* tendencies within the American political and
economic systems had made any such solution impossible.[30] The very
success of Roosevelt's neo-corporatist policies to underwrite investment
and reconstruct the financial system on a much sounder base of Federal
government support ensured that those who desired a more interventionist
role — as enshrined in the National Industrial Recovery Act and the
Tennessee Valley Authority — would be defeated. Nevertheless, the period
between 1933 and 1936 did witness the creation of the regulatory system

which has been the basis of the state's role in the financial system since 1945. The major bodies created were the Reconstruction Finance Corporation (which aimed to divorce investment from commercial banking and to restrict interest rate competition); the Securities and Exchange Commission (to regulate the Stock Market and limit concentration and risks) and the Federal Deposit Insurance Corporation (to insure national and state bank deposits). The Federal Reserve Board was also given extensive new powers to set limits on interest rates, and to regulate the conditions of credit and the overall money supply.

As Owens argues, however, while this was an extension of the state's role, the system was still one very much dominated by the private capital markets. The Federal Reserve Board had new powers but it was not the Central Bank which some people desired at the time. The Fed was not able to draw all smaller banks into the system and the private banks involved could still operate very much on their own commercial criteria in relation to international or domestic business. Similarly, there was no creation of special credit institutions to encourage the commercial or investment banks to favour export industries − despite the role of the US Import-Export Bank − or to provide 'soft' loans to essential industries. In this sense the American system became what Owens calls a cartelised system. The commercial banks were limited to short-term loans: only the investment banks were able to make long-term loans. The savings and loans and mutual savings banks proliferating in the states were confined to loans to consumers and for mortgages.

This cartelised system worked passably well − or so it appeared − during the 1950s and most of the 1960s. By the end of the 1960s, however, the United States began to wake up to the fact that its policy of Keynesian and regulatory policies was no longer working effectively. The economy was faced with increasing international competition, technological backwardness, a low level of capital formation, a relatively low GNP growth rate and, comparatively, one of the worst unemployment records in the West. The most glaring example of this realisation of economic decline was the massive import penetration in the 1970s into those industries − textiles, cars, steel, shipbuilding and consumer electronics − in which the US had led the world. Since then the relationship between the state and the financial and the industrial sectors has once again become a key topic of debate. There have been those who academically (Thurow and Reich) and politically (Gary Hart) have argued for a more extensive state role of a corporatist kind.[31] This has clear connections with the New Deal strategies of the 1930s but, as Owens shows, it has not had much impact on the activities of the state in its relationships with the financing of industry. The major debate has in fact been between those who want to see a further deregulation of the financial sector and those who desire the maintenance of the state's regulatory role and an *ad hoc* Federal response to particular industrial problems.

It would appear that since the late 1960s there has been something of a stalemate between these two approaches. As Reich has argued, the state has not developed an industrial policy as such. Rather the state has reacted to an *ad hoc* fashion with loans, one-off aid packages, tax concessions, tariff quotas and import restrictions to industries in rapid decline. On one or two occasions this has meant the bailing-out of particular firms regarded as essential to the economy. The Lockheed, Chrysler and Continental Illinois rescues are clear examples of this. None the less, this has not been a coordinated approach to the planning of industrial policy or the financing of industry.[32] Indeed, in so far as the state's role in the financial sector is concerned, the bias has been in favour of deregulation of the 1930s system rather than any moves to enhance the state's directive and coordinating role. As Owens shows, there has been continuous pressure from the banking and other financial institutions to encourage the deregulation of interest rate policies, the ending of the cartelisation of institutions, and demands for greater freedom for the provision of services and geographical location. As Owens contends, this has not always been due to pressure from new demand, rather it has been a response by financial institutions to the increasing competition they have faced from international and domestic competitors.

Nevertheless, Owens shows that deregulation will be piecemeal and never be fully effective because there are aspects of regulation which all actors in the market desire. Regulation underwrites the stability of the system itself at a time when banking failures (e.g. Penn Square National Bank in 1982) are rising to the highest levels since the 1930s. Indeed, the regulatory agencies may well be forced to intervene even more actively due to the incidence of dubious investments by many banks in agriculture, real estate, oil exploration and overseas government debts. Investments which may well have been encouraged by the recent deregulations of interest rate policies, which have in turn led to a concentration of resources into the national commercial and investment banking institutions at the expense of the local and state banking system. This may have deleterious consequences for American industry as small local businesses (the engine of American growth) find it increasingly difficult to raise loans on a long-term basis from national banks which have little historic or practical experience of industrial banking.

In conclusion then one might argue that in the period of the post-war long boom the American regulatory private capital market system appeared to serve the industrial system well. In reality, while the banks and financial institutions made large profits for themselves, the underlying poor performance of the US economy, which became apparent in the late 1960s and 1970s, questioned this assumption. Recently some academics and politicians − although a minority − have realised that the lack of capital formation indicates that the financial system may very well have been making short-term and overseas profits at the expense of the long-term strength of the domestic economy. This pinpoints the problem of relying on private capital markets and regulation alone: when a recession occurs it is already too late to do anything about it. One is, in other words, forced to rely on actors who are normally more concerned with short-term profitability for themselves than the long-term viability of the enterprises they do and do not support. Only the West German banks, having an industrial banking tradition, are the major exceptions to this rule. A further problem for those who would attempt to provide for a more directive state role is, of course, that in a private capital market system the financial and industrial institutions become key political actors as a result of their economic power. The ability of the state, then, to build political coalitions around a more directive role for Federal influence over the financing of industry is undermined by the multiple points of access and veto which the American federalist and pluralist political system affords to economic actors with money and clout.

If the American approach has had numerous problems since the 1960s, some of which may very well have been a result of the lack of a state-led or negotiated strategy to the financing of industry, the underlying size and strength of the American economy have ensured that, even in the absence of a high-growth performance, the per capital income and standard of living of most Americans has been one of the highest in the world. That America could do better, as some now recognise, is not in doubt. Nevertheless, the American system appears as an example of a relatively successful private capital market system when compared with the case of Britain.

Like the Americans the British have relied on a private capital market approach to the financing of industry. Ironically, however, this system has been at once less subject to effective government regulation (there is as yet no equivalent of the Securities and Exchange Commission to regulate the Stock Exchange which is left to self-regulation), and yet more prone to attempts by the government to interfere in industrial policy. In this sense the British case is an example of the worst of all possible worlds. Historically, and particularly since 1945, governments in Britain have attempted to influence industrial policy and the actions of firms without either regulation or controlling the financial system directly. On the contrary, the financial system has been defended as sacrosanct and the paragon of all the virtues of profit-making. Industry, on the other hand, has been the site of constant adversarial interventions by governments. Since 1945 the state in Britain has pursued limited planning, Keynesian, neo-corporatist and *laissez-faire* policies which have undermined any continuity in industrial planning by firms or by government. Thus the British have pursued contradictory financial and industrial policies. It is hardly surprising, therefore, that Britain's post-war economic and industrial performance is one which is characterised by a deterioration in relative economic growth compared with most competitors, increasing decline in the share of world trade, inflationary instability, rising unemployment, declining relative living standards and extremely low capital-formation.

There seems little doubt, despite the arguments to the contrary from the British financial institutions and their supporters in the Conservative Party, that the excessive reliance on private capital markets to fund industry has been one of the major causes of Britain's relative economic decline. The British banking and financial system has had very little historical involvement in the financing of British industry as industrial bankers in the West German tradition. Ingham and Hu both point to this phenomenon. They argue that Britain's dilemma arises from the fact that Britain was both the first industrial nation and, at the same time, a very successful mercantilist and trading nation.[33] This gave investors and bankers two possible sources of investment. On the one hand, they could choose to invest in the new industrialising industries in the North, or they could continue to finance the explosion in world trade which gradually attended the industrial revolution and freeing of trade in the mid-nineteenth century. Ingham argues convincingly that, historically, the wealthy aristocratic investors and merchant banks associated with the City of London normally opted for the latter, more profitable investments. The nascent giants of the industrial revolution had to rely on retained profits, the good financial sense of local landowners, or the short-term loans which the small county banks were forced to limit themselves to by the Bank of England.[34]

British industry did not throughout most of the nineteenth century suffer seriously from this lack of interest by the City of London in domestic manufacturing industry. British industry had the advantage of dominating international markets because it was the first to industrialise: it also had a large captive colonial market to trade with. There was, as a result, no real need for the state to become involved in a process of channelling investment into industry on a continuous basis. It appeared to contemporaries that the reliance on private capital markets, with a limited state role, was the reason for Britain's success. The City of London's role generated massive overseas invisible earnings; the manufacturing sector provided visible exports to most of the rest of the world. By the latter half of the nineteenth century, however, there were those who had begun to recognise that British industry was no longer able to complete effectively with the newly industrialising nations. It was out of this realisation that politicians from such disparate ideological, political and economic backgrounds as Joseph Chamberlain, Randolph Churchill, Bernard Shaw and the Webbs began to discuss the need for an end to free trade and a more active and directive role for the British state in guiding industrial investment.[35]

Despite shifts in the state's welfare role in the years before the First World War no political coalition was built to implement such a radical policy by the British state. The country which had given *laissez-faire* to the world and benefited mightily from it in the nineteenth century has clung to free trade for most of the twentieth century, despite the obvious deleterious consequences of this approach for domestic industry and economic performance. Only in the 1930s did Britain adopt protectionism, and then only as a consequence of import controls being used against its own products. The British state did not intervene coherently to resolve problems of economic decline or to channel resources into industry. In a sense this was surprising because, as early as 1931, the Macmillan Committee had argued that there was a yawning gap in the financing of industry. The Stock Market was clearly more interested in government debt and overseas investment (especially for railway construction) than in the provision of medium and long-term finance for small and medium-sized business. This Committee found that large and successful firms were able to raise loans from the commercial and merchant banks easily enough (or use retained profits); the problem was that if there was any risk involved the banks and financial institutions were not really interested because they could always find safer sources of investment overseas.[36]

As Lisle-Williams shows (Chapter 7), the problem has remained and has dogged all post-war attempts by government to assist industrial performance and economic growth. At no time has any post-war government — Labour or Conservative — ever seen the need to intervene directly to control credit and change Britain from a financial system dominated by private capital markets. Governments have tried to negotiate with industry and have even intervened with agencies to assist industry. Ironically, however, since the nationalisation of the Bank of England after the war there has been very little constructive thinking — apart from outright nationalisation by the Left — about the structure of controls and incentives which the state might adopt to shape and mould the financial system in the service of domestic industry.

Britain suffered after 1945 from being one of the victorious nations. It did not have to rethink fundamentally its industrial, financial and economic needs as France, Japan and West Germany did. It had also been heavily influenced both before and during the war by Keynesian economic thinking and became one of the leading exponents of this indirect demand-side approach to economic management after 1947. This approach denied the need for any directive state role in supply-side problems (like the financing of industry or the allocation of limited resources to key firms or industrial sectors). On the contrary, Keynes, in his attempt to defend capitalism and as much of the *laissez-faire* system as possible, argued that by maintaining effective demand governments could underwrite capitalism without the need for extensive state controls. The maintenance of effective demand would allow the private capital markets and privately-owned firms to act freely to choose which goods to produce and who should rationally receive investment funds.

This system would have worked well if the Keynesian approach had been able to ensure that an increasingly international financial system would be concerned mainly with the domestic needs of manufacturing industry but, as Lisle-Williams shows, this has not been the case in the post-war period. The historic attachment to short-term lending and commercial rather than nationalistic criteria of profitability amongst British financial institutions has persisted. This was not a visible problem in the 1950s and early 1960s, as the long post-war boom and government attachment to Keynesian demand management continued to provide Britain's antiquated, unproductive and non-competitive manufacturing industries with relatively assured demand. In this environment it did not matter very much that the financial institutions would only provide short-term finance, firms could always use retained profits and raise loans or equity finance (large firms) or short-term overdraft facilities (all firms). Unfortunately, these conditions did not last and by the end of the 1960s, as trade competition increased, interest rates rose and profitability declined, all firms have been faced with the dilemma of having to look increasingly to external rather than internal sources of funding to finance research and development and − in an increasing number of cases in the 1970s and 1980s − survival.

But Lisle-Williams argues, persuasively, that it is in these conditions that Britain's attachment to traditional private capital market practices has revealed fundamental problems for the financing of industry. It is not only that there has been no tradition of industrial banking and a reliance on short-term lending in Britain, the Stock Exchange itself has never been a particularly effective source of industrial finance. The Stock Exchange in Britain is primarily a market for trading existing securities; its role as a device for raising new money for industrial development is very much a secondary function. Hu has argued that even the massive increase in share dealings since 1945 by the financial institutions has not resulted in very much new money passing to firms. On the contrary, the boom in institutional shareholding has been through a transfer of ownership of existing shares from private households to the institutions. The actual purchase of shares by the public has, in fact, declined, to be replaced by institutional ownership - an institutional involvement which is more geared to the buying and selling of securities than as a source of long-term equity ownership in particular companies. Furthermore, any increase in public involvement in recent years has normally been for short-term speculative gains (as in the case of privatisation sales under the Thatcher government) rather than long-term investment.[37]

This anti-industrial trend has been reinforced by the development of the City of London as a large off-shore financial centre related to the expansion of the Eurodollar market. This has encouraged large multinational firms to enter the money markets as lenders and borrowers and reduced the reliance of the commercial and merchant banks on domestic business as a source of profitable investment. Relatedly, the declining profitability of domestic manufacturing industry, when compared with overseas and property investment, has resulted in personal savings being located increasingly in financial institutions and building societies. This has, on occasions, had almost catastrophic consequences for the City of London and industrial investment. Given the tax and financial incentives granted to property ownership in Britain by all post-war governments, this has become one of the major sectors of the economy for personal savings and institutional investment. It has been argued that this has been to the net detriment of investment in industry and, in the early 1970s, almost led to the collapse of the integrity of the City of London due to profligate institutional investment in property speculation.[38]

Nevertheless, as Lisle-Williams contends, it is too easy to blame the financial sector alone as the main culprit for Britain's lamentable industrial performance. In fact, as he shows here, industry itself has been slow to react to changed trading conditions and has failed to adapt in the light of new technological conditions. This has surely been − with the lack of financial interest in the needs of domestic industry − one of the main causes of Britain's poor economic record. Yet it must be accepted that the role of governments has also been a further contributory factor. Lisle-Williams argues that one of the fundamental problems facing the financing of industry has been the continuous endorsement by all post-war governments of the legitimacy of financial self regulation and self governance. The fact that the financial sector has been unwilling to accept responsibility for the wider industrial consequences of its own actions has reinforced this tendency.

The fundamental problem for the British economy has been that there has been a disjuncture between the post-war state's attitude to industrial and financial policy which has compounded the consequences of the reliance on a self-regulating financial system. The private capital markets, left to their own devices, have pursued commercially and organisationally rational policies which have resulted in money being invested more in property, overseas industry and government debt than in domestic industry. This is understandable but it is a tendency which has been compounded by the failure of post-war governments to realise the need to control − whether directly or indirectly − the activities of the financial institutions.

Unlike many of its competitors the British state did not act after 1945 to take a directive role in the financing of investment. While one special credit institution was created − the Industrial and Commercial Finance Corporation (ICFC) − in 1945, this body was independent of government control despite a 15 per cent shareholding by the Bank of England. The London and Scottish clearing banks were involved but they traditionally took all plum industrial investments for themselves and underfunded ICFC.[39] Even the windfall of Marshall Aid was misappropriated. Rather than following the lead given by other nations who used Marshall Aid to reconstruct and revitalise industry, most of this money was used to redeem government securities and debts incurred during the war. The first post-war Labour government might have been seen as a socialist government at the time because it imposed import and exchange controls, experimented with manpower planning, restricted new capital issues and nationalised key heavy industrial sectors and the Bank of England. In reality, however, this government was hardly as radical as contemporaries might have assumed, and this was no more apparent than in its handling of the relationship between the state and the financial system. After the financial crisis of 1947 the government gave up its plethora of war-time controls and adopted a Keynesian approach to the economy, which involved allowing self-regulation of the private capital markets. The Bank of England then became the mouthpiece of the City of London in government rather than the other way around. The attachment to defending the reserve role of sterling, which necessitated endless destabilising stop - go policies for industry throughout the 1950's, was ample testament to this fact.

It is in this sense that the 1950s have been seen as wasted years. When the state − either through negotiation or direction − might have been using the opportunity of a boom to restructure, industry and the financial sectors were left to their own devices. It was not until the relative decline of the economy became apparent in the 1960s that governments − both Conservative and Labour − began to recognise the need for a more involved role in the supply side of the economy. Ironically, when this reappraisal came about it did not involve a more active state role in the financial sector. This sector was left very much to its own devices while an adversarial political battle has raged ever since between the two major political parties over more or less state intervention in industry itself. It is at this point that the disjuncture between financial and industrial policy has become most glaringly apparent.

While there has been fundamental disagreement between the parties over industrial policy, for much of the period after 1960 until 1979, there was something of a consensus in industrial policy in practice. The main lines of this policy − as Lisle-Williams shows here and has been documented elsewhere [40] − were faltering attempts to construct a bargained corporatist structure with indicative-style planning structures. The bias of this approach was not directed towards the creation of special credit institutions or the provision of powers for the state to control credit in quantity; rather the financial system was left to its own devices, while the state created new Ministries, Industrial Reorganisation Corporations, Development Agencies, Enterprise Boards and sector working parties. These bodies sought to work in cooperation with business and labour to fashion a consensus over industrial policy. Unfortunately, this approach failed. There were a number of reasons for this. First of all, the government was unable − due to its lack of effective controls over the financial institutions − to find sufficient funds to restructure British industry. Most of the funds earmarked for these interventionist bodies relied on public expenditure which, in the 1970s and 1980s, became impossible to finance at a time of declining growth and political resistance to increasing tax burdens. Secondly, much of industry rejected trade union and government intervention as a form of backdoor nationalisation and looked to *laissez-faire* solutions. The labour movement itself was also unable to deliver the goods due to its own attachment to voluntarism and the pursuit of individual union self-interest. Their willingness to accept fundamental industrial restructuring was always predicted on any government first maintaining high levels of social welfarism and job protection, both of which were becoming increasingly difficult to finance due to economic decline and popular aversion to increasing tax burdens. As a result industrial strategy failed to generate any national consensus and corporatist experiments continuously collapsed with recriminations on all sides.

It is at this point that one can see the fundamental disjuncture in state, finance and industry relationships in Britain. The state, in its corporatist phases, never provided itself with the necessary instruments to provide effective control over the supply of credit for industry which were essential to the success of its strategy. The history of special credit institutions in Britain is ample testament to this fact. As we saw, ICFC had been created in 1945 but it had failed to develop either close relationships with government or to create a major role for itself in long-term lending to industry. This failing continued throughout the 1960s and 1970s, despite an attempt by the Heath Government to enhance its role in 1973 as Finance for Industry.[41] The Labour governments which followed Heath after 1974 paid little attention to this agency and concentrated instead on their own National Enterprise Board. This agency was intended to take equity ownership in existing profitable industries and provide long-term state funds for new industry. In practice, due to public expenditure constraints, it was underfunded and in response to the cumulative electoral, ideological and political pressures exerted on the Labour government, spent most of its resources bailing out 'lame duck' industries − notably British Leyland.

Here in microcosm is the failure of the British state - finance - industry relationship. Fearing the consequences for sterling and confidence that any radical nationalisation or state intervention in the financial sector might occasion, the government was forced to leave the financial sector to regulate itself while at the same time failing to provide an active industrial policy for winners rather than losers. The consequences of this disjuncture are now self-evident in the de-industrialisation and continuing poor economic performance of the British economy. This is surely evidence both of the deleterious consequences of continuous political conflict and a failure to develop a national consensus over industrial and financial policy. It is also testament to Zysman's original point that no state can hope to be an effective economic actor with a financial structure which is inimical to an active state role. The British reliance on a private capital market structure clearly makes it impossible for the state to implement an active industrial policy.

It is, however, at this point that one has to be cautious. It might be logical to argue that the only effective solution is for the British state to recognise its own weakness and only adopt policies which are consistent with the prevailing financial structure. This in a sense, is the logic of Zysman's argument. The difficulty for Britain and the United States is that the recent Thatcher and Reagan administrations have indeed adopted this scenario. The Americans have moved haltingly under Reagan to deregulate their financial systems and the Thatcher government has adopted a similar approach. Since the Conservatives came to office they have ended exchange controls and moved to end the traditional cartelised nature of the Stock Exchange to encourage a more effective overseas penetration of British capital markets. Similarly the interventionist agencies of the state have been swept away and greater reliance has been placed on the ability of the private capital markets to finance industry, the government's role being confined, largely, to managing the supply of money in global terms and attempting to reduce public expenditure – particularly through the sale of profitable public enterprises to domestic and overseas financial institutions.

The major question is, of course, whether or not this approach, which fits the state's role to that which accords with the structure of the financial system, is likely to generate a more effective financing of industry. At present it may be too early to tell but there are indications that such an approach may not be successful. Owens' chapter shows that there are problems with such an approach in the USA. It is, however, in the British context that the major problems with this approach may be most evident. Since the ending of exchange controls billions of pounds have flooded overseas to take up the more profitable investment opportunities available abroad. The state of manufacturing industry – crippled by high interest rates policies and the resulting artificially high currency value before 1982, which seriously affected export competitiveness – has not proved to be a particularly favourable location for the fund managers of British financial institutions or commercial banks. The dilemma for Britain and America is therefore apparent. It makes little sense for the state to pursue interventionist industrial policies when the underlying financial system is uncontrolled by effective quantitative controls over credit. On the other hand, by relying on institutions and banks which are not concerned fundamentally with the wider national consequences of their own corporate behaviour, the state has given up any claim to be in control of the nation's economic destiny. That destiny is squarely left in the hands of institutions which must put their own corporate and investors' interests ahead of the nation as a whole.

The Reagan and Thatcher governments are thus left hoping that these actors will regenerate the industrial base. Like Pontius Pilot they have, in a real sense, washed their hands of responsibility. This is the ultimate stance of governments which choose a minimal regulatory role in financial systems dominated by private capital markets. Such governments cannot complain if, in the absence of the expected recovery, they find themselves ejected from office by disgruntled voters. The problems do not, however, end there. As Lisle-Williams indicates if a government comes into office committed to financing industrial investment it can no longer rely on mouthing platitudes about industrial policy and ignore the constraining structure of the financial system. In a very real sense any future government which rejects reliance primarily on private capital markets will have to become involved in providing itself with the instruments of control and negotiation which will enable an active state role to be fulfilled. The question which remains, given our survey of the practices and problems experienced in other major advanced industrial countries, is whether there is a model which might be adopted which minimises the dysfunctional consequences of a statist approach and yet provides a mechanism by which financial institutions might be directed towards assisting domestic industry without any serious consequence for their own corporate and financial viability.

IS THERE A BEST MODEL FOR STATE, FINANCE AND INDUSTRY RELATIONSHIPS?

The simple answer to this question is no. As we have seen, there are many permutations of state, finance and industry relationships and the six countries studied in this volume provide evidence both to support the claims of particular approaches and to reject them. The simple truth is that there is no one best model which can be applied to all countries regardless of their historical traditions and political and economic structures. Yet it would be fallacious to argue that our study has not pointed to some clear lines of approach which must be adopted if any model is to be attempted. Similarly, this volume hopes that the relative merits of particular structures and relationships will be become more apparent. It seems clear, for instance, that the British and American reliance on private capital markets is one which denies the state any ability to control its own economic destiny directly. Thus, such an approach is not likely to commend itself to those nations or political actors who desire some effective control over their national industrial future. But, for those who believe that the market, left to its own devices, will generate sustainable economic growth a private capital market system is the only desirable model.

In the real world, however, elected governments find it difficult to adopt such an approach for long. This is because governments normally have to concern themselves with the political and electoral consequences of corporate behaviour. Even the Reagan administration has experienced difficulty in relying exclusively on the private capital markets. Running a massive budget deficit with high interest rates and a strong dollar has ensured that American industry has found difficulty in maintaining trade competitiveness. This has resulted in import penetration and recent moves by Congress to introduce protectionist legislation to assist American industry against what is seen as unfair competition from more nationalistic governments, like Japan, who are prepared to protect their own markets against foreign competition.

The problem for the Reagan administration is, of course, that being unable to reduce the budget deficit fundamentally or intervene drastically in the financing of industry, it is forced − as in the autumn of 1985 − to rely on *ad hoc* measures, such as one-off currency revaluations and interest rate subsidies for firms competing internationally, in order to ward off congressional demands for full-blooded protectionism; the fear being that any such drastic action might well result in counter-protectionist moves by America's trading partners, which could undermine the free trading system which is crucial to the growth and expansion of the capitalist economic system. Even more worrying, of course, is the likelihood that any closure of American markets to the commodities produced by developing countries will result in those countries being unable to finance the crippling interest charges which they have incurred through the profligate lending policies of western − and in particular American − banks. The consequence of Third World countries defaulting on their loans might well be a cataclysmic series of collapses in the international banking system.

There is, then, a clear dilemma for nation-states. How do they provide a conducive environment for their own industries to prosper without generating a protectionist backlash from countries which are less successful in financing industry? While we cannot provide a simple answer here to the international ramifications of this question — such an issue requires a book-length study of its own — in the remaining pages of this introduction it is possible to point to some general conclusions as to which approaches do provide governments with some degree of effective control over their own economic destinies. One way of approaching this is to ask whether the current proposals being worked out in the British Labour Party to create a more viable state - finance - industry relationship are likely to work in practice. This is useful because, as we saw, the British case has been one of the most intractable of the countries analysed here. Furthermore, there seems little doubt that, in the absence of a more involved state role, the financing of British industry will remain problematic.

What does the Labour Party propose? One thing at least has been learned by Labour since 1945: it now recognises that no future government can base its industrial policy on state expenditure and negotiation alone. The traditional approach has been found wanting and has been rejected. Interestingly, however, Labour also seems to have rejected the traditional statist model traditionally associated with its left wing as well. The left's approach has normally been to demand the nationalisation of the commercial banks and key financial institutions. Such an approach would fundamentally change the financial structure in Britain. It would provide for a state-led, credit-based system similar to that found in France. Unfortunately, for those who believe in planning and statism it is clear that such an approach — whatever its economic and political symmetry — is electorally and financially impossible in Britain. It is not just that the majority of the people reject nationalisation as a solution. The real problem for any government adopting this approach is that the British state does not possess the independent, economically rational bureaucratic tradition of the French and Japanese kind, which might be able to operate such a system free from the debilitating effects of social, political and ideological considerations. In the time it would take to create and staff such a directive planning agency and the necessary special credit institutions to implement policy, there is little doubt that the consequent crisis of confidence that would be generated amongst domestic and foreign investors would lead to a sterling crisis of a magnitude as yet unseen. The consequences for the standard of living and the electoral future of such a statist government are obvious. Such a government would not last long.

There are, of course, other reasons why this approach would fail in operation. As the French case reveals, it is one thing to nationalise the banks; it is altogether another thing to change the behaviour of those who run them. The French discovered in 1945, and again after 1981, that without a tradition or expertise in industrial banking the personnel of the nationalised banks were simply unable to act as the government might have wished. This problem might be solved by changing the personnel but, even if this were attempted, it is unlikely that even the new personnel would be able to do very much against the fundamental constraint which this approach faces, that is, the loss of confidence internationally any such actions would occasion. The further nationalisation of French banks and concomitant crises for the franc in 1982 and 1983 are ample testimony to this fact.[42] The crucial issue is, then, not whether banks are nationalised, but whether the financial institutions which exist can be encouraged to adopt national as well as purely commercial criteria in their corporate behaviour. The Japanese and West German cases are particularly salient here. Each of these economies possesses privately-owned banks which, either through indirect state control of credit or through negotiation, do accept some domestic responsibility for their corporate behaviour.

It is interesting, in this light, to recognise that recent proposals from the Labour Party do seem to show that the Party has learned part of this lesson. Rather than attempting to create a state-directed and nationalised credit-based system of the French type, Labour now proposes to create a National Investment Bank.[43] The basic idea is that this bank would be publicly-owned and act as a special credit institution to provide funds for those industrial sectors which are earmarked for special assistance through a tripartite negotiation structure between government, business and labour. Development agencies nationally and locally would play a crucial role in making bids, with local industry, for state investment funds. The money for this bank would not come from public expenditure as such, but from a new indirect system of exchange controls. Instead of returning to direct quantity controls on the export of capital the idea is that a future government would allow the financial institutions to invest freely overseas. But, if they invested more than 5 per cent of their assets overseas, the government would impose harsh tax penalties on the institutions and use the money so generated as a source of finance for the NIB. The bulk of NIB's money is intended to come, however, from the requirement that the financial institutions will have to invest 10 per cent of their assets in the NIB. The hope is that not only will money invested overseas since 1979 return to the country but that it will not then find its way into property and Stock Market speculation. On the contrary, the intention is to force the institutions to become more involved in investing in industry domestically (presumably as industrial bankers) and have a fail-safe sum available to the NIB for such domestic investment from the 10 per cent charge and the tax on excessive overseas investment.

Relatedly, the proposals also offer the prospect of NIB acting for the first time as a long-term lender to industry, the basic idea being that NIB would lend to industry on a preferential long-term basis. This would be through a refinancing role. NIB would provide loans (and some equity shareholding) at rates below the existing commercial rate and on a par with those being provided to competitor industries abroad. But because this might lead to a situation in which NIB loans did not generate returns commensurate with the profits which the financial institutions might be able to achieve operating abroad or at commercial rates of interest, the government would guarantee commercial returns for the institutions. Thus the funds from institutions would be invested as NIB loan stock carrying rates of return commensurate with commercial rates and backed by the Bank of England. Any subsequent deficits would be funded as a charge on the Treasury. The clear intention behind this approach is to ensure that pension funds and insurance companies do not suffer as a consequence of being forced to invest in the long-term future of British industry. Similarly, because firms, individuals and institutions will still be able to invest overseas if they wish, it is hoped that there will be no fundamental loss of confidence and sterling crises when such an approach is implemented.

We can see that this approach is very different from the statist proposals of the past. In general terms the idea is to create a half-way house between the Japanese system of credit controls and the negotiated West German approach. It is as a result, a much more sophisticated approach to the financing of industry by the state than any government has attempted in the past. It attempts to provide an indirect state role without fundamentally changing the structure of private capital markets. Rather, it is an attempt to graft the strengths of the Japanese, French and West German systems onto the existing financial structure. The overall system would be one which was negotiated, but with reserve powers — through the NIB —

to ensure that, in the absence of the banks and financial institutions operating as industrial bankers, the state would have sufficient funds and instruments to direct investment into domestic industry. In this crucial way the proposal meets the charge which Zysman and Lisle-Williams have directed at British financing of industry in the past. The state would have the power to ensure some leverage on the financial system even though a negotiated private capital market system would now be in operation. The state's industrial policies would not be left entirely in the hands of autonomous and domestically irresponsible actors.

Nevertheless, while the scheme shows a sophisticated appreciation of the constraints of the real world and an ability to pick and choose from the experiences of other countries, there are a number of problems with the practical adoption of such an approach in Britain. These operate at two levels. The first is electoral and perhaps the most difficult to overcome. There is no national consensus in Britain about the state's proper role in the economy. The Labour Party is tarred both with the brush of the failure of neo-corporatist policies of the past and a left wing committed to statist solutions. This, plus its continuing reliance on trade union finance, and commitments to high public expenditure, are all factors which have diminished support for the Party amongst the electorate. Many voters and, more importantly, businessmen and financial institutions, perceive the Party as a vehicle for backdoor nationalisation, and incapable of pursuing economically rational policies when in office. Thus, while there is no doubting that the NIB proposal − a policy emanating clearly from the nationalist and social democratic wing of the Party - is intended to invigorate British industry, many people doubt the capacity of a future Labour government to implement such a policy without falling into the trap of bailing out lame duck industries for social, ideological or electoral reasons.

Fearing this it is understandable why many voters and key economic actors prefer the devil they know − Thatcher, and the freedom to pursue their own self-interest − rather than the devil they do not. It is hardly surprising that the financial institutions should be sceptical of the viability of this scheme given the record of Labour governments in the past. Furthermore, the burgeoning support for the Liberal Social Democrat Alliance reinforces this lack of national consensus. The Alliance have had little to say about the financing of industry. They appear to be still locked into the replication of the failed neo-corporatist incomes policy approach of the past. This provides the financial institutions and their supporters with an effective bolt-hole from the possibility of a more directive state role. Since any Alliance success electorally would probably lead to a fundamental emasculation of the NIB proposal in favour of a negotiated approach, the institutions would still be left with no effective control over their corporate behaviour. Given that an election in the near future is unlikely to provide a clear Labour majority, then the major constraint facing this approach will be the adversarial nature of the British political system and the failure to agree a national consensus over the state's role in the economy.

Assuming, however, that a future Labour government − or indeed an Alliance coalition − adopted this approach, it would appear that there are a number of serious problems with it in practice. From the lessons to be learned from our study, it would appear that there are both sins of commission and omission in the scheme. One of the major problems in the British context is the proposal to finance any shortfall between NIB loans and commercial loans as a charge on the Exchequer. Given that loans will be made over a lengthy period to industries which may take sometime to operate profitably - or, indeed, which may fail - then in the short to medium term the charge on the Exchequer may well be extremely high. The problem here is that any consequential rise in public expenditure would provide ammunition for opponents to deride the financial soundness of the scheme. While there is little doubt that MITI and West German and French banks have taken risks and made losses, and that such a shortfall in the first years of such a scheme would be inevitable, these bodies have not suffered from the continuous adversarial political nature of British politics. Because MITI has been able to operate continuously it has been able to overcome these problems and point in the long term to its success. Given the volatility of British politics and the likelihood of continuing economic decline in the future, the NIB exercise is likely either to be ridiculed long before it has had time to work in practice, or be scrapped by a later government opposed to it ideologically.

There is a further cause for concern in the proposals relating to the process by which loans would be granted. We saw that, in part, the success of the Japanese system was the way in which those responsible for operating state directive policies have been protected from political interference and able to operate primarily in terms of economic rationality. The West German banks, being formally autonomous of the state, have also been able to act independently of social and ideological pressures, and have rejected the bailing out of lame duck industries. Yet we also saw that one of the problems for the French — especially under the

Socialists — was the way in which state directive agencies have become increasingly prone to political interference undermining economic and commercial criteria. The problem with the NIB proposal is that the mechanism which is proposed to allocate funds is likely to be prey to similar pressures. Given that Labour intends to grant trade unions, local authorities and businessmen a crucial role in allocating and bidding for funds, there is every likelihood that investment decisions will be as much prone to social and political considerations as they have been in the past. Since there is no intention of creating the NIB as a commercially autonomous body free of these pressures, it is inevitable that its investment decisions will become politically contested. If this happened the proposals would fail to ensure that industrial winners were chosen and a return to the financing of industrial decline would be ensured.

There are further problems associated with what the scheme fails to create. The NIB would become a major investment bank in time but it would still be dwarfed by the financial resources residing in the privately-owned financial institutions. Only 10 per cent of their assets would be invested in the NIB and they could gamble that investing overseas was still less risky than investing at home, even with the tax penalties the government might impose. This would be a perfectly rational approach because they could also gamble on the return to office of a government committed to abolishing the NIB. But there is an additional problem which would arise even if the NIB operated for a very long period. In Japan and France the strength of the state's role was seen to be less in its planning, investing and ownership functions, rather it arose from the state's ability to control credit quantitatively. This forced banks and institutions to rely on the state for liquidity — especially as the state also plays a crucial role in channelling private savings from households to the banking system. This ensured that the financial institutions had to become involved with domestic industry or face liquidity problems. The problem with the NIB approach is that personal savings would not be channelled by the state directly; they would continue to flow to the private financial institutions due to the tax benefits granted to them. Thus there would be no effective way for the state to ensure that these institutions used the remaining 90 per cent of their assets as industrial bankers. The funds — even if forced bank to Britain by tax penalties — might simply be invested in property and speculation on the Stock Exchange. While the NIB might still act as an industrial banker, the proposals provide no mechanism by which the state can force the financial institutions to become industrial bankers lending on a long-term basis.

Despite this there is little doubt that the NIB proposals are an extremely interesting attempt to learn the lessons of the past and to adopt the traditional structure of the British financial system to the needs of national economic recovery. If some of the failings documented here could be avoided — particularly the impact of social and political pressures on investment decision-making — then it is possible that the NIB offers the British state a mechanism which will allow some state direction of investment in industry without doing fundamental damage to the traditional strengths of the City of London. While it is clearly too much to expect the financial institutions to change their behaviour fundamentally, the proposals offer at least a glimmer of hope for long-term funding of industry which may be embryonic and therefore highly risky. One could suggest further measures — such as quantitative controls and the direction of savings by the state — but, given the liberal traditions predominating in Britain, it is likely that these would be to push the state far too close to a statist approach which is electorally damaging. Indeed, it may very well be that even the NIB approach will be more than the financial institutions and the British voter are prepared to stomach given the generalised antipathy in this country to state intervention in the economy. To achieve something like the NIB may be the best that one can hope for given the context of British politics and the way in which private capital markets are seen as sacrosanct. If the NIB is not created there seems little doubt that the deindustrialisation of British industry will continue unabated.

By way of conclusion it is worth restating the point we made earlier. The British case reveals that a statist model of the French type will not work successfully in Britain. Similarly, it is doubtful that the Japanese approach of an insulated super-Ministry dictating to government, industry and financial sector would operate successfully in the other countries analysed here. The West German model is perhaps the only approach which might in theory be acceptable to all of the countries. This arises because it is a negotiated system in which private firms and financial actors are relatively free to pursue their own interests. Similarly the government and labour are also provided with an important voice in deliberations over state policy. The problem is that such an approach can only be adopted if all of the actors involved are prepared to accept the logic of economic and commercial rationality. Furthermore, it required that the financial institutions must themselves recognise a national as well as corporate responsibility. As we saw, this system does not work well in Italy and it is unlikely to work well in countries like Britain and America where there has been no tradition of industrial banking and ample opportunities, historically, for financial institutions to take advantage of the benefits of their respective countries international economic roles. Given the profits to be made overseas it is impossible to countenance these actors taking on a domestic responsibility in the absence of state directives or incentives to the contrary.

The lesson from this study is, therefore, that while countries can fundamentally restructure their state, finance and industry relationships, they cannot do just as they please. Statist solutions appear to offer little prospect for the effective management of capitalist economies. This is not because the theory is wrong in ideal terms; rather it arises from the inability of the state itself to control the international flow of money and credit on which its currency values and short-term standards of living depend. Beyond this any of the approaches described in this volume are possible strategies for countries to adopt. As the articles in this volume and the discussion here hope to reveal, however, the adoption of any of these strategies does not end political conflict, even in relatively successful economies. This is so because any of the strategies adopted will have costs and benefits which can only be mediated by the creation of a national consensus over the desired state role in the economy.

Indeed, if any lesson can be drawn unequivocally from this study it is that those countries which have worked out a national consensus over the need to underwrite the long-term financing of industry, within the logic of capitalist trading relationships, have also been those with the most successful post-war record. This implies that the development of a national consensus is a necessary prerequisite of a viable state, finance and industry relationship. It is not, however, a sufficient condition. Beyond this it is imperative for the consensus to be directed towards both economically rational and domestically sensitive policies and relationships. Which particular model is then adopted is then not really important so long as it works to sustain that consensus within the peculiar cultural, political and social environment operation in individual countries. The message to be gleaned from reading the country studies which follow is that some nation-states have achieved this much more effectively than others.

NOTES

1. Yao-Su Hu *Industrial Banking and Special Credit Institutions: A Comparative Study* (London: Policy Studies Institute, October 1984), pp. 28-9
2. J.K.Galbraith, *Money: Whence It Came, Where it Went* (Harmondsworth, Middlesex: Penguin, 1981) provides a stimulating introduction to this problem.
3. Geoffrey Ingham, *Capitalism Divided: The City and Industry in British Social Development* (London: Macmillan, 1984), pp. 62-78.
4. This argument is implicit in much of the otherwise excellent account of John Zysman, *Governments, Markets and Growth: Financial Systems and the Politics of Industrial Change* (Oxford: Martin Robertson, 1983), *passim*.
5. For an introduction to possible state roles see the useful sort summary in Jacques Leruez, *Economic Planning and Politics in Britain* (London: Martin Robertson, 1975), Introduction.
6. For further details of the range of policies which governments might utilise see: John Pinder, 'Causes and Kinds of Industrial Policy', in John Pinder (ed.), *National Industrial Strategies and the World Economy* (London: Croom Helm, 1982), pp. 44-52
7. For an introduction, See Phillipe C. Schmitter and Gerhard Lehmbruch, *Trends Towards Corporatist Intermediation* (London: Sage, 1979, esp. Chapters 1, 2 and 3.
8. For a discussion of some of the problems experienced in Britain and France, see Andrew Cox and Jack Hayward, 'The Inapplicability of the Corporatist Model in Britain and France: The Case of Labor', *International Political Science Review*, vol. 4 no.2 (1983), pp. 217-40.
9. Gerhard Lehmbruch, 'Introduction: Neo-Corporatism in Comparative Perspective in Gerhard Lembruch and Phillipe C. Schmitter (eds), *Patterns of Corporatist Policy-Making* (London: Sage, 1982), pp. 1-29.
10. For a summary on the United States, see A.D. Chandler, 'The United States, Evolution of Enterprise', in P. Mathias and N.M. Postan, *The Industrial Economies* (Cambridge: Cambridge University Press, 1978). On the transformation of the British state, see Stuart Hall, 'The Representative - Interventionist State, 1880 - 1920s' (Unit 7 States and Society Open University, 1984).
11. Zysman, *op.cit., passim*.
12. Ibid., pp. 78-80.
13. Ibid., pp. 16-18.
14. Ibid., pp. 75-80.
15. Ibid., pp. 93-4.
16. Yao-Su Hu, *National Attitudes and the Financing of Industry* (London: PEP, vol. XLI, Broadsheet no. 559, 1976), pp. 37-8.
17. Hu, *Industrial Banking. op.cit.*, p.19.
18. Hu, *National Attitudes, op.cit.*, p. 18.
19. Ibid., pp. 23.
20. Hu, *Industrial Banking, op.cit.*, pp. 21-26.
21. Cox and Hayward, *op.cit.,Passim*
22. Jack Hayward,'France: the Strategic Management of Impending Collective

Impoverishment', in Andrew Cox (ed.), *Politics, Policy and the European Recession* (London: Macmillan, 1982), pp. 111-40.

23. For further details see Howard Machin and Vincent Wright (eds), *Economic Policy-Making under the Mitterand Presidency, 1981-1984* (London: Frances Pinter, 1985), esp. Chapters 1, 3, 4 and 7.

24. Hu, *National Attitudes op.cit.*, p. 8.

25. Hu, *Industrial Banking op.cit.*, p. 16.

26. Hu, *National Attitudes op.cit.*, pp. 8-12.

27. Ibid., pp. 13-16.

28. Ibid., p. 38.

29. For an extended treatment, see J.K.Galbraith, *The Great Crash 1929* (London: Andre Deutsch, 1979).

30. For a discussion of the Strength of these tendencies see Robert H. Salisbury, 'Why No Corporatism in America?', in Schmitter and Lehmbruch (eds),*Trends Towards Corporatist Intermediation, op.cit.*, pp. 213-30.

31. Robert Reich, *The New American Frontier* (New York: Times Books, 1983; and Lester Thurow, 'The Road to Lemon Socialism', *Newsweek* 25 April 1983), p. 63.

32. Robert Reich, 'Making Industrial Policy', *Foreign Affairs* (Spring 1982), pp. 855-64.

33. Ingham, *op.cit.*; and Hu, *National Attitudes op.cit.*, pp. 26-7.

34. Ingham, ibid., pp. 40-6.

35. Hall, *op.cit.*

36. Hu, *National Attitudes op.cit.*, p. 29.

37. Ibid., pp. 29-32.

38. For details of this see Andrew Cox, *Adversary Politics and Land* (Cambridge: Cambridge University Press, 1984), pp. 155-75.

39. Hu, *Industrial Banking op.cit.*, pp. 23-4.

40. On the failures of the British experience see Andrew Cox, 'Corporatism as Reductionism: The Analytic Limits of the Corporatist Thesis', *Government and Opposition*, vol. 16 no. 1 (Winter 1981), pp. 79-95.

41. Hu, *Industrial Banking op.cit.*, pp.23-7.

42. Howard Machin and Vincent Wright, 'Economic Policy under the Mitterrand Presidency, 1981 - 1984: an Introduction', in Machin and Wright, *op.cit.*, pp. 20-1.

43. *Investing in Britain* (London: Labour Party, September 1985).

2 The State, Finance and Industry in Japan
Bernard Eccleston

In attempting to explain Japan's spectacular economic expansion since the 1950s many writers have stressed the crucial role of the state, but the way this role has been interpreted has varied remarkably. Neo-liberals see Japan as a model for non-interventionist economies where the state merely guides market trends and promotes healthy competition. By contrast, there are other explanations which use the term 'Japan Incorporated' to signify the existence of a national commercial unit headed by a Central Board made up of the elite leaders of big business, the bureaucracy and the ruling LDP politicians.[1]

The focus of the debate in the literature of Japan is not particularly helpful because it brings into sharp relief the difficulty of using crude and ambiguous concepts with which to assess the state's influence. A common quantitative technique used to assess the impact of the state in the economy is to measure the relative share of government spending in GNP. If we compare Japan with the other major capitalist economies in the OECD, we find that in the three decades from 1953 the government share in Japan was equivalent to only 15 per cent of GNP in contrast to over 30 per cent in the OECD as a whole. If this is then related to the evidence that productivity and growth rates in Japan were *double* the OECD average, then it is not difficult to see why neo-liberals place such emphasis on the advantages of free-market capitalism.

However, this approach does seem to put too much weight on the link between direct state *control* of resources and the extent of the state *influence*. For example, as we shall see, the Japanese state does not actually own commercial banks, but that non-ownership hardly lessens state influence. In practice, the commercial banks in Japan are encouraged to lend beyond their means to companies, but in so doing they are in turn dependent on the Central Bank of Japan for short-term credit. There is thus a chain of dependency from the state, through commercial banks to individual companies. This dependency clearly allows the state to influence the flow of credit and, even though the influence is 'indirect', it is hardly less influential. So by concentrating too much on direct state ownership of resources it is all too easy to exaggerate the difference between direct and indirect influences.[2]

Equally, the exponents of the Japan Incorporated view tend to exaggerate the cohesion and uniformity within elite groups. A crude Marxian view of state monopoly capitalism in Japan underestimates the extent of competition between large companies, or the rivalries within and between the bureaucracy and LDP politicians. This view assumes a monolithic dominance of big business over the state which does not reflect the reality of protracted processes of mutual adjustment. The pluralist version of Japan Incorporated sees the state as a neutral, unifying institution which maintains the national interest using traditional values of loyalty and trust in authority as a source of legitimacy. But even these socio-cultural explanations can easily exaggerate the cultural stereotype of a dutiful, deferential population which hardly squares with the visual images of student riots or popular protests. Too often this stress on cultural factors confuses consensus with conformity.[3]

It is the emphasis on consensus *management* by the Japanese state that seems to me to offer the most fruitful approach. Quite apart from the specific techniques which the state uses to implement industrial policy there is a clear attempt to shape a national consensus which places industrial expansion as *the* main economic objective. This objective has been *the* consistent priority in post-war Japan in contrast to other capitalist economies which have tried to juggle full employment, stable prices, rising living standards, counter-cyclical policies, the balance of payments *and* economic growth. There are examples, of course, when recessions have been policy-induced because of rapidly rising prices or deficit foreign balances; at other times the state has been forced to divert resources in order to control the appalling social and environmental costs of the Japanese 'economic miracle'. But, looking at the whole post-war period, the state has constantly and consciously managed to promote the belief that long-term national prestige needed rapid economic growth. It is vital then to recognise the way the state in Japan has interpreted the national interest in terms of faster rates of industrial expansion, and has tended to relegate other economic objectives to second-order priorities.[4]

Not all sectors of Japanese society by any means have benefited from growth-maximisation policies, and throughout the post-war period the state has has to mediate conflict which could threaten what at times seems to be a fragile social consensus. From the late 1960s policy adjustments were necessary to meet the challenge of environmental protest groups, and in the 1970s pressures became stronger to increase state welfare provision. In response, the state did increase pollution controls and social security spending but only after prolonged efforts to keep these items off the political agenda. Changes were made, but with well-publicised reluctance on the grounds that excessive state interference might hold back the overall levels of growth. Economic growth was given a major political dimension as the key factor in guaranteeing Japan's independence and national prestige following the disaster of the Second World War. National survival objectives were translated into economic priorities by the state in order to maintain the social consensus on growth-maximisation.[5]

It is, of course, easy to reinforce policy *objectives* by using nationalistic sentiments, but it is quite another matter to translate these into economic growth rates. If we consider the devastated Japanese economy in the early 1950s, what seems to have been crucial were the decisions to adopt an industrial strategy which emphasised the growth potential of capital-intensive manufacturing processes, and especially in large firms. This emphasis on the role of large-scale conglomerate companies was not new because the whole industrialisation programme in the later nineteenth century had been based on state-supported *zaibatsu* (industrial and financial holding companies). But the depths of post-war economic dislocation and the need to promote self-reliance heightened the need for a *speedy* recovery. Large firms were encouraged to expand their production of high value-added goods in order to break out of the Asian pattern of labour-intensive output. These key industries would render important external economies through input/output links; they would be able to utilise the backlog of technical improvements that had been developed in the West since 1940; finally, they would have better long-term export prospects.[6]

Elite firms in engineering, shipbuilding, steel and motor vehicles were given state aid on a massive scale and were protected from the ravages of competition by import tariffs. Such firms were also to be protected from cyclical recessions by state-organised cartels with the result that the state further institutionalised a dualistic structure of production with a small number of giant firms, and a vast array of small dependent subcontractors. This economic dualism has persisted into the 1980s, as a key platform for economic growth. All capitalist economies have some such differences in firm size, but in Japan's case the sheer scale of the differences between manufacturing firms is remarkable. Even in 1980

58 per cent of manufacturing output is supplied by firms employing less than 100 people compared to 16 per cent in the UK, 17 percent in the US, 18 per cent in West Germany and 23 per cent in France.[7]

State industrial assistance is, then, conspicuously concentrated on larger firms where technical efficiency is greatest, and therefore value added per employee is largest. To a large extent these bigger companies are insulated from excessive competition by state support, and because they can transfer the burden of output adjustment onto smaller subcontractors who are therefore much more prone to bankruptcy. By institutionalising dualism the state underlines the sovereignty of large producers who have the greatest long-term growth potential.

But the implications of state-sponsored dualism extend deeply into the social fabric of Japan partly because the large firms dominate the organisations of state - business coordination. This in consequence divides manufacturers on the basis of firm size and the degree of insulation against market recessions. More importantly *labour* is divided, because employees of larger companies have guarantees of lifetime employment, higher wages and much better non-wage benefits in the form of company housing and welfare schemes. In contrast to the western stereotype of Japanese industrial relations, only *one-third* of labour are given lifetime employment status, and these guarantees are extended predominantly to male workers. The other side of the bargain as far as large firm employees are concerned is that they tend to be much more flexible, pliable and committed to their companies - not least because they have so much to lose if they do not cooperate, as lifetime employment status would be lost if labour moved between companies.[8]

In a very real sense this development of a dualistic structure of production gives Japan a much greater degree of flexibility in adjusting to market trends. Capacity and product changes are facilitated by state assistance and worker docility, but also because adjustment burdens can be transferred to sub-contractors or to temporary employees (mostly women) of large companies. There *is* intense competition between large firms for market shares etc, but the competition is controlled by the state to allow the survival of the fittest. Although a Fair Trading Commission was established by the US Occupation Administration, the chief activity of the FTC 'seems to be the sanctioning and registering of *exceptions* to the law rather than enforcing it'.[9] The national interest in Japan seems to involve 'healthy competition between oligopolists.

Without actually owning a large share of Japan's national resources the state has managed to build up a responsive industrial structure which has achieved remarkable rates of economic growth. Within this responsive structure there is intense competition between large firms, but with a safety net of state support and small subcontractor dependence. Worker cooperation and loyalty in large firms has been bought by lifetime employment guarantees and a state-sponsored system of company unions. Small capitalists and their employees are excluded from such support, but the state has managed to retain the support of these excluded groups for the national growth objectives. Such continuing support has never been satisfactorily explained, but it seems clear from psephological studies that such excluded groups are rarely the ones who turn out to support those parties in Japan who oppose growth-maximising policies. Small-firm employees were not significant supporters of the citizen's environmental protest groups, nor of welfare rights movements.[10]

The key role of the state in Japan then seems to have two aspects: first, to promote and protect large firms with the best long-term prospects. But secondly, to convince those sections of society excluded from specific state support that their sacrifice is needed for the overall achievement of national economic success.

THE STATE AND THE FINANCIAL SECTOR SINCE 1945

The US occupation of Japan from 1945 to 1952 witnessed a major drive to reform social institutions within a liberal democratic framework. Universal franchise was imposed, military groups disbanded, the absentee landowning system abolished, more effective trade unions were encouraged, and the power of giant conglomerate companies undermined. Pre-war industry was dominated by *zaibatsu* groups which combined commercial, finance and industrial capital through interlocking directorships and holding companies. US policy was to dissolve the links which held the *zaibatsu* together. Vast changes were proposed but their complete implementation was, in some ways, diverted by Mao's victory in China and the Korean conflict. External exigencies forced the US to change the emphasis towards speedily reforming Japanese capitalism to provide a more effective anti-communist ally in Asia.

Amidst the social and political turmoil of the early 1950s the bureaucracy was the only group that remained largely intact, as political parties were in disarray and many business leaders had been purged because of their links with militarism. The continuity of elite economic bureaucrats ensured that as administrators of US policies they played a key role in economic recovery. Although integrated *zaibatsu* units were broken up, the larger city banks remained intact but were totally dependent on Bank of Japan support for their continued solvency.[12]

During the 1950s the Ministry of International Trade and Industry (MITI) emerged as the driving force behind the use of heavy industry expansion to support national economic independence. By integrating trade and industry, MITI was able to control the purchase of imported materials and capital goods through trading licences. This meant that favoured large firms could be given direct priority.

However, even in these early years of recovery MITI's authority was hardly absolute. Budget expenditure was closely controlled by the Ministry of Finance (MOF) and Bank of Japan (BOJ) officials, who were obsessed with the need to adopt a conservative, balanced budget after the inflationary ravages of 1945-49. In the protracted friction within the state bureaucracy, expansionist MITI policies were frequently implemented through circuitous off-budget channels, but conservative state finance priorities generally forced MITI to use more vigorous 'indirect' policies to ensure an adequate supply of investment finance.

Rapid industrial expansion clearly led to a vigorous demand for investment finance, but Japanese companies had few reserves of their own to finance such expansion. By breaking the close institutional links of the *zaibatsu*, US policies further exposed the weakness inherent in grossly inadequate equity capital markets. Investment needs were indeed immense and it is well known that investment in Japan has been regularly double the average OECD levels at not less than 30 per cent of GNP. It is also widely appreciated that savings ratios are also higher in Japan, but from the early 1950s the state moulded the growth of financial institutions to keep savers and investors separated, thus reserving a key intermediary role for state agencies.[12]

One outstanding feature of Japanese society is this high savings propensity, and for households the most important form of deposit is in the Post Office system. Local savings through post offices have been vital in Japan since industrialisation began in the mid-nineteenth century, but their importance has been strengthened as a source of deposit collection. Tax exemption on interest paid by the Post Office is given automatically, and the constraint of maximum limits on each individual account can be evaded by opening different accounts in other names. Returns from Post Office savings are therefore very lucrative, but the ubiquitous distribution of post offices even in rural areas adds advantages of access. The accounts themselves are very flexible with a variety of very competitive rates offered to depositors for short and long-term deposits and a national system of cash dispensers to facilitate withdrawals. These advantages are compounded by restrictions on the ability of other financial institutions to compete as deposit collectors, for example through controls on commercial bank branching. [13]

Saving propensities are undoubtedly influenced by the absence of effective state welfare payments, the tendency to pay biannual productivity bonuses in lump sums, and by rising incomes. However, these explanations of Japanese frugality are clearly influenced by the relative underdevelopment of consumer credit and mortgage finance institutions. Access to financial markets for consumption is restricted, and consequently the level of individual financial liabilities is low in comparative terms.

In these ways the growth and flow of household savings are guided through Post Office accounts, but the use of these funds for investment is channelled through separate institutions. The state has maintained this fragmentation to ensure control over allocation. Aggregate savings ratios are also high in the corporate and state sectors. Obviously, companies find it cheaper and easier to finance their own investment and very rapid growth has increased their ability to use retained profits. In common with the capitalist economies Japan offers a range of tax exemptions on self-finance; equally important though, is the tendency for city banks to require larger deposits as loan collateral.

Self-finance by companies was clearly crucial once expansion was underway, but in the 1950s the state's own savings were vital in getting the expansion started. Lower social spending and fiscal drag were key factors in translating conservative state budgeting into substantial state surpluses up to the mid-1970s. These direct savings, and the use by the state of Post Office deposits, provided the resources for direct industrial assistance, but equally important was the state's role as a financial intermediary.

City banks are the principal source of short-term and trade finance for industry by placing restrictions on the ability of city banks to collect deposits or issue bank bonds, the state limited their independence. The role of city banks as aggressive lenders to industry was actively encouraged, but in view of limits placed on their deposit-taking role this placed heavy burdens on their liquidity. Such burdens were relieved through Bank of Japan finance which created a massive level of dependency on the Central Bank. This dependency was not mediated through market mechanisms of reserve asset and interest rate adjustment however, but through direct credit rationing. Market mechanisms were thought to be far too uncertain, and given the insulation from international money markets, the Japanese authorities have long preferred more specific allocation of credit. If, for example, the BOJ wanted to restrict credit then less emphasis was placed on raising interest rates or increasing reserve ratios, instead quantitative credit ceilings were imposed to force city banks to cut back loans.[14]

Only since the late 1970s has credit rationing been replaced by limited market mechanisms, and even then the forced sale of state bonds to city banks has constrained freedom of adjustment. Thus the liquidity burdens on city banks is still critical given their tendency to over-lend relative to deposits.

Coordination between the BOJ and city banks is exceptionally close given the extent of dependence on BOJ support, and this is extended to the ways city banks implement changes in loan ceilings by reallocating loan priorities between competing borrowers. These relatively 'indirect' methods of investment allocation were further supplemented by directly channelling state surpluses through other specialist banks. Loans and subsidies for controlled licences to export or to import crucial materials and capital goods were given through the Export-Import Bank. Long-term equipment loans were supplied through the Japan Development Bank. State support was largely financed from Post Office savings through the Fiscal Investment and Loan Plan (FILP) which could supply resources to these quasi-public corporations. As only quasi-public institutions, FILP support lay outside rigid budget balancing restrictions placed by MOF and Diet authorities, and such loans provided up to one-third of key sector borrowing in the early years of economic recovery.[15]

Even this level of support underestimates the state's importance, because if a company received FILP support this acted as a seal of approval for further loans from private banks. If MITI 'designated' a firm or an industrial sector, then this approval acted as a guarantee for further loans which were frequently syndicated via quasi-public companies.

Credit availability was thus controlled in a variety of ways by the state, and the principal beneficiaries were large firms where long-term growth potential was greatest. Not only was credit allocation protected for larger companies, but also the cost of borrowing was constrained. Until the second oil shock of the later 1970s the macro-economic priority was to keep interest rates low in order to maintain high levels of industrial investment. BOJ support for city banks meant credit was allocated at an interest rate *lower* than short-term market rates thus removing any financial motive for city banks to reduce their over-lending. Equally, there emerged a hidden subsidy for larger companies in the form of preferential interest rates. In a nation of surplus savings it was not difficult to keep depositors's interest rates down, especially when competition in deposit collection was controlled to favour post offices. But the other side of the coin for non-designated smaller firms, would be higher interest rates and secondary loan priority.

At the macro level the state in Japan has managed the financial markets by controlling the links between savers and investors in a fragmented and specialised structure. City banks are encouraged to over-lend to maintain the expansion of industry, but in the process they become dependent on the BOJ. This dependence allows much greater coordination in day-to-day lending activities, but the ultimate threat of withdrawing short-term Central Bank support is known to be unlikely. City banks gain the prestige of being associated with leading national firms and the advantage of paying lower rates for Central Bank support. The state has an immensely powerful lever for its priorities on industrial investment, which it supplements with inter-agency personnel transfers especially of early-retiring officials.

Such intimate levels of dependency have obviously been challenged in the 1980s by the international pressures to liberalise financial markets. Such pressures have been impossible to resist given the continuing trade frictions between Japan and the West. But liberalising markets in Japan has been shrouded with safeguards so that there are still important provisions in the legislation to suspend freedom of capital flows in exceptional circumstances, which in the usual Japanese manner were not specified.

Amongst conservative Japanese politicians an even bigger danger to the operation of financial markets is seen in the form of the substantial growth in budget deficits since 1975/76. This trend has removed the flow of state surpluses, and there are fears that financing such large public sector deficits will crowd out private sector investment by absorbing an increasingly large share of savings. It is difficult with such recent trends to isolate the effect of increasing state deficits, but there has been an increased drive to improve the terms and flexibility for Post Office depositors in an effort to bridge the fiscal gap. Private sector investment has dropped from the peak levels of the early 1970s, but it is clear that companies are not as keen to increase capacity as fast as in earlier years because of the world recession. Consequently, it is doubtful whether sluggish investment levels in the early 1980s are solely due to excessive state deficits.[16]

INDUSTRY AND THE FINANCIAL SECTOR

The corollary of city bank over-lending in Japan is seen in corporate sector over-borrowing which extends the chain of dependency to individual companies so that city banks are 'merely a channel through which the Central Bank feeds industry with funds'.[17] Given the enormous increase in corporate investment which would have been impossible to finance through their own savings, Japanese companies rely to a larger extent on external funds than is usual in the West. What really distinguishes Japanese experience though, is the extent of dependency on bank borrowing.

International comparisons of corporate financial flows are extremely difficult to standardise, but it does appear that corporate borrowing from banks in Japan provides over two-thirds of finance needed compared to only one-third amongst other OECD economies. External finance is important elsewhere - for example, in West Germany - but in Japan banks rather than other financial institutions predominate. Equity share markets never really developed in Japan because *zaibatsu* groups coordinated in-house industrial finance, and equity stock markets were not a priority for the state in the early post-war reforms. Other financial institutions were very slow to develop because of the way the state consciously directed city banks into extensive and aggressive industrial lending.

Company asset and liquidity ratios appear to be much lower in Japan which gives an impression of a risky fragile financial structure because external or indirect sources of finance are thought to be much more uncertain and difficult to manage. However, terms like 'indirect' or 'external' are ambiguous concepts not least where extensive bank-industry cooperation - or even joint management - is present. Although explicit *zaibatsu* links were broken and exclusive in-house banking prohibited, close coordination between banks and their major customers is very common in Japan. Institutional factors like city bank illiquidity reinforces this cooperation; where large loans are made to individual companies the banks are perforce interested in the financial management of their big borrowers.

Personal exchanges are key avenues of close consultation as they are between the Central and city banks. BOJ support is closely related to the achievements of prestige companies and it is therefore logical for city banks to engage in day-to-day consultation at management level. Even for those firms who depend less on bank loans and more on their own savings, the established norm of bank - industry cooperation persists, placing Japan closer to the German or French models of industrial banking practices.

Joint financial management greatly helps larger firms to adjust capacity quickly especially because large parent companies act as a funnel guarantor of their dependent subcontractors. Credit restrictions may be transferred to smaller firms by extending the repayment periods on post-dated credit notes, which account for over a half of small firm revenues.[18] Thus the web of dependency is completed from the state to the very smallest of family workshops.

Corporate over-borrowing and city bank over-lending have been reinforced in importance as key characteristics of Japanese finance by the sharp fluctuations in the rate of economic growth. Orchestrated and coordinated spurts of capacity growth have induced further excess lending and borrowing trends. Recessions have been the burden of adjustment passed down the line to have the greatest impact on financially dependent subcontractors and their unprotected work-force. Japanese industry is able to climb quickly out of recessions because dualism continues to be supported by state protection for large firms who are in the national interest 'too big to fail'. In contrast 'one third of companies with less than 20 workers go bankrupt every five years, and one half every ten'.[19]

THE STATE AND INDUSTRY

The depth of financial interdependency within Japanese industry is one key factor which makes it difficult to distinguish direct from indirect state intervention. Explicit and detailed instructions to companies concerning output of investment are relatively rare, but there are a wide variety of consultative organs which coordinate decisions on economic activity amongst the prestige companies. It is as misleading to think of this coordination as state prescription as it is to suggest that it allows free-market adjustments. MITI in particular seeks to provide a forum within which reactions to market trends can be organised to ensure, workable competition' for large firms, thus maintaining national priorities on economic growth.

What this has meant in practice in that MITI has guided the response of industry to both short and long-term economic change. Long-term needs have meant the identification of whole industrial sectors as priority areas for expansion or contraction. For example, the earliest MITI advise in the 1950s was to contract labour-intensive sectors like textiles or food-processing in favour of capital-intensive sectors like chemicals, metals, engineering and motor vehicles. In turn, the 1970s saw the shipbuilding and metals sectors designated as 'throw-away' industries to be replaced by knowledge-intensive industries such as microtechnics. It is the vast commerical intelligence gathering aspects of MITI's work that generates the flow of information on market trends and potential. Through MITI's leadership of a variety of consultative institutions this intelligence is pooled among larger companies.[20]

This kind of state support is not unknown in other western economies, but there is a sharp difference in the extent to which MITI coordinated the flow of information on technical and product changes in competitor states. Accusations of industrial espionage have been frequently aimed at MITI as the Japanese tend to devote fewer resources to basic R/D, but more to the improvement of engineering techniques developed overseas. MITI's own research facilities help to socialise the risks of technical change for Japanese companies, and overseas missions assist in the purchase of patent rights. R/D expenditure is thus made more effective, and the colossal gambles of prestige projects like Concorde or gas-cooled atomic energy are avoided.

Long-term aims are embodied in economic plans produced by the Economic Planning Agency, although the specific output targets mentioned in such plans are thought to be as unreliable as long-range forecasts.[21] In fact, the consistency with which planning targets underestimate private sector growth and overestimate public sector performance have given rise to the view that Japanese planning through the EPA is merely a cosmetic exercise. Five year plans are however a useful medium through which MITI can set the agenda for consultative groups, particularly when sector changes are designated. The ability and willingness of firms to switch to different product lines is an unusual feature of Japanese capitalism, which highlights market adjustment through diversification of existing firms, rather than the entry of new ones. 'Throw-away' sectors are designated to encourage firms to plan the process of diversification early, rather than wait for losses to force change.

Administrative 'guidance' by MITI of industrial change is implemented through a wide range of consultative agencies where requests, suggestions and encouragement may be backed by more positive financial promises or threats. Incentives to change are hardly different from those used for example in the EEC: depreciation allowances, tax exemptions or credit on new processes, state loans or subsidies. But what does differ is the thoroughness with which MITI orchestrates the use of investment incentives through city bank dependence on the BOJ.

Short-term adjustment to capacity is coordinated through a similar mix of consultation and financial inducements. But in recessions rationalisation cartels supplement MITI's 'guidance'. In industries like steel, shipbuilding and petrochemicals economies of scale are so immense that small subcontractors have a smaller share of capacity and cannot be used to bear the burden of reducing output. Therefore to combat the threat of cut-throat competition between large firms, MITI organises the reduction of output shares on a quota basis which makes adjustment more orderly and guarantees the survival of market leaders. Knowing that cartel quota allocation will be largely determined by market shares though, encourages more vigorous competition for markets in expansionary phases. Thus the intensity of the upswing is increased, but the consequences of recession are mediated by cartels.[22]

These operations give important clues to what MITI means by workable competition: maximum flexibility for large companies to assist in Darwinian selection processes for firms and facilitate long-term growth potential. This interpretation of competition does appear to operate in direct contravention of anti-monopoly legislation, and the plethora of exceptions and amendments negotiated in this area indicates the relative strength of MITI *vis à vis* other bureaucrats especially in the FTC. 'Workable competition' involves promotion of market-share rivalries between large firms but with a recession safety-net of state support and guidance. Although this has generally been coordinated through mutual cooperation, increasing liberalisation of foreign markets has given some companies the strength to offer resistance to MITI priorities.

This more independent stance by big business was especially noticeable in the reaction of companies to the first oil shock in 1974, when a wave of speculative price increases and profiteering swept Japan. At the same time as companies resisted MITI's guidance, LDP politicians were attempting to reduce MITI's economic role in favour of greater Diet control. The public reaction to the impact of freer markets and the controversial links between Tanaka and the Lockheed bribery scandal seems to have boosted MITI's longstanding claims as protector of the national interest because, in the second oil shock in 1979, MITI was able to reclaim a supervisory role: 'Given the general development imperatives of post-war Japan, the public has been willing to accept the trade-off between bureaucrats occasionally exceeding their mandate and quicker more effective economic administration'.[23] Hence MITI's guidance is projected as the legitimate route to integrating national economic priorities through 'workable competition'.

Big business undoubtedly gains from their close cooperation with MITI's long-term policies especially in terms of their penetration of world export markets. The instances of guidance resistance by Japanese companies are not extensive and overall, the benefits of cooperation appear to outweigh the occasional periods when MITI's advice is perceived as a threat.

THE PROBLEM OF LIBERALISATION IN THE 1980s

Japanese finance markets appear to have several interrelated features based on over-borrowing by city banks from the Bank of Japan, over-lending to companies, a high proportion of external finance from bank loans and the separation of savers from investors. In comparative terms this may appear to be a fragile structure, but in practice the reality is for the state to 'pool, socialize and diversify risk',[24] for city banks and for large firms. The risk of relying on external loans are mediated through joint financial management, and the financial problems for city banks in relying on BOJ support are ameliorated by lower interest rates paid for these support funds. In a clear fashion the state holds the key intermediary role.

There have been changes in recent years to some components of the system. Interest rate adjustment is more important; foreign capital flows more liberalised; the issue of public deficit bonds has grown dramatically and the extent of FILP assistance has fallen. Superficially it could be argued that the state plays a more indirect role, but the constraints on freer financial markets are still important. The Japanese state has never conceded that market forces always operate in the national interest, and freedom for capital flows is hesitantly conceded because of the potential effects on exchange rates and the balance of payments. Qualifying clauses have been inserted into the legal framework on free competition because 'this method of distributing the benefits of high growth stifles the conditions for growth'.[25] Such 'conditions for growth' have plainly been interpreted as 'workable competition' for prestige companies in post-war Japan. Thus even with less overt state intervention in investment allocation it remains vital to guarantee the financial prospects of market leaders. Daily links through city banks are maintained to socialise the risks of investment in industrial plant. Such an intermediary role is not unusual, but what distinguishes Japan from other capitalist economies is the concentration on the needs of industry rather than housing or social expenditures.

How significant is the change to what appears to be a more indirect role? It is clear that FILP funds take a smaller share of private investment, but the state have moulded the financial institutions to match the needs of large manufacturing firms so state direction could now be said to work on an automatic pilot. Where necessary, the state will intervene directly to protect large firms, but financial structures have been so carefully programmed to make this a rare occurrence. In many ways the direct/indirect distinction is tangled up with normative judgements made by western economists on the role of market allocation versus planning in liberal democratic economies. G. C. Allen puts it this way: 'although government has fostered growth by various devices it certainly did not and could not prescribe the policy to follow. Therefore it is misleading to say the Japanese economy is centrally planned'.[26] 'Prescribe' is the key word because the democratic process appears to conflict with the potential of the state to use its authority to enforce policies.

In financial terms the state does have the power to prescribe, because of the levels of dependency which link the Bank of Japan to individual companies through city banks. The fact that the BOJ has rarely used outright threats to enforce policy does not negate the potential to do so. What matters is that financial dependency is an important institutional feature which reinforces the search for mutually acceptable allocations of finance. One might agree with Allen that the state *tends* not to prescribe policy for firms, but one could also dispute the assessment that it *could* not.

By linking state intervention in Japan with the term 'central planning', liberal economists draw two false trails concerning the ability to prescribe in a democracy, and the relatively low levels of state industrial ownership.

There is no doubt that the Japanese state spends a smaller share of GNP than in the West, but by itself this aggregate can be misleading. In fact, the main disparity has been in the area of lower Japanese current government *consumption* and welfare transfers rather than state *investment*. FILP funds have declined relative to private investment, but even a small state loan acts as signal of approval for private financial institutions. These signals are much more important than the persistently unreliable EPA targets, but this does not imply that state control is inadequate because other bureaucrats encourage private expansion beyond targets, whilst finance officials constrain public spending below targets. Planning by the EPA has a political and cosmetic function which has frequently been overridden by competing national priorities.[27]

It is common to measure the degree of state influence along a spectrum from market capitalism to socialist planning on the basis of government shares of GNP, but this is a very crude measure. The Japanese state has endeavoured to manage its budget so as to reduce future commitments to social spending, or to prop up loss-making lame ducks. It does spend less in aggregate but expenditure in concentrated in industrial sectors where growth potential is greatest.

Neither the deficiencies of indicative planning nor the lower levels of state spending in Japan in any way diminish the economic importance of state intervention. But does this intervention contravene the spirit of representative democracy?

If Japan Inc. is interpreted as a conspiratorial business committee of the bourgeoisie, then the examples of rivalries within big business, the bureaucracy and the LDP seem to cast doubt on the adequacy of Japan Inc. as an explanation of state intervention. It is certainly difficult to pinpoint an independent locus of power, be it big business or the bureaucracy. But the existence of pluralist-style rivalries cannot diminish the impact of the continuing promotion of industrial growth as an ideology by elite groups. Economic or commercial supremacy has replaced military dominance as the unifying national goal and the state has played a key role in maintaining a consensus on this overarching objective.

It is too easy though, to take cultural preferences for group harmony as *the* defining feature of social consensus, because this explanation implies national conformity. What is more important is the creative role the state takes in mobilising and managing consensus values especially when conflict is apparent. The state has led the moves to convince groups who have been marginalised by the economic miracle, that their sacrifices are worth bearing for the long-term national interest.[28]

For example, western images of industrial relations in Japan are dominated by the unusual degree of company loyalty and deference to authority. This pattern of work relations is said to be based on Japan's unique social values but 'like other peoples the Japanese are not averse to inventing traditions'.[29] Company unions and lifetime employment guarantees were initiated on a limited scale in the 1920s to combat rapid labour turnover, and the advantages of this system of labour relations were actively promoted by the state through Employers' Federations in the early 1950s. Company unions develop levels of dependence which directly counteract the power of industrial unions and reduce the strength of militant workers. Hence the privileged third of workers who have employment guarantees also become tied to a growth-maximising ideology which promotes their own long-term individual interests through the rising incomes and benefits that are associated with large company expansion.

The remaining two-thirds of the labour force are less well paid, less unionised, more subject to unemployment, etc. , but their inferior position is justified by their educational background and gender. Sexism is deeply embedded in Japanese employment structures so that women are relegated into a flexible reserve army because 'men are superior beings entitled to many rights not granted to women'.[30] In a similar way, male workers who are not the top graduates of the top universities cannot gain access to lifetime employment status in large firms, but are 'encouraged to make sacrifices as a matter of course to serve the national interest in catching up with and surpassing the West'.[31] Small capitalists are exhorted to bear their uncertainties because they are not so efficient as their parent companies. The most they can hope is that their cooperation with major contractors will be rewarded with orders whenever expansion of output is needed. Small employers do tend to form the backbone of LDP political support in urban areas, so it seems that conservative anti-communist policies compensate for their inferior economic position.

There are many other 'creatively applied weapons in the conservative arsenal'[32] such as the way household savings are projected to be part of the Japanese tradition of family self-help. Such cultural supports tend to maintain the flow of Post Office deposits as well as justifying the lower levels of state welfare. In the early 1980s the spectre of 'the British disease of low productivity and higher state welfare' was raised to divert pressures for increased public social security payments.

There have been examples when even the LDP's brand of creative conservatism has not maintained consensus. Despite fierce resistance to environmental pollution controls the scale of protest was such that in the early 1970s Japan moved from being the worst to the most protected society. But three things are interesting about this switch: (1) how MITI fought to resist the control legislation; (2) how the LDP took credit for the environmental legislation and for appearing to be stronger than MITI; and (3) the way the oil crises 1974-79 widened the gap between legal principles and implementation.

Over the whole post-war period there have been close personal connections between members of the LDP, big business and the bureaucracy based on the homogeneous social and educational background. Personnel transfers are common at mid-career levels because civil servants tend to retire early on relatively low pensions and need to find employment. This movement, know as *Amakudari*, (or descent from heaven(!)) is to some extent institutionalised by the organisation of controlled lending spots in firms, banks or public companies where connections with Ministry interests are strong.[33] Early retirees also go into the Diet as MPs; and ex-MITI bureaucrats often emerge as MITI Cabinet Ministers. These transfers clearly add to the potential for future cooperation although there are sufficient examples of interest conflict to cast doubt on the existence of a monolithic Japan Inc.

By selectively interpreting Japan Inc. as a monolithic organisation pluralists do ease the task of undermining the explanatory value of the model. If we see Japan Inc. as a creative conservative ideology though, we can allow for short-term adjustments and rivalries, but maintain the long-term priority for economic growth. Even the violent opposition of environmental groups confined their resistance to abstaining from LDP support rather than positively supporting opposition parties. Creative conservatism gives the appearance of mutual adjustment between interest groups when in reality access to state coordination varies markedly. If the term 'corporation' is to be used in Japan it should, as Pempel suggests, be corporatism without labour - and we could add, without small business.[34]

When measured in economic trends of productivity or industrial growth rates, the Japanese economic miracle can been seen starkly in terms of its rise to the top of the world economic league table. Clearly the way the state has selectively promoted the development of leading companies through its role as a financial intermediary has been fundamentally important. Equally intriguing is the way the state has managed the conflicting interests of groups who have suffered the social consequences of rapid economic growth.

Whether we define state intervention as direct or indirect, the role of the state is enormously important. Even if we accept the term 'administrative guidance' as a description of state involvement it is as well to remember that this is translated as *yudo kisei*, where *yudo* means stronger force as in *yudo bakudan* - a guided missile!

NOTES

1. A useful review of the literature on Japan Inc. can be found in the chapter by Harushiro Fuki in *Policy-Making in Contemporary Japan* (Cornell University Press 1977) ed. T. J. Pempel. Two issues of *Technology Review* (July 1981; July 1983) are also good general surveys of views of Japan Inc. and management practices.

2. Yoshio Suzuki, *Money and Banking in Contemporary Japan* (University Press, Yale 1980) is helpful for a survey of finance in general, but it is now a little dated given recent changes in monetary policies.

3. The role of social and cultural values in Japan is developed by N. Glazer in *Asia's New Giant*, ed. H. Patrick and H. Rosovsky (Washington Brookings Institute, 1976). An alternative approach may be found in J. V. Koschman, *Authority and the Individual in Japan* (University of Tokyo Press, 1978). The latest attempt to relate a cultural focus to Japan's economic miracle is Michio Moroshima, *Why Has Japan Succeeded? Western Technology and the Japanese Ethos* (Cambridge University Press, 1982)

4. An excellent introduction to the role of the state in Japan's economic development is C. Johnson, *MITI and the Japanese Miracle* (Stanford University Press 1982).

5. On environmental policy changes, see S. R. Reed, 'Environmental Politics', in *Comparative Politics* (April 1981). For protest groups, see M. McKean *Environmental Protest and Citizen Politics in Japan* (University of California Press, 1981). Welfare changes are an important aspect considered by J. C. Campbell, 'The Old People; Boom and Japanese Policymaking', in *The Journal of Japanese Studies 5* (Summer 1981).

6. Johnson, *op. cit.*, ch. 6.

7. The most detailed assessment of the impact of dualism in Japan in F. Twaalfhoven and T. Hattori, *The Supporting Role of Small Japanese Enterprises* (Holland Indivers Research, 1982).

8. See R. E. Cole, 'Permanent Employment in Japan: Facts and Fantasies', *Industrial and Labour Relations Review* 26 (1972). An alternative Marxian view is offered by R. Stevens, 'The Japanese Working Class', *Bulletin of Concerned Asian Scholars* 12, 3 (1980).

9. E. M. Hadley, *Antitrust in Japan* (Princeton University Press, 1970, p. 445.

10. See S. C. Flanagan and M. B. Richardson, 'Japanese Electoral Behaviour', *Contemporary Political Sociology* 2 (1977); and R. Benjamin and K. Ori, *Tradition and Change in Post-Industrial Japan* (Praeger, 1981).

11. Johnson, *op. cit.*, ch. 5.

12. A good introduction to aggregate savings and investment patterns can be found in A. Boltho, *Japan an Economic Survey* (Oxford University Press 1975), ch. 4.

13. E. Sakakibara and R. A. Feldman, 'The Japanese Financial System in Comparative Perspective', in *Journal of Comparative Economics* 7 (1983), pp. 15-17.

14. Andreas R. Prindl, *Japanese Finance* New York: J. Wiley & Sons, (1981), ch. 3.

15. C. Johnson's *Japan's Public Policy Companies* (Washington Hoover Institute, 1978) contains an excellent review of FILP operations.

16. Quantitative studies of public sector deficits have been a main feature of annual *Economic Surveys* of Japan issued by OECD in the 1980s.

17. G. C. Allen, *The Japanese Economy* (London Weidenfeld/Nicolson, 1981), p. 59.

18. Twaalfhoven and Hattori *op. cit.*, p. 31.

19. J. Greenwood, 'Darwinian Selection in Japanese Business', *The Times* 25

November 1974.
20. See *Industry and Business in Japan* ed. K. Sato (Croom Helm, 1980), Ch. 4. and Johnson, *op. cit.*, ch. 6.
21. A critical review of Japanese planning can be found in T. Watanabe, 'National Planning and Economic Development', *Economics of Planning*, 10, no. 1 (1970). For the bureaucratic view, see R. Komiya and K. Yamamoto, 'Japan: the officer in charge', *History of Political Economy*, (13 March 1981).
22. The operation of cartels is usefully described in R. Komiya 'Planning in Japan', in Morris Bernsteid (ed.) *Economic Planning East and West* (Cambridge, Mass., 1979).
23. Johnson, *op. cit.*, p. 273.
24. Sakakibara and Feldman, *op. cit.*, p. 20.
25. Johnson, *op. cit.*, p. 256.
26. Allen, *op. cit.*, p. 192.
27. Watanabe, *op. cit.*, p. 48.
28. See T. J. Pempel and K. Taurekawa, 'Corporations without Labour', in *Trends Towards Corporatist Intermediation*, ed. G. Lembrusch and P. Schmitter, (New York Sage, 1976).
29. K. Okochi, B. Karsh and S. B. Levine, *Workers and Employers in Japan* (Princeton University Press, 1973) p. 13.
30. Susan Pharr, 'Women in Japan', in L. Austin (ed.), *Japan the Paradox of Progress* (Cambridge: Yale University Press, 1976) p. 305.
31. H. Khan, *The Emerging Japanese Superstate* Harmondsworth: Penguin, 1973), p. 132.
32. T. J. Pempel, *Policy and Politics in Japan, Creative Conservatism* (Temple University Press, 1982) p. 298.
33. C. Johnson, *Public Policy Companies* ch. 5.
34. Pempel and Taurekawa, *op. cit.*

3 The State, Finance and Industry in France
Diana Green

It is often said the French do not love their industry. . . To be accurate,
it is the market economy, rather than industry, whose necessity the
French question. . . they accept competition only when it is tamed,
that is, when it can do them no harm. They tolerate profit, but only
when profiteers are sanctioned. It's true, French Society has not
assimilated the modern industrial culture.

(J. D. Lefranc, 1983 p. 159)

France, like Britain, is nominally a mixed economy in which a substantial
public sector exists alongside a predominantly privately-owned industrial
structure. Yet French capitalism differs from the Anglo-Saxon model in
a number of important ways. First, French capitalism is state-sponsored
capitalism. H. Luthy (1955) suggested that it is 'synthetic capitalism'. This
is perhaps going too far, but does draw attention to the fact that French
capitalism is profoundly anti-market. State intervention is a very long-
standing tradition in France. Since Colbert drew up the first industrial
plan in the seventeenth century, governments have tended to 'guide'
industrial development. This predilection for 'administered industrialisation' springs from a deep-rooted mistrust of market forces. The market
is too blunt and too ineffective a tool to be entrusted with the delicate
task of managing industrial change. Secondly, the French have never fully
accepted the logic of free trade. Indeed, they believe that such a philosophy
is both irrational and damaging. Their logic is deceptively simple: if the
overriding aim is to increase the nation's productive power, the domestic
industry has to be protected. State protection, initially in the shape of
tariff barriers, was therefore seen as the logical means of assisting the
growth of domestic industries. France thus acquired a reputation for being
the most highly protected and cartelised economy in the West - a reputation
which it has proved difficult to shake off.

The French tradition is mercantilist. The mercantilist creed called for
the state to promote national economic power and create a unified national

economy. Whereas mercantilism was repudiated in Britain (by Adam Smith and the classical economists), in France the state continued to play this role and guided the economy through the period of industrialisation. While the English bourgeoisie saw the government as a constraint from which little if any good would come, the French saw the state as both a necessary agent for the protection of established positions, and a means of creating new wealth. (Zysman, 1977). Mercantilist principles shape economic and industrial policies in France even today.

A critical determinant of, and prerequisite for, state intervention of this kind and on this scale is the centralised nature of the French administrative system. The French state is a bureaucratic structure invented by Napoleon and imposed on a recalcitrant and fundamentally anarchic populace. The creation of this centralised, hierarchical system (modelled on the structure of the army) was arguably an attempt to eliminate politics by bureaucratising it. As Thoenig (1973) points out, centralisation in the French context is not simply the concentration of power in the hands of a small social élite. The French state is not a monolithic entity; the commanding heights of the polity are stratified and caste-ridden. Within the administration, the key figures are the mobile meritocratic élites known as the *grands corps*. These officials who are seen - and see themselves - as the privileged interpreters and guardians of the 'general interest', provide an essential corrective to the systemic rigidity and compartmentalism (Suleiman 1974; Hayward, 1983). The close ties developed during their years at the élite training institutions (the Ecole Polytechnique, Ecole Nationale des Mines, Ecole des Ponts et Chaussees, and *ENA*, the National Administrative School) create and sustain vital 'old boy networks' which are the back-bone of coordination within the civil service. More importantly for our purposes here, the tradition of *pantouflage* ensures that *grand corps* members leave the civil service at mid-career and take up senior management positions in public and private corporations, in the financial sector or go directly into politics. Thus, at the personal level, financial and industrial capital are linked to the state, facilitating state interference and control.

STATE OWNERSHIP AND CONTROL: THE NATIONALISED SECTOR

Even before the 1982 nationalisations, the state had a substantial stake in both the industrial and financial sectors. Since the first nationalisation in the seventeenth century, the extension of the state ownership has been continuous but sporadic. Although the 1936 Popular Front regime was reponsible for a major phase of nationalisation, public ownership has not been exclusively associated with the left. It was under de Gaulle's aegis, immediately after the Second World War, that a further extension of state ownership took place, together with the introduction of national economic planning. More recently, under the neo-liberal Giscardian regime, the state took control of a blocking minority in the Dassault Aerospace corporation and effectively nationalised the bankrupt steel companies, Usinor and Sacilor (Green, 1981). Before 1982, then, nationalisation was dictated by a wide variety of motives; from rationalisation (the public utilities) to the creation of state-owned agencies in strategic sectors (The Atomic Energy Commission) or, more prosaically, to bail out lame ducks.

It is impossible to determine precisely where the boundaries of the French public sector lie *inter alia* because the number of concerns in which the state owns (directly or indirectly) a minority shareholding fluctuates. Worries about 'creeping nationalisation' prompted a Senate investigation in 1976: this found that, although the number of parent companies had fallen by about 22 per cent over the previous 18 years as a result of privatisation, the number of subsidiaries held by the public enterprises (which escape parliamentary control) has increased by something like 135 percent over the same period.[1]

The pre-1982 nationalised sector was characterised by two main types of public enterprise: the public service monopolies (the grandes enterprises nationales or GEN) and industrial and commercial corporations (such as Renault and the aerospace groups, SNECMA and SNIAS) which were run like private sector firms. The public service monopolies have played a vital role in capital accumulation throughout the whole of the post-war period. After 1973, the nuclear energy and telecommunications programmes fulfilled a counter-cyclical function, compensating for the stagnation of private sector investment. The investment of the GEN accounted for about 25 per cent of total capital investment between 1973 and 1980.

Most of the firms in the market economy public sector have experienced relatively little direct interference on the part of government. This is particularly true of Renault which, by managing to combine commercial success with social responsibility, was seen as a model for other public enterprises to follow (Green 1981a). The oil companies, Elf-Aquitaine and Total-CFP, have been less fortunate. Although, ostensibly, these are joint enterprises, governments have continuously asserted their management rights and interfered in commercial decisions, despite having minority holdings.[2]

In the financial sector, the state increased its potential control by nationalising the four major deposit banks and a number of insurance companies in 1946. The behaviour of these banks (reduced to three in 1966) has differed little from that of the private, commercial banks; their networks, both at home and abroad have been extended with the minimum of governmental interference. Before 1982, then, nationalisation effectively constituted the cornerstone of state capitalism.

The socialist government's 1982 nationalisation programme was dictated by political considerations (a manifesto commitment) even though this was played down. Nationalisation was presented as part of an industrial strategy which accords public sector investment a 'locomotive' role, mobilising economic growth and creating jobs. State ownership was to be extended into competitive advanced technology sectors (such as information technology) which should take over and continue the investment effort previously carried out by nuclear energy and telecommunications. Since nationalisation was also a means of rescuing a number of lame duck groups,[3] the economic and financial logic was questionable from the outset.

The 1982 nationalisations did, however, significantly increase the size of the French public sector: state-owned companies now account for 18 per cent of industrial employment, 25 per cent of industrial investment and turnover, and 32 percent of exports.[4] Public enterprises now account for 95 per cent of steel production, 35 percent of chemicals, 84 per cent of aerospace production, and more than 40 percent of electronics. In the financial sector, state-owned corporations account for 87 percent of bank deposits and 81 per cent of credits in metropolitan France.[5]

NATIONAL PLANNING

The French have operated national economic planning since the end of the Second World War. The first, and arguably the only 'true' Plan, marked both an increase in the scale and a change in the nature of state intervention (Kuisel, 1981). The aim in these early years was to reconstruct, then modernise and develop, the structure of industry. In this very basic sense, national planning exemplified an approach to what is today called 'industrial policy'. It is important to emphasise here that planning was not, and is not, concerned with the management of resources on a day-to-day basis. Put another way, despite various attempts to link it more closely with the state budget (Green, 1980; Hayward, 1984) its relationship to and impact on, macro-economic policies has always been tenuous. The fact that the Planning Commission has no executive authority and no financial resources of its own puts the onus of Plan implementation on the 'spending' ministries and the Finance Ministry.

In the early post-war years, the planners were influential. They helped allocate Marshall Aid funds to underwrite the reconstruction effort and had some control over private sector investment. Modernisation and liberalisation (after France joined the EEC) weakened this influence. From the Second Plan onwards, although the Plans contained 'normative projections' (macro-economic and sectoral), there was no attempt to ensure that these targets were met. During the 1960s, the Plans lost their central role in the detailed allocation of investment and acquired an informational and hortatory function. The emphasis was on the Plan's usefulness as a means of reducing market uncertainties (Masse, 1975; Estrin and Holmes, 1983). After 1970, even this role was questioned in the face of economic crisis. The belief that the state could 'guide' the development of the entire industrial sector was explicitly abandoned as the Plans became 'strategies for development'. The political commitment to planning reached its lowest ebb during the preparation of the Eighth Plan, when the cynical subordination of planning to the needs of political expediency (in the run-up to the 1981 presidential elections) was accidentally exposed (Green, 1980; Hayward, 1983).

The Socialists, who have long been committed to a more ambitious conception of planning, were determined to 'revive' it. As a result of their 1981 victory the Eighth Plan (which had not been ratified by Parliament) was abandoned. An 'Interim Plan' (1982 - 83) allowed them time to reform the planning process, as well as ensuring that the Ninth Plan would coincide with the last five years of Mitterrand's term of office 1984 - 88) (Hayward, 1983; 1984).

The legislative procedure has been reformed to a bid to give the Plan more 'teeth' without compromising its indicative nature. Institutional and procedural reforms have tackled the problem of making planning more democratic. The core of the Ninth Plan is a series of medium-term public investment programmes. It breaks new ground in that their implementation is, in principle, tied more closely to the annual budgetary process. *Prima facie*, socialist planning merely confirms the trend started by Giscard D'Estaing: transforming the Plan into a vehicle for public expenditure planning. We can only speculate why the state assumed a dominant role in the process of industralisation. One feasible and rather seductive explanation relates to the fact that French industrialisation took place somewhat later than in Britain. The French are obsessed with league tables, and their position in these, relative to their main competitors. A common theme of statements about industrial development and a justification for state action is French industrial and technological backwardness. Andrew Gerschenkron (1962) has argued that in those countries which develop relatively late, a 'sudden burst' is essential if obstacles to development are to be overcome. This means that the more backward the country is, the greater the need there is for *organised direction*. Such organisation inevitably involves the suppression of market forces and the conscious planning of industrial direction.

In the rest of this chapter, we shall examine in more detail the ways in which French governments have attempted to realise their aim of creating a powerful, modern industrial state, focusing on the relations between the financial sector, the private industrial sector and the state. We shall show that:

a. the state has been able to exercise influence over private sector investment decisions not only as a result of its control over the banks and financial institutions but also because its presence has, until recently, stunted the growth of alternative sources of finance (Notably the private capital market);
b. state intervention has been facilited *inter alia* by the structure of industry and behavioural phenomena such as the historic reticence of the banks in the face of industrial risk and the traditional preference of the French saver for liquid assets.

THE STATE AND THE FINANCIAL SECTOR

In France, as in other market economies, financial intermediaries and financial institutions fulfil the function of matching the demand and supply of capital. France differs from other modern industrial economies, however, to the extent that in the process of adjustment and transformation the role of the market is dominated by that of the state.

Until the mid-1960s, the French financial system rested on a complex arrangement of financial 'circuits' each of which was separate from and superimposed on the others. These circuits ensured that designated instruments (each with its associated fiscal or financial advantage) were mobilised for the realisation of some specific objective. Selected agencies or networks also enjoyed a monopoly over the collection and/or distribution of these instruments which were generally reserved for specified client groups. Thus, the savings institutions had a monopoly over tax-exempt

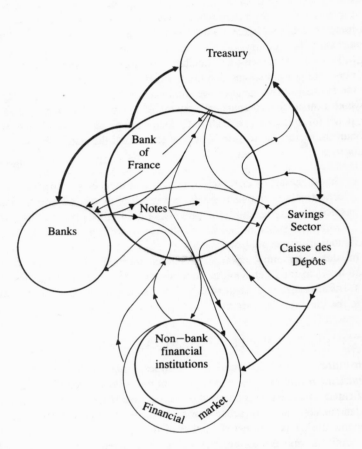

Figure 3.1; The financial circuits
Source: P.Patat, *Monnaie, Institutions financières et politique monétaire* (Paris:
Economica, 1982).

savings instruments and their funds were utilised to finance local authority construction and public sector housing (see below),

The interrelationship of these four circuits is shown schematically in Figure 3.1. Clearly the role of the Central Bank - the Bank of France - is crucial. All the flows pass through or terminate in the Bank and it is the Bank which provides the sole means of communication between the four circuits, in the shape of accounts opened at the Bank.

The Bank of France
The Bank of France was initially set up, as a private venture, by two financiers in 1800, for the specific purpose of providing direct finance for industry and trade. Having secured state support from the outset, however, the Bank grew rapidly and, by 1803, had secured the monopoly of note issue in the Paris region. By 1848, this monopoly had been extended to the whole of metropolitan France. During the second half of the nineteenth century, the Bank gradually assumed a second important role, as banker to the commercial banks. Two further functions were added after 1914. First, the need to finance the war effort and the growth of the state's role in economic life meant that governments increasingly turned to the Bank to borrow funds. The Bank thus gradually assumed the role of the state's banker. Secondly, the Bank assumed greater responsibility for managing foreign exchange operations. State control over the Bank was increased in 1936, in recognition of the growing importance of its economic role, and it was fully nationalised in 1945.

During the post-war period, the Bank's role has continued to evolve. It now no longer provides industrial and commercial credit, directly, but indirectly through its refinancing of the banking system. The decision to concentrate on its role as lender of last resort has necessarily altered its relationship to the commercial banks. Increasingly, the emphasis has been placed on *control*, both for regulatory purposes and more specifically, credit control, one of the main instruments of French monetary policy.

The Central Bank, The Treasury and Monetary Policy
Although the Bank of France has managed to escape total governmental control, it has never enjoyed the influence and independence accorded to its West German counterpart, The Bundesbank. The French government borrows from the Bank and the Bank holds the state's current account. Unlike some Central Banks, it is not responsible for managing the public debt.

Monetary policy is the joint responsibility of the Treasury and the Bank, although the former is clearly the senior partner. This 'condominium' (Hayward, 1983) is exercised through four committees, the National Credit Council, (Conseil National du Crédit) the Banks Control Commission (Commission du Contrôle des Banques), the Stock Exchange Commission (Commission des opérations de la Bourse) and the Franc Area Monetary Committee (Comité Monétaire de la Zone Franc). The most important of these is the National Credit Council, which is formally presided over by the Minister of Finance. The CNC, which was set up by the 1945 law to advise the government on monetary policy and credit control, has a membership of 45, with representatives drawn from the main economic Ministries (including the Planning Commissioner), the banking and non-bank financial sectors, industry and trade unions. It is effectively the Bank's managing board. Executive authority is invested in the Bank's general credit directorate with the Governor playing a key role in monetary policy decisions.

The main instrument for regulating the money supply in France is a system of credit ceilings, (the *encadrement* system) which involves the rationing of credit to the banking sector. The present system was introduced in 1976[6] in a bid to cope with a rapid expansion of the money supply after 1970.[7] What matters here is not the efficacy of credit ceilings as an instrument of monetary policy,[8] so much as the reasons for choosing this form of credit control. *Encadrement* was chosen because it provided a means of controlling monetary growth but at the same time it left the monetary authorities free to set interest rates. Qualitative control was given priority over quantitative controls.

The ability to manipulate interest rates is essential to French governments for both practical and strategic reasons. First, structural weaknesses mean that uncontrolled interest rate fluctuations are likely to disrupt the financial system[9] and exacerbate the financial weakness of the corporate sector (Pollin, 1984). Secondly, control of interest rates is a vital industrial policy instrument: the provision of cheap credit (via subsidised interest rates) has traditionally constituted the basic building-block of all industrial policy schemes. The *encadrement* system reinforced the state's ability to steer credit to designate priority areas by the simple expedient of exempting those areas from the general credit ceilings.[10]

The French Banking Sector

As has already been indicated, the French financial sector is institutionally complex. Financial institutions fall broadly into two main categories: those which are banks and those which are not. Their functions and the scope of their various activities are statutorily determined.

The banking system has been traditionally subdivided into three main categories: the commercial banks (including the 'Big Three' national banks, nationalised in 1945); the cooperative and mutual sector (including a large network of agricultural banks) and the savings banks.

In addition to, and quite separate from the banking sector are a number of non-bank financial intermediaries. The 'Financial Establishments' (Etablissements Financiers) comprise a group of specialised financial agencies which raise funds by means of loan and share capital, provide loans (generally 'soft' loans) and investment on the Bourse (Stock Exchange). Most of these specialise in specific types of business (e.g. leasing, finance for industry). We shall examine the non-bank financial intermediaries in more detail later in this chapter. For the moment, it is important to note that the main source of innovation (in the form of new financial facilities and new financial instruments) during the post-war period is the non-bank financial sector. It is the state which, either directly or through the non-bank financial intermediaries has fulfilled an entrepreneurial role, stimulating savings, extending credit and thus facilitating economic and industrial growth.

Of the three categories of 'banks' referred to above, only the commercial banks are technically classified as banks to the extent that they are 'listed' (*inscrites*) by the Bank of France.

The Cooperative and Mutual Sector

Whether the cooperative and mutual institutions should be classified as banks is a controversial issue. Structurally, this sector resembles the savings sector more closely than the commercial banking sector: networks of local agencies are linked hierarchically through regional agencies to a national *caisse*. Each network is functionally specialised to the extent that it was set up to provide financial services for a specific socio-economic group (e. g. Crédit Agricole provides cheap finance for farmers, while the Banques Populaires were set up to provide funds for artisans). The local and regional agencies are cooperatively owned and have traditionally benefited from access to funds at subsidised rates of interest and special tax regimes. The national *caisse* supplements the resources of the affiliated banks by issuing bonds in its own name. The *quid pro quo* of this preferential treatment is state interference; notably in their lending policies, through the national *caisse* whose Managing Board includes central government Nominees.

Despite this control, the activities of the cooperative and mutual agencies have altered to such an extent that it is increasingly difficult to sustain the distinction between them and the commercial banks. Thus Crédit Agricole has built up an overseas network and offers a wide variety of financial services to its clients, including a credit card. It has also extended its client base and now provides loans for the agro-food industry. Measured by the size of its assets, Crédit Agricole is now one of the largest banks in the world.

The Savings Banks

The French savings sector is actually composed of two parallel networks. The Savings and Provident Agencies (Caisses d'épargne et de prévoyance) are semi-independent organisations at the local level. Their Managing Boards are democratically elected (including employees) but their activities are regulated and they are supervised by the Treasury. The National Savings Bank (Caisse Nationale d'Epargne) is a public agency set up by and working through the Post Office's branch network.

The savings bank network has traditionally collected the lion's share of personal savings in France. In 1983, deposits totalled 550 billion francs, the major part of which was transmitted to the Caisse de Depots et Consignations (CDC).[11] The cartelisation of the French banking sector is evident here too, to the extent that the savings institutions have traditionally concentrated on providing housing finance. Since the late 1970s, however, they have begun to diversify their operations, competing with and behaving like the commercial banks. They now offer a wide range of short and longer-term products, including bonds, unit trusts, cheque books, cash cards and a credit card.[12] Whether they will eventually turn into fully-fledged commercial banks operating at the regional level (and thus fill an important gap in the French banking system) is a moot point. For the moment, the pace of despecialisation is being carefully controlled by the state using devices such as differential ceilings on deposits, differential interest rates and differential tax arrangements.[13]

The Caisse des Dépôts et Consignations

The Caisse des Dépôts et Consignations, like the Bank of France, is a Napoleonic creation, dating back to 1816. Its importance in the French financial sector can be gauged by the size of the total funds it manages which, in 1983, was of the order of 1026 billion francs. It draws these funds partly from the savings banks and life insurance companies (nationalised in 1945) as well as managing a number of pension funds.

The Caisse invests in bonds and equities which are quoted on the Stock Exchange where it is one of the most important institutional dealers.[14] It collects the dividends accruing from the state's shareholdings and may act as a holding company for the state. Traditionally, the Caisse has directed most of its funds into local authority construction programmes and subsidised housing. In 1983, 45. 5 billion francs was advanced to local authorities. It also provides loans for the productive sector, via the specialised non-bank financial institutions and to the Treasury to help finance public expenditure programmes. In the same year, it advanced 20 billion francs and 23. 6 billion francs, respectively for these purposes.

The Lagrange Report, commissioned by the incoming Socialist government in 1983, was critical of the Caisse for its 'excessive centralism . . . and technocratic structures', and for being 'introverted and too often out of touch with the concerns of the local authorities'. The Report prompted a redefinition of the Caisse's role and a reform of its administrative structure. The emphasis is now on the Caisse as a tool of financial decentralisation. An administrative reorganisation has produced two major changes. A new division has been created specifically responsible for stimulating local development. It aims to enter into financial and technical partnerships with local authorities and has initiated new modes of intervention of local development (e. g. participation in agencies providing loan and equity finance at the local level).[15] Secondly, the various technical subsidiaries of the Caisse (which together employ some 20, 000 staff) have been reorganised and grouped under the umbrella of a holding company, the Caisse des Dépôts Developpement (C3D). It has adopted an entrepreneurial style and announced that given the collapse of housing under the impact of the recession, more emphasis will in future be given to technological development, especially in the communications field. Recently, C3D announced the creation of a subsidiary specialising in consultancy and finance for local authorities wishing to invest in Cable TV.[16]

The Commercial Banking Sector

Despite a gradual liberalisation, during the post-war period, functional specialisation is still the hallmark of the French commercial banking sector today. To date, 'mixed' or 'universal' banking such as is found in West Germany has not emerged in France (Economists Advisory Group, 1981). Until the late 1960s, the structure of the system rested on the corporatist laws of 1941 and 1945. These laws had transformed the pattern of specialisation which had emerged before the war into a principle of rigid separation, turning the *de facto* division between deposits, loan capital and share capital into a *de jure* division. This meant that the commercial banking sector was sub-divided into three functionally different categories:

1. deposit banks were discouraged from taking shares in companies and from offering any more than sort-term loans;
2. banques de'affaires (investment or merchant banks) were discouraged from taking deposits; and
3. the medium and long-term credit banks were not allowed to take deposits and were to concentrate on providing medium-term credit (i.e. over two years) in the form of loan capital (Morgan and Harrington, 1977).

By the mid-1960s, there was considerable pressure for changes in the organisation of the French banking system and the rules governing banking behaviour. This was the period of very rapid economic growth: demand for investment finance, from both the public and private sectors, increased sharply. The volume of savings was inadequate to meet this additional demand. In the business sector, self-financing capacity was constrained *inter alia* by the growing burden of debt servicing as firms turned increasingly to the banks for short-term credit. In the personal savings sector, the growth of savings was affected by the impact of high (and continually rising) inflation and the limited range of savings instruments (Patat, 1982).

Reforms were introduced in 1966 and 1967 in a bid to remove the bottleneck and, more generally, involve the banks in the modernisation of the economy by encouraging them to provide more finance for industry. These marked the start of the despecialisation of French banking: deposit banks were allowed to provide credit over any time-period, and banques d'affaires allowed to collect deposits. A tentative step in the direction of deregulation was taken, too: the limits placed on the size of the system (especially the number of branches which could be opened) was relaxed, and the need for authorisation to open new branches was scrapped.

The results of this loosening of control were immediate and dramatic. They were evident in four main ways. First, there was a significant increase in banking activity. The number of permanent bank branches doubled between 1970 and 1975 (from 4340 to 9508) and there was a sharp increase in the number of deposits. Bank credits doubled in five years (from 0.9 billion francs in December 1977 to 1.9 billion francs in December 1982), while the banking sector's share in medium and long-term loans to industry increased by 6 per cent (from 43.4 percent in 1976 to 51.5 per cent in 1982).[17]

Secondly, the combination of deregulation and competition (especially from aggressive new foreign entrants) precipitated structural change. The number of French banks fell from 444 in 1946 to 326 in 1973. The subsequent increase in the total number of banks (399 in 1982) is explained by the increase in the number of foreign banks, (attracted by the expanding economy and the more liberal climate) which, in 1980 accounted for 6.4 per cent retail deposits. Concentration produced a number of large banking groups (e.g. Credit Industriel et Commercial (CIC)) which have progressively increased their share of banking business in France. Thus, whereas a dozen of these groups accounted for about 70 per cent of the business of the listed commercial banks in the 1950s, by 1973, six groups accounted for 80 per cent on this business. Even before the recent nationalisation (see below) the French banking system was more highly concentrated than that of West Germany and the US, but less concentrated than that of the UK.[18] Thirdly, the geographical distribution of the banks changed. The decline in the number of regional and local banks accelerated as an increasing number of banks concentrated their activities in Paris.

The growth of French banking activity is not limited to metropolitan France. A fourth indicator of the change in French banking practice is the spectacular growth of overseas business, especially after 1970. France now has the second largest overseas network in the world, with banks in 100 different countries. Three French banks are today listed among the ten largest world banks. Although a number of banks have a long history of involvement with foreign trade (e. g. Credit Lyonais's overseas activities date back to 1860, the internationalisation of French banking has accelerated since the 1960s. The removal of barriers to trade after France signed the Treaty of Rome had opened the way for expansion. A further impetus was provided when banking activity in the domestic market stagnated after 1975. Since 1980, it is their foreign operations which, for many banks, have been their most profitable activity.

Bank Reforms
Since the late 1970s, a number of official reports have examined savings and credit in France resulting in reforms which have affected the structure and functioning of the banking sector and the relationship between the state, the banks and industry. Two of these reports will be mentioned here.[19]

The first of these, the Mayoux Report,[20] commissioned by the Barre government was strongly critical of the banking structure and banking practice. It suggested that over-centralisation and credit control were severely constraining the government's regional and industrial policy aims. It also drew attention to the deteriorating financial structure of French firms and, more specifically, the difficulties experienced by the small business sector in getting access to investment funds. Its recommendations upset the banks (which felt threatened) and the government (whose monetary policy was criticised) and was therefore largely ignored. A small number of piecemeal reforms did result, however, including the creation of a financial agency designed to facilitate the access of small firms to loan finance. The CEPME (Credit d'Equipment des Petites et Moyennes Entreprises), which was set up in 1980, has a decentralised structure (in reponse to Mayoux's criticism). Despite being hailed by the press as a 'bank for the small business sector', it is para-public credit agency, and as such represents a further extension of the panoply of state-controlled financial institutions. Its creation also underlines the fact that despecialisation has not spread beyond the banking sector: in the para-public sector, segmentation is still the order of the day.

Whereas the Mayoux Report had focused on credit, the Dautresme Report turned its attention to savings.[21] It highlighted the seemingly intractable problem of reconciling increasing demand for investment funding with a falling supply of savings given the structural and behavioural characteristics of the French financial system. It was particularly critical of the rigidity of the system which is exacerbated (if not explained) by the traditional preference for administered relationships (the 'financial circuits') and concomitant scepticism about market mechanisms. Attention was also drawn to the limited range of savings instruments (especially longer-term savings and the relative paucity of venture capital) compared with other countries. This again is at least partly attributable to strict control of the financial intermediaries. Dautresme recommended changes not only to the structure of savings but also reforms designed to change the habits of the French saver. These included new, index-linked savings instruments and the development of collective savings in the form of short-term mutual funds (FCP - Fonds Communs de Placement), unit trusts (SICAV) and life assurance, all of which (in deference to the conservative habits of the French saver) combined liquidity with potentially greater profitability and low risk. The Report was also critical of the cartelisation of savings (i. e. the extent to which certain instruments were available to specific groups of savers through specific savings agencies). It was suggested that greater competition between the different agencies would lead to a greater volume of savings and thus help to plug the gap between savings and investment.

The Dautresme Report was well received, given the Socialist government's aim of expanding the underdeveloped capital market. It has been followed by actions designed to stimulate both long and short term savings. More generally, its publication coincided with (if not prompting) a period of unprecedented expansion and innovation (by French standards). A range of new financial instruments was introduced either index-linked like the 'Popular Savings Book' (LEP or *Livret Rose*) or offering a high yield together with a low-cost realisation such as the SICAV and the CEA (Compte D'Epargne en Actions), an equity-based savings account. Perhaps the most interesting of these is the CODEVI, an industrial development savings account introduced in October 1983. As its name implies, this was a calculated attempt to persuade the ordinary saver that he can profitably invest in industry.[22] Moreover in a bid to increase competition in the savings sector, (following Dautresme's recommendation), the CODEVI are offered to the public by both the commercial banks and the savings banks. The introduction of the CODEVI thus marks an important stage in the progressive de-specialisation of the French banking sector. The CODEVI proved highly attractive to French savers. Close analysis suggests that rather than leading to an expansion of savings overall, their introduction resulted in *switching* between instruments as savers sought to take advantage of the tax exemption offered by the CODEVI. It should be noted that the state, rather than the banks, was the source of these initiatives.

The Banks and Industry

A series of bank failures in the nineteenth century, largely attributable to bad debts as a result of over-investment in high-risk industrial enterprises, prompted the banks to adopt a cautious set of guidelines for future action: credit should only be extended when risks were low and a return was guaranteed. As far as industry was concerned, this meant that finance should only be available in the form of short-term loans for specific projects. This attitude to industrial risk still prevails today and partly explains why the French commercial banks have, like their British counterparts, tried to avoid becoming entangled in the affairs of their industrial clients.

French banks have always experienced a greater degree of political interference and tighter control than their counterparts in other western countries. Control and influence are exerted by formal mechanisms (the system of *tutelle*) and informally (direct pressure on the bank chairmen) within a regulatory framework which controls the pace and direction of change. The decision by the Socialist government to nationalise the banks in 1981 focused attention sharply on the issue of managerial autonomy, highlighting a basic conflict between the notion of a bank as a business free, within certain limits, to pursue its main aim of maximising profits in an international market and thereby subject to the discipline of the market; and a more 'political' conception of a bank as an instrument of government policy, subject to the rules laid down by its political masters.

Nationalisation

The three largest commercial banks have been under state control since they were nationalised in 1946 (although some private capital was introduced when a small quantity of shares was offered to employees in 1973). The decision of the Socialist government to nationalise 36 private banks together with the two investment groups (Paribas and Suez) was dictated by a mixture of ideological and practical considerations. First, nationalisation appeased the Communist Party (their partners in government) and the hard left of the Socialist Party, and was symbolic of the break with the past. Secondly, it was seen as a means of extending the state's access to, and control over, the funds needed for modernising industry. Specifically, it provided the state with more leverage over the banks which had to be persuaded to place less emphasis on short-term profits and more on serving the wider national interest (by supporting industry and creating jobs). Thirdly, as in the case of the industrial nationalisations taking place at the same time, nationalisation served as a means of rescuing a number of the banks which were in serious difficulty.

The 1982 nationalisation law nationalised 36 private banks with deposits over 1 billion francs and the two private investment groups. The 'Big Three' national groups were 'renationalised'. This considerably increased the importance of the state-owned banking sector which now comprises 135 out of the 399 listed banks. A large part of the banking sector escaped nationalisation, however. In the case of the banking groups, for example, only the parent company was nationalised. Important subsidiaries like the Compagnie Bancaire (a subsidiary of the Paribas group which is quoted on the Stock Exchange) were not affected. The cooperative and mutual banks (including Crédit Agricole) escaped, as did the foreign banks.

Nationalisation presented the Socialist government with an opportunity of radically reshaping the banking structure and transforming the banks into a tool of industrial policy. This has not happened. Various scenarios were considered; there was a mild flirtation with the idea of creating a National Investment Bank[23] but this was rejected as being too 'socialist' a solution for either the moderates within the Party or the financial markets. A less radical proposal, which would have reduced the national-ised banking sector to some ten groups, was similarly rejected. The government has opted for a gradual restructuring which, after a series of mergers, is expected to reduce the total number of nationalised banks to 20. An analysis of those changes which have taken place to date suggests that, over and above the need to rescue those banks which are in difficulty, the mergers and de-mergers have been determined by the same sort of technocratic compulsion to 'redistribute the cards' in the interests of some higher/neater logic as the re-shuffles in the industrial sector. A recent Senate report suggests that the long-term viability of some of the groups is questionable as a result of these changes. Moreover, nationalisation has increased the rigidity of the banking system and prevented rather than setting in motion the changes which are essential for the development of a modern and competitive system: 'The real danger of nationalisa-tion is not what it has done but what it has prevented from being done'. (p. 138).

The Bank and Lame Ducks

In almost all western economies, the banks have found it increasingly difficult to remain on the sidelines while the number of lame duck indust-ries and firms escalates under the impact of adjustment in a continuing recession. In France, the *dirigiste* tradition means that the banks have always been drawn into such problem cases at a much earlier stage than in countries such as Britain and West Germany. Even the more 'liberal' Giscardian regime was not averse to putting pressure on the banks to ex-tend their lines of credit or to join the state in rescue operations, providing soft loans for the steel industry and troubled companies, like Boussac in the textiles sector (Green, 1983b).

As has been shown, nationalisation was seen as a means of increasing the state's leverage over the banks. The first attempt to exercise this was in July 1982 when the nationalised banks were instructed to provide capital injections for the newly nationalised industrial groups to the tune of 6 billion francs. A bitter confrontation ensued as the banks complained, vociferously and publicly, about being pressurised to depart from the rules of prudential banking practice, jeopardising their own financial situation and their reputation in international financial markets. The exercise has not been repeated.

Nevertheless, behind-the-scenes pressure on the banks to take a softer line with their industrial clients continues. The actual extent of bank exposure to industrial risk is impossible to determine. All the banks have increased their provisions against bad risk. For example, the Banque Industrielle et Mobilière Privée (BIMP) whose annual report for 1982 specifically mentioned the 'growing number of firms in a critical situation', increased its net provisions to 29.5 million in 1982, compared with 8.5 million in 1981 - an increase of 247 per cent

Some idea of the size of the problem can also be gleaned by examining specific cases. First, the rescue of the French newsprint group, La Chapelle- d'Arblay, this was justified on the grounds of the strategic importance of the industry and the social consequences of its collapse. Significantly, one of the group's plants was in the Rouen area which happened to be the constituency of the Industry Minister. As in all rescue cases, financial restructuring had to be linked to a credible industrial plan. After all attempts to find a domestic buyer failed, the management of the group was taken over by a Dutch group, Parenco. The rescue plan also involved the rationalisation of the group's activities (which were to be eventually concentrated in the Rouen area) involving the loss of some 3000 jobs between 1984 and 1988. The total cost of the rescue (including planned investment of 1 billion francs) was put at 3. 2 billion, 900 million of which was provided by the Banks.

Another long-running problem is that of Creusot-Loire, the private sector engineering conglomerate which first got into difficulties in 1981. The first rescue plan failed to resolve its fundamental problems (which stem mainly from its loss-making steel activities) and a further financial crisis forced the search for a more radical solution in the autumn of 1983. The second rescue plan involved the breaking-up of the Creusot-Loire group, transferring most of its loss-making steel activities to the nationalised steel groups (Usinor and Sacilor). Its holding in the highly profitable Framatome (which has a monopoly of nuclear plant construction) was to be reduced from 70 to 50 per cent. The accompanying financial package involved a partnership between the state, the shareholders and the banks, with the latter providing some 2 billion of the total 6 billion package.[24] By May 1984, a further crisis threatened and the chairman indicated that the group would need a further 2.3 billion francs cash injection to stave off bankruptcy. The government refused to consider this appeal unless Schneider, the parent group, was prepared to provide an additional 800 million in equity funds. When Schneider refused to comply, the creditor banks (essentially BNP, Crédit Lyonnais and Société Générale) offered to reschedule the debt they had outstanding to Creusot-Loire (3 billion francs) in return for a stake in one of the financial holding companies of the Schneider group (as a means of guaranteeing the proper use of their funds). This was rejected by M. Pineau Valencienne as an attempt to nationalise the Schneider group. Creusot-Loire was then placed in official receivership.

The collapse of Creusot-Loire sparked off one of the most vitriolic and public battles between the state and the chairman of a private sector group ever witnessed in France. At issue are the terms of which the state (and the nationalised banks) are prepared to bail out the company and what can be extracted from Schneider, the parent group, in return. The problem is exacerbated by the Socialist government's concern about 'backdoor nationalisation' which, politically and financially, it cannot afford. Unfortunately, given the strategic importance of the group's nuclear interests, and the heavy involvement of the banks, all the feasible scenarios involved some extension of state control

The Banks after Nationalisation

Of the 36 banks nationalised in 1982, only seven showed net profits in 1983 at a level higher than in 1981. The largest banks appear to have been most severely affected, particularly the banking groups, four of which announced net losses in 1983. The profitability of the three largest national banks has declined too, as has that of the investment groups.

It would be wrong to attribute this poor performance wholly to nationalisation. Even before 1982, several of the banks were in difficulty. Thus Credit du Nord's difficulties stemmed mainly from its attempt to prop up the Ribourel construction group over a 20 year period. The French banks also suffer from being generally undercapitalised by international standards. Although their poor performance after 1982 is partly explained by the continuing recession and their increased exposure to international lending (a problem which confronts the wider international banking sector), it has also been affected by a number of specifically French phenomena. Thus, the system of credit control (*encadrement*) has severely constrained the banks' profitability on domestic operations and restricted competition between the banks and their ability to innovate. Secondly, the burden of taxation falling on the banks has increased significantly, representing 200 per cent of net profits in 1981 compared with 140 per cent in 1973. During the 1980s a number of windfall taxes were levied, too. Nationalisation compounded the bank's financial weakness, depriving them of access to essential equity capital by barring access to the financial markets. Ironically, the Socialist government found itself being called on to provide financial assistance for the very banks whose resources it hoped to plunder!

The government has resolved this problem in a surprisingly pragmatic and non-ideological way. First, in a bid to strengthen the banks' balance sheets, the government reduced its call on their resources (in the form of dividends and contributions to the state's nationalisation compensation fund). Secondly, the banks have been allowed to increase their provisions (on both domestic and foreign risk). Thirdly, in a paradoxical move, the government decided to allow the banks to return to the Stock Exchange and raise funds by means of new financial instruments, the titre participatif (TP); and the certificat d'Investissement (CI). TPs are non-voting certificates, half-way between a share and a bond, offering a yield partly indexed to bond market rates. The CIs are non-voting preference shares. Not surprisingly both instruments (which arguably constitute a form of privatisation at odds with both the spirit and the letter of the 1982 nationalisation laws) have proved attractive to the banks as a means of strengthening their capital base.

Nationalisation has neither radically altered the structure of French banking nor transformed the banks into mere instruments of government policy. There are signs, however, that the campaign to change the bank's attitude to industrial risk is beginning to bear fruit. A number of the larger banks have announced that they are extending their services to include 'marriage-broking' or, more generally, advice and assistance to firms seeking shareholdings, takeovers or joint ventures. At the same time, the banks have taken the lead in setting-up venture capital funds and organising management buy-outs. French banks, like their British counterparts, are still wary of taking equity participation in industry, a cautious attitude which has been reinforced by the experience of some of the West German banks which have recently got their fingers badly burnt. Arguably, the growth of these new activities is explained by the combination of deregulation and increasing competition, however, and has taken place despite rather than because of nationalisation.

The State and Industry

If the ultimate aim of French industrial policies during the post-war period has been industrial leadership, the proximate aim has been a problem-solving one: to remedy the structural weakness and technological backwardness which are the consequences of belated industrialisation. The persistence of these problems explains the fundamental continuity which characterises industrial intervention in France, despite the rhetoric of change. Specifically, governments have pursued four main objectives. First, they have attempted to direct the pace of industrial change, restructuring declining industries and assisting those regions affected by structural adjustment by financial assistance and incentives to new industrial investment. Secondly, they have promoted a belated specialisation, especially in advanced technology industries and products, based on intensive basic research (supported *inter alia* by public purchasing policies) or the 'Frenchifying' of imported technology. Thirdly, merger promotion in designated key sectors has ensured the creation of 'national champions', large enough to compete with other (non-French) transnational companies in international markets. At the same time, care has been taken to encourage the growth of new firms and maintain an innovative small and medium-sized industrial sector to support future expansion. Finally, efforts have been made to encourage French entrepreneurs to extend their efforts beyond national boundaries to export and eventually, to invest overseas (Green, 1981a and b). French governments have deployed both general and selective industrial policy measures to achieve these aims. Indeed, they have been particularly inventive on this score. According to one recent estimate, there were some 300 industrial policy mechanisms in 1982 including 150 different forms of industrial subsidy.[25] A common feature of many of these schemes is the subsidisation of interest rates. Rather than attempt an analysis of them, we shall examine state intervention in industrial investment decision from two different angles: first, via the nature of the state/firm relationship; and secondly, via some of the administrative agencies involved.

Clearly, the ability of any government to pursue an industrial policy hinges on the nature of its relationship to the firm (or firms) which comprise particular industries. The ability of government to influence investment decisions depend on such factors as the size and number of firms in an industry, the nature of their ownership, and their dependence on external funding. In the absence of state ownership, compliance depends on the extent to which firms can be persuaded to trade a loss of managerial autonomy for financial favours. In the French context, it is important to distinguish between independent industrial groups and small (often family-owned) concerns.

A characteristic feature of the French economy is the interpenetration of public and private capital: linkages between state and financial and industrial capital are cemented by a complex mesh of cross-shareholdings. As has been indicated, the state has both majority and minority holdings in a large number of companies, directly or indirectly through the agencies it owns or controls. Morin (1977) found, for example that the Caisse des Dépôts had shares in 170 French firms in 1976. In such cases, the state may have a passive but can hardly have a neutral role. Morin also found that, although the commercial banks had a relatively limited interest in industrial shares, a number of industrial companies had banking subsidiaries, including Renault. Cross-shareholdings were also a feature of inter-bank relationships. Industrial participation has traditionally been the preserve of the merchant banks (including those owned by the three banks nationalised in 1946) and the two investment groups, Indosuez and Paribas, which were nationalised in 1982. Indosuez has holdings in a number of the industrial groups nationalised at the same time (Saint-Gobain, Thomson-Brandt, Rhône-Poulenc and CGE) while Paribas, whose industrial holdings had an estimated value of 7 billion francs in 1983, is heavily involved in the oil industry and is one of the leaders in providing venture capital for the biotechnology industry.

A number of the industrial groups resulted from a concentration process orchestrated and underwritten by the state (e. g. CII-HB, the mainframe computer company, Peugot-Citrôen the motor group). Having sponsored the creation of these national champions, the state has used them to spearhead its industrial policies. A confidential government report in 1976 (the Hannoun Report) which was leaked to the press, revealed the extent to which a number of these groups were being kept afloat by government funding.

The notion of a partnership of public and private capital for the achievement of some agreed national goal is the cornerstone of the French approach to active intervention. This was first formalised in a number of state-sponsored programmes (e.g. nuclear energy, Concorde, the TGV), in the shape of 'programme contracts' within the framework of the National Plan. The discretionary nature of state/firm contracts rendered them potentially attractive as a means of securing specific industrial objectives, even to the neo-liberal Giscardian regime. The original concept was therefore refined and sanctions (for non-performance) were introduced. From the state's point of view, the contractual approach was financially as well as ideologically attractive. Since contracts were only available to efficient firms, the state was able to maximise the catalytic effect of its interventions at the minimum cost: 'helping the strong' was a particularly economical way of using public funds. At the same time, the arm's length nature of the contractual relationship was a politically attractive way of moblising investment. The contractual relationship was also welcomed by the business sector. The agreements not only spelled out the conditions of the state's financial involvement in the firm's investment plans, they also indicated that, within certain mutually agreed and specified limits, managers would be allowed to manage.

State/firm contracts were a prominent feature of the industrial policies pursued by the Giscard regime: 'growth contracts' and 'development contracts' were used to promote investment in priority advanced technology sectors like electronics. They have been continued by the Socialists, in a modified form.

The political nature of these contracts was underlined by the inclusion of performance targets which arguably square ill with the profit-maximising aims of a commercial concern (e.g. job-creation and balance of payments targets). As Le Franc (1983) suggests, this form of bureaucratic intervention implies a confusion of roles: it is the civil servant who takes control and defines industrial strategies while the entrepreneur justifies his request for subsidies by arguing that he is acting in the national interest.

The small business sector has presented French governments with a different problem. Their independence and the concomitant fear of losing control tends to make entrepreneurs in this sector as wary of state assistance as they are sceptical of seeking additional capital via new shareholders. Under-capitalisation, low profit margins, high taxes and social charges have been a continuous constraint on the self-financing capacity of these firms (see Figure 3.2). They have increasingly resorted to external finance, for investment (and to ease cash flow problems), mainly in the shape of short-term banking loans. The growing debt burden has further weakened the financial structure of this vital sector. Governments have attempted to tackle this problem in two main ways. First, they have created a number of para-public agencies specialising in the provision of loan and equity capital for smaller firms. Secondly, procedures have been decentralised in a bid to improve their access to financial assistance.

The Role of the Treasury

The activities of the Treasury department of the Finance Ministry provide a good guide to the nature and scale of state intervention in industrial decision making France. In addition to monetary policy, its supervises the non-bank financial intermediaries and is responsible for stock and bond market policy, housing policy and the management of the public debt. The Treasury has always been heavily involved in industrial policies,

Characteristic Ratios of the Financial Situation of Companies and Quasi-Companies (other than large National Firms) in % Value Added.

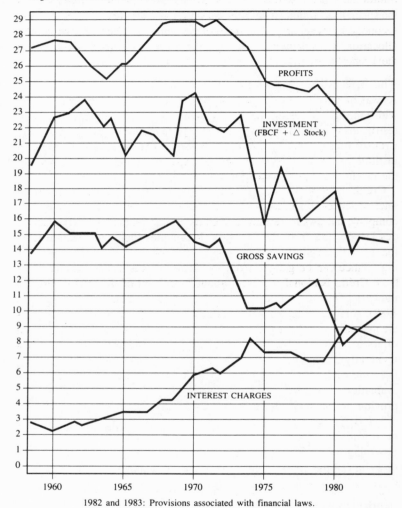

1982 and 1983: Provisions associated with financial laws.

Figure 3.2: The deteriorating financial structure of French firms

Source: Ministère du Plan et de L'Amènagement due Territoire, *Le Financement des Entreprises* (Paris, 1983).

too, to the extent that a large part of investment funding in both the public and private sectors is subject to its approval. Its promotional role has traditionally been exercised in two main ways: first, via supervision of the specialised financial institutions which provide industrial credit, and secondly by servicing a number of committees which determine the allocation of investment credits and the access of foreign businesses to the French market.

The Specialised Financial Intermediaries

As was indicated above, *encadrement* has provided French governments with a means of directing the flow of credit into designated priority sectors, restructuring industrial sectors (e.g. steel) and industrial groups (e.g. BSF, Creusot-Loire) and to promote exports. The specialised financial institutions act in an entrepreneurial capacity on behalf of the state to the extent that they finance these operations.

Crédit National is the most prominent of these specialised intermediaries concerned with industrial investment. Originally a private company, it draws its resources from the money market, from the Caisse des Dépôts and from the Treasury. It provides long and medium-term loans, both from its own resources and on behalf of the state. Its importance can be gauged from the scale of its activities: direct loans from Crédit National represent about 5 per cent of the total of French industrial finance and about 10 per cent of loan finance (Cohen *et al.*, 1982). Analysis of its portfolio shows that about 85 per cent of its activities are in industry, with the rest in trade and the service sector. Crédit National offers a range of types of loan finance, at subsidised rates of interest (generally 2-3 per cent below the market rate). During the 1970s, it has been increasingly called upon to provide industrial analysis and project evaluation. A number of its officials are seconded to the Treasury and provide on-the-spot advice on all rescue operations.

The BFCE (Banque Francais du Commerce Extérieur) is another source of subsidised credit. It has specialised in helping exporting firms, providing long and medium-term loan finance on its own account and on behalf of the government. It also finances exports indirectly through a number of specialised subsidiaries.[26]

Equity Finance

The under-capitalisation of the corporate sector has been a source of concern throughout the post-war period. The policy response has been to create a number of para-public equity financing agencies, to plug what is seen as a gap in the private capital market.

Historically, the first of these were the SDR (Sociétés de Développement Régional) set up in 1955 to provide loan and share captial for small and medium sized firms at the regional level. The creation of IDI (the Industrial Development Institute) in 1970 was indicative of their lack of success. IDI is the most visible of French equity capital agencies and provided the model for later ventures. Although the state has a majority holding (directly and through institutions it owns or controls), IDI has fought to preserve managerial autonomy, and the right to act according to commercial rather than political criteria. Its attitude to lame duck firms has been a source of perennial irritation to successive French governments. Indeed, it was directly as a result of disagreement about the rescue operation of the BSF group that the Chairman, M. Dominique de la Martinière resigned in 1983. Despite persistent financial difficulties IDI appears to have answered a real need. Focusing on medium-sized companies,[27] it has had some success in helping the expansion of under-capitalised firms, some of which have been successfully introduced to the secondary market. At the same time its small scale and flexible mode of operation have facilitated its second major task, that of solving 'problems of succession' (by finding new shareholders, arranging mergers or takeovers).

Promoting and Coordinating Industrial Intervention

The Treasury claims to be the *de facto* source of industrial policy despite the existence of an Industry Ministry (recently redesignated the Ministry of Industrial Redeployment). Although the MIR has managed to increase its importance and autonomy in the policy area (as a result of administrative reforms which have increased the size of its intervention budget), the Treasury exerts influence and control via its intervention in and servicing of a number of interministerial committees concerned with industrial investment. Historically, the first and most important of these is the FDES (Economic and Social Development Fund), whose management council advises on and coordinates the major national investment decisions (i.e. those that will be supported in connection with the National Plan). Although there was a progressive reduction of the amount of investment financed through the Fund during the 1970s, it still provides the Finance Ministry (which authorises the allocation of funds) with control over the volume and distribution of a substantial amount of industrial investment (Hayward, 1984).

During the late 1970s, a number of committees were set up to deal with the problem of capital formation in the context of the post-oil shock recession which had posed particular problems (structural, technological and financial) for the French productive sector. The first and most controversial of these was the CIASI (Interministerial Committee for the Adaptation of Industrial Structures now renamed the CIRI, Interministerial Committee for Industrial Restructuring), created in 1974 to bail out industrial lame ducks. As has been indicated elsewhere (Green 1983b and c), rescues are joint operations between the state, the bank involved, and the firm's shareholders. To the extent that collapse is attributable to poor management, problems of succession or under-capitalisation, CIRI's activities clearly overlap with those of the IDI. A sharp increase in the number of problem cases after 1981, coupled with the incoming Socialist government's desire to decentralise decision-making, resulted in the establishment of six additional committees (CORRI) at the regional level.

Three other interministerial committees, modelled on the CIRI were established during the last years of the Giscard's presidency (Green 1983b). The FSAI, a 3 billion franc special adaptation fund was set up in 1978 to assist conversion in the depressed regions dominated by the steel and shipbuilding industries. Financial assistance was provided in the shape of capital grants and a new form of industrial subsidy, *prêts participatifs*. These are subordinated loans (i.e. loans which are counted as additional equity), with repayment partly geared to (expected) profits. 'Participatory loans' were subsequently generalised as a tool of selective financial assistance. A second committee, the CIDISE (Interministerial Committee for the Development and Maintenance of Employment), was set up in 1979 to provide risk capital for small successful firms, especially exporters. As its title implies, the aim was to combine the promotion of industrial 'winners' with job creation. The third of these committees, the CODIS (Committee for the Orientation and Development of Strategic Industries) was set up in the same year to steer the growth of a number of 'strategic' industries during the 1980s. Specifically, it aimed to encourage indigenous technological development in a limited number of areas (initially six). The committee, which had no budget, selected the 'strategic areas', defined the strategies, found suitable firms (i.e. those which would agree to spearhead the investment effort with state backing) and coordinated administrative action to ensure realisation of the strategies. Despite its limited jurisdiction, the CODIS inaugurated systematic and detailed industrial planning of a type never before seen in France.

The only one of these committees to survive under the Socialists is the CIRI. The FSAI proved inappropriate to the task: the timing of the decision to abandon the principle of tying regional subsidies to specific job-creation targets proved disastrous, given that the number of regions affected by structural decline (and unemployment) was increasing dramatically. The Socialists have introduced new forms of regional assistance, including a scheme whereby designated 'Poles of conversion' benefit from additional incentives in a bid to attract new investment. CODIS and the CIDISE also disappeared. They have been replaced by the FIM (Industrial Modernisation Fund) which was launched in September 1983 to promote innovation in products and processes. It breaks new ground in a number of ways. First, although the Fund is formally administered by the Ministry of Industrial Redeployment (rather than the Treasury), applications for assistance below a ceiling of 5 million francs have been delegated to the regional delegations of the ANVAR (which promotes innovation). It is hoped that this will speed up administrative procedures and improve access for small firms. Secondly, the FIM procedure spearheads the Socialists' attempt to persuade the public to invest in industry. Its resources are drawn from the CODEVI deposits lodged with the savings banks (see above). Financial assistance takes the form of subordinated loans ('technological participatory loans') with 7-10-year term, covering up to 70 per cent of the cost of the investment. The loans are available at a subsidised rate of interest, initially 9.75 per cent (compared to a market rate of 16-18 per cent in 1983) and will eventually be tied to the interest rate paid on the 'A' Savings Account.[28] By January 1984, loans from the FIM had been agreed or allocated to the tune of 3.5 billion francs. Although most of these have been channelled to small firms, a substantial proportion has been received by the troubled motor industry.[29] Some 9 billion francs' worth of loans are expected to be distributed in 1984, to promote innovation in 'niches' such as the energy-saving car, advanced technology equipment, the office of the future, 'smart cards' (e.g. credit cards with a built-in memory), biotechnology, and the micros-in-schools programme.

FRENCH INDUSTRIAL PERFORMANCE

During the post-war period, and especially after 1958, the French economic and industrial structure was radically altered: the shift from agriculture to industry accelerated, concentration reduced the fragmentation producing a number of large industrial groups, and there was a gradual, if belated, specialisation, mainly in the consumer goods industries and those with a low-skill requirement and high capital content (e.g. volume cars). Changes in the pattern and volume of trade also took place, with a shift away from the old French empire towards European countries (Green 1981c).

If the period before 1974 was characterised by rapid industrial development, the period since then has been marked by decline and crisis. The combination of two oil shocks in the 1970s and the consequent recession has revealed the continuing weaknesses of French industry and precipitated a period, since 1981, of painful and accelerated structural adjustment. The 'modernisation' of industry has become a government priority. The severity of the problem can be gauged by examining a few key indicators.

Table 3.1: Capital accumulation in France, 1973−83 (%)

	1973	1974	1975	1976	1977	1978	1979	1980	1981	1982	1983
Investment rate:											
SQS[a]	20.3	20.1	19.1	19.7	19.0	18.6	18.1	18.9	18.5	18.2	18.0
Other SQS	18.7	18.2	16.4	17.0	16.0	15.3	14.5	15.2	14.9	14.5	14.4
GEN[b]	37.5	42.1	47.6	47.2	50.8	51.8	54.1	54.5	52.3	57.8	49.9

Notes: a. Companies and quasi-companies.

b. Grandes Entreprises Nationales: the eight major public enterprises (GDF, CDF, EDF, SNCF, RATP, Air France, Air Inter, PTT.)

Source: *Le financement de l'industrie*, vol.4 preparatory reports for the 9th Plan, *La Documentation Francaise* (Paris 1983).

The growth rate of industrial production fell from 6.1 per cent between 1969 and 1974 to 1.1 per cent between 1974 and 1981, and by 1982 was as the same level as eight years before. The share of industry in total value-added, which grew from 23.3 per cent in 1959 to 29.4 per cent in 1975, fell back to 27.4 percent in 1981. Industry's share of gross fixed capital formation declined too, from 32.2 per cent in 1975 to 25.1 per cent in 1981. As Table 3.1 shows, public sector investment has accounted for the lion's share of total investment for the last decade, while private sector investment has stagnated. In 1981, investment fell by 12 per cent to a level 5 per cent below the 1970 level, with a further decline in 1982. The consequence of this is progressively ageing capital stock.[30] Industrial jobs are disappearing at a faster rate than new ones are being created. The increase in unemployment (which passed the politically sensitive threshold of 2 million in 1981) has been exacerbated by a combination of industrial collapse and de-manning in industries which were previously job-creating (e.g. volume cars). Moreover, a change in the *nature* of investment over the last few years, to increase productivity and competitiveness, has inevitably had a deleterious effect on employment levels.

From 1963 to 1974, the export of French manufacturers, by volume, grew rapidly (Table 3.2). Since 1974, export growth has slowed (to an annual rate of 4.6 per cent between 1974 and 1980), and there has been a significant loss of market share. Penetration of the domestic market by foreign products increased at the same time as exports decreased: the share of imports in the domestic market rose from 21.8 per cent in 1973 to 28 per cent in 1980. This trend is partly due to the specialisation which has taken place as a result of the French economy's increasing openness to trade.

Table 3.2: Export performance of French manufacturing industries

	Annual Average 1974 1980 1963 1974	From previous year 1975 1976 1977 1978 1979 1980
Growth of markets[a]	9.4 6.1	0 10.9 5.9 6.0 8.3 5.8
Volume growth of exports	11.2 4.9	−4.1 9.0 7.8 5.1 9.9 2.7
Gains (+) or losses (−) of market shares	+1.7 −1.2	−4.1 −1.9 +1.8 −1.0 +1.6 −3.1

Note: Growth of markets calculated from volume growth of imports by each trading partner weighted by trade in manufactures in 1977 (SITC sections 5+6+7+8+9).

Source: OECD Economic Surveys, *France* (Paris, January 1982).

This deterioration is partly explained by relative costs and prices. Although productivity has improved, unit labour costs in manufacturing rose sharply between 1973 and 1980 (10.3 per cent per annum on average, compared with 3.5 per cent during the previous decade). Analyses seem to suggest that the growth of wages and social security charges, which together make the French worker one of the highest paid in the industrial world, largely account for this acceleration (Table 3.3).

Table 3.3: Comparison of hourly wage costs, including social charges in manufacturing industry in 1981

Country	Hourly wage (incl. social charges, francs)
West Germany	61.20
US	55.09
Canada	48.84
France	48.06
Italy	46.20
Japan	36.24
GB	36.10

Source: EEC and national sources.

CONCLUSION: STATE VERSUS MARKET

As this chapter has shown, a key factor explaining rapid industrial development during the post-war period was the partnership between the state, and financial and industrial capital. The private capital market was (until recently) relatively underdeveloped, and industrial investment decisions have traditionally been subjected to substantial state intervention. While these two phenomena are related, we are not necessarily dealing with cause and effect: there is no proof that the weakness of the private capital market is attributable to state intervention. Conversely, it does not follow that a healthy capital market would have developed in the absence of state intervention. The volume and direction of industrial investment have clearly been influenced not only by fiscal and monetary policies but also and more importantly by the provision of targeted aid. Governments have subsidised interest rates, for example, to promote investment in areas or products deemed to be vital to the national interest. In so doing, they have effectively paid the political premium demanded by the private capital market for risks which are unduly high and/or where returns are uncertain. Similarly, para-public agencies like the IDI, and committees like the CIRI, correct for the failure of the market to recognise the value assigned by government to investment projects (or firms or industries) by implicitly accepting lower (or negative) rates of return. It could also be argued that given the traditional preference of the banks for sort-term loan finance, the state has compensated for market failure in the shape of longer-term investment funding. The shift from fixed to variable rates of interests during the 1970s clearly had an impact on both the source of investment funding and the volume of investment. For the banks, variable rates proved an attractive means of shifting industrial risk back to their clients. From the point of view of the firm, investment appraisal became more difficult (since the cost of external funding could not be assessed). Given the reliance by a large number of firms on bank finance, the shift to variable rates could partly explain the collapse of private sector investment. For those firms prepared to trade some measure of managerial autonomy, the long-term fixed rate loans provided by government clearly represented an attractive, and relatively safe, alternative.

The nature of state intervention in industrial investment decisions also gives cause for concern. Contractual schemes may represent a useful check on the use of public funds, but they also constitute an incursion into the decision-making processes of the firm. In such partnership arrangements, the state shares both the cost of the investment but also the associated risk. The extent to which the state is *substituting* for the entrepreneur can be gauged by the proportion of the costs and risk it assumes. In the case of the industrial modernisation fund (FIM), for example, assistance is available for up to 70 per cent of the cost of the investment project via subordinated loans of up to 10 years' duration. These 'participatory loans' are not simply a more sophisticated form of long-term loan finance. Despite the nod in the direction of the market (to the extent that repayment is geared to expected profits), they effectively constitute a state guarantee for projects which, at the market price, would not be viable. By such mechanisms and, more generally, its manipulation of interest rates, the state effectively distorts the calculation of risk and returns. At the same time, by rationing credit, it inevitably increases the cost of credit, and this constrains the economic and industrial development it wishes to secure.

The modernisation of the financial sector provides a good illustration of the French government's dilemma. The root of the problem is that the state is attempting to reconcile a number of conflicting objectives. If the banks are to help ease the state's financial burden, they must be profitable. Profitability depends, *inter alia* on the ability to adapt to changes taking place in the wider international financial sector, i.e. the freedom to respond to the pressures of competition (in the shape of structural changes, manpower reductions, diversification of operations, and so on). The banking profession is currently coming to grips with changes which are undermining traditional organisation and practices. Thus, computerisation is revolutionising banking procedures and is likely to lead to important changes in the organisation of banking as an activity. The growth of home banking is only one example of changes which could have important consequences for the future size and shape of banking networks. Similarly, pressure on the banks to provide a wider range of financial services coupled with increasing competition amongst the financial institutions for a greater share of the market is already leading to large-scale restructuring and the emergence of 'financial supermarkets'.

The rigidity of the French financial system, the persistence of segmentation, and the continuation of tight state control constrain innovation in the domestic market and inhibit the bank's ability to respond to changes taking place in the international system. Moreover, the continuation of controls and poor profitability in the domestic market are likely to have a perverse effect (as far as government is concerned) in that the banks will inevitably seek to shift a greater part of their activities to the more profitable foreign markets.

The Socialist government's notion of using the banks as an instrument of industrial policy proved to be a non-starter. The U-turn in their relationship with the banks can be seen as part of the more general conversion from Socialism to realism (Green 1984a) - a conversion precipitated not least by the shock of realising that political interference in the banks' activities would undermine the banks' standing abroad.

It is in the financial sector, the the ambivalence of the Socialists about the market is most marked. Paradoxically, the Socialist government has set itself the object of revitalising and expanding the underdeveloped French capital market. The motives are mixed: on the one hand, the government would like Paris to become an international financial centre, rivalling the City of London. At the same time, and at a more practical level, a revival of the capital market is seen as an essential means of increasing the flow of capital to industry (and thus a prerequisite of the 'Modernisation' of French industry). Its actions have been remarkably successful: bolstered by the fiscal incentives introduced by the government in 1983 in a bid to boost investment in securities, and encouraged by the Government's adherence to more orthodox economic policies since the last devaluation, trading on the Paris Bourse (Stock Market) has boomed.

The development of a modern financial system is crucial if France is to continue to play an active role in the international capitalist system. It is also imperative if the growth of the service sector is to compensate for the decline of manufacturing. As its actions in both the industrial and financial sectors show, the French state too readily fulfils the function of a Maginot line, delaying, for as long as possible, the process of essential adjustment and change. For how much longer French industrial investment decision-making will be politicised, and how soon market forces will be allowed to carry out essential modernisation, is impossible to predict.

NOTES

1. Report on the Senate Finance Committee under the chairmanship of E. Bonnefous, October 1977. Those subsidiaries in which the state had a minority shareholding were excluded from the calculation
2. A recent, and well-publicised example was when the Barre government vetoed Elf's bid to take over the American company, Texas-Gulf.
3. The state took over nine groups: PUK (metal products), Rhone-Poulenc (chemicals), Saint-Gobain (basic materials and electronics conglomerate),

Dassault, Matra, (aerospace), Thomson, CGE, CII (electronics), CGCT (telecommunications). The nationalisation of the two steel groups, Usinor and Sacilor, which were bailed out by the previous government was completed.

4. M. Sauzay, 'Journees de travail sur la politique industrielle de la France' (15-16 November 1982)

5. Blin Report *(Rapport d'information sur le controle des entreprises publiques: banques nationalisees par le loi no. 82-155 de 11.2.82)* Senat, no. 375 (Paris, June 1984).

6. Credit ceilings were operated on three occasions prior to 1972: February 1958-February 1959; February 1963-June 1965, and November 1968-October 1970. Prof. J.P. Pollin, *Money versus Credit: Insights from French Policy Experience*, paper presented at Conference on Monetary Policy, (Brasenose College, Oxford, September 1984).

7. The French-money supply grew by 15 per cent from late 1969 to late 1970, by 17 per cent from 1970 to 1971 and by 18 per cent from 1971 to 1972.

8. See *Cahiers Economiques et Monetairs de la Banque de France*, nos. 17 and 18 2nd term (Paris, 1984).

9. Some deposit-taking institutions are effectively lenders on the money market while the financial institutions rely on the money market to raise loan and share capital. Interest rate fluctuations therefore affect them differently.

10. Industrial and exports credits are excluded, as are funds for housing and agriculture.

11. Under the Minjoz Law of 1950, the savings banks are authorised to use up to 50 per cent of their annual net balances in the shape of loans to the local authorities through the CDC. Since 1972, they have been authorised to use a proportion of this 'Minjoz contingency' as they wish.

12. The savings banks have recently joined the PTT, the *Banques Populaires* and the commercial banks in offering the *Carte Bleue* credit card.

13. The main instrument offered by the savings banks is the 'A' passbook savings account which currently has a ceiling of 68,000 francs and pays interest at the rate of 7.5 per cent, tax free. *Credit Mutual* offers a Blue Passbook Account *(Livret Bleu)* which is roughly equivalent. The Popular Savings Book (LEP or *Livret Rose*) introduced in 1983 for the lower paid, has a ceiling of 30,000 francs. It attracts an interest rate of 8.5 per cent, tax free, but is indexed. Deposit accounts such as the savings banks' 'B' account and the deposit accounts offered by the commercial banks are subject to taxation.

14. It has been estimated that the Caisse absorbs about 30 per cent of new bond and 20 per cent of new stock offerings. See S. Cohen *et al.*, 'Rehabbing the Labyrinth: the financial system and industrial policy in France', in S. Cohen and P. Gourevitch, *France in the Troubled World Economy* (London; Butterworths, 1982)

15. The Caisse has taken shares in Regional Participation Institutions (IRP) in five French regions. In 1984, it announced an agreement to take shares in the Regional Development Societies (SDRs).

16. See Diana Green 'Cable TV in France: a non-market approach to industrial development', *National Westminster Bank Review*, August 1984.

17. Blin Report *op. cit.*, p. 10.
18. In France, West Germany and the US, the three main banks had respectively 10.9, 4.7 and 1.7 per cent of the total number of branches. These banks account for 22.4 per cent of the total activity of the financial sector in France compared with only 8.2 per cent in the case of their West German counterparts (Blin Report, p. 11).
19. Studies of the French financial sector were also carried out during the preparation of the 8th and 9th National Plans: *Rapport du Commite Financement* (Paris, La Documentation Francaise, July 1980; Rapports de Mission au Ministere d'Etat, Ministre du Plan et de L'Amenagement du Territoire, vol. 4: *Le Financement des Entreprises; L'Allocation des Ressources Financieres*, Paris, La Documentation Francaise, January 1983. The Working-Group on Monetary Policy (for the 9th Plan)) also looked at the inadequacy of savings (personal and corporate) and the financial difficulties of the business sector.
20. *Le Developpement des Initiatives Financieres Regionales et Locales* (Mayoux Report) (Paris, La Documentation Francaise, 1978).
21. *Le Developpement et la politique de L'Epargne* (Dautresme Report) (Paris, La Documentation Francaise, 1982).
22. The CODEVI deposits raised by the banks and savings institutions are to be earmarked for industry. Of the 70 billion francs expected to be collected during 1984, approximately half (34 billion francs) will be channelled into industry in the shape of cheap loans through the commercial banks or through the specialised financial agencies such as *Credit National* (routed through the Caisse des Depots). A small proportion (8 billion) will be channelled into Industrial Modernisation Fund (FIM), managed by the Ministry of Industry and providing cheap loans for industrial innovation.
23. See *L'Imposture Monetaire* (Paris, Editions Anthropos, 1981), produced by a working party attached to the Economic Committee of the Socialist Party.
24. Schneider, which indirectly holds 50 per cent of Creusot Loire's shares, put up 720 million francs.
25. *Aides a l'Industrie*. Report of the Commissariat General au Plan (Paris, 1982).
26. For example SOFININDEX, which is jointly owned by a number of financial institutions, assists the expansion of expanding firms by providing share capital. See Diana Green, *The Export Imperative: French policies to promote overseas trade*. Unpublished report for the Department of Industry, 1981.
27. Intervention in small firms is now carried out by SOPROMEC-IDI a joint subsidiary of IDI and the Banques Populaires, set up in 1978.
28. Leasing companies also have access to subsidised loans from the FIM.
29. Renault received 500 million francs towards the launch of an energy-saving car and the modernisation of its plants at the beginning of 1984.
30. The average age of equipment was six years in 1973. This fell to seven years in 1982.

116   *State, Finance & Industry*

REFERENCES

Blin Report (1984). Rapport d'information sur le contrôle des entreprises publiques: banques nationalisées par la loi no. 82-155 du 11.2.822 (Senat, Paris, June).

Cohen, S. and Gourevitch, P. (1982).*France in the Troubled World Economy* (Butterworths, London.

Bruneel, D. and Fraco, J.M. (1984). 'Financial Innovation and Monetary Policy in France' in *Financial Innovation and Monetary Policy* BIS, Basle March pp. 57-90.

Dautresme Report (1982). *Rapport sue le Development et la Protection de l'Epargne* (La Documentation Francaise, Paris).

Economists Advisory Group (1981). *The British and German Banking Systems: a comparative study* (Anglo-German Foundation, London).

Gershenkron, A. (1962). *Economic Development in Historical Perspective* (Harvard University Press, Cambridge, Mass., 1962).

Green, D.M. (1980). 'The Budget and the Plan', in P.Cerny and M.Schain, *French Politics and Public Policy*, Francis Pinter, London).

Green, D.M. (1981a). *Managing Industrial Change? French politics to promote Industrial Adjustment* (HMSO, London).

Green, D.M. (1981b). *The Export Imperative: French policies to promote overseas trade* (unpublished report for the Dept. of Industry).

Green, D.M. (1983a). 'France: enlisting the aid of the private sector', in B.Hindley (ed.), *State Investment Companies in Western Europe* (Macmillan for the Trade Policy Research Centre, London).

Green, D.M. (1983b). 'Strategic Management and the State: France', in K.Dyson and S.Wilks (eds.), *Industrial Crisis* (Martin Robertson, Oxford).

Green, D.M. (1984a). 'Mitterrand: From Socialism to Realism', in *Economics Affairs* vol. 4, no. 3 (April-June 1984), pp. 23-7.

Green, D.M. (1984b). 'Cable TV in France: a non-market approach to industrial development', *National Westminster Bank Review* (August 1984).

Loi Bancaire. (Paris, January 1984).

Morgan, M. (1984). *The Politics of Banking* (Macmillan, London).

Morgan, E.V. and Harrington, R.L. (1977). *Capital Markets in the EEC* (Economists Advisory Group, London).

Patat, J.P. (1982). *Monnaie, Institutions Financieres at Politique Monetaire* (Economica, Paris).

Harrington, R.L. (1974). 'The Importance of Competition for Credit Control', *Issues in Monetary Economics*, eds. H.G.Johnson and A.R.Horbay (Oxford University Press).

Hayward, J. (1983). *Governing France: The One and Indivisible Republic* (Weidenfield and Nicolson, London).

Hayward, J. (1984). 'From planning the French economy to planning the French state: the theory and practice of Priority Action Programmes', *Continuity and Change in France*, ed. V.Wright (George Allen and Unwin, London).

LeFranc, J.D. (1983). *Industrie: le peril francais* (LE Seuil, Paris).

Luthy, H. (1955). *The State of France*, trans. Mosbachery, E. (New York, Praeger).

Kuisel, R.F. (1981). *Capitalism and the State in Modern France* (Cambridge University Press).

Mayoux Report (1979). *Le Development des Initiatives Financieres Locales et Regionales* (le Documentation Francaise, Paris).

Patat, J.P. (1982). *Monnaie, Institutions Financieres et Politique Monetaire* (Economics, Paris).

Pollin, J.P. (1984). 'Money versus Credit: Insights from French Policy Experience', Paper presented at Brasenose College, Oxford (September).

Suleiman, E. (1974). *Politics, Power and Bureaucracy in France* (Princeton University Press).

Thoenig, J.C. (1973). *L'Ere des Technocrates: Le cas des Ponts et chaussees* (L'Editions d'organisation, Paris).

Zysman, J. (1977). *Political Strategies for Industrial Order* (University of California Press, Berkeley).

4 The State, Banks and Industry: The West German Case

Kenneth Dyson

Amongst the central attributes of the twentieth century is our recognition that the power of a state is linked to its economic prowess, and that its political stability is shaped by its capacity to satisfy the material aspirations of its people. It is, therefore, scarcely surprising that observers, at home and abroad, have been fascinated by the extraordinary rate of growth of the economy of Imperial Germany between 1871 and 1914 and then of the Federal Republic of Germany after 1949. The question of whether German capitalism possessed 'an efficient secret', became a very practical one for states threatened by Germany's emergence as Europe's *économie dominante*. Answers to this question have been various, ranging from ideological factors like the 'social market economy' (*Sozialmarktwirtschaft*) to industrial relations based on 'social partnership' (*Sozialpartnerschaft*) and a rationally organised trade union movement. Such answers tell us more about the Federal Republic and indicate the discontinuities caused by the Third Reich, total defeat and a competitor communist 'Germany' in the East. Other observers argue that *Modelldeutschland* has deeper historical roots; that the banking system and its close links with industry and its role in economic diplomacy is 'the efficient secret' of German capitalism and suggests a major continuity. For Karl Hilferding Germany was a system of 'finance capitalism', the banks having become 'industrial capitalists'[1] for Andrew Shonfield the West German economy was a system of 'coordination by banker', the banks acting as a surrogate for state planning of investment.[2]

Judgements about the nature and role of German banking reveal considerable misunderstanding, wishful thinking and simplification that fails to do justice to a complex and changing reality - in part because the search for 'the efficient secret' is foreclosed by the desire to find a ready-made answer. This chapter analyses the nature of the relationship between state, banks and industry in the provision of investment finance in West Germany, trying to identify continuities and changes. The behaviour of

German banks, and their peculiar importance both at the micro industrial level and in economic diplomacy, must be seen as the outcome of two factors: first, economic and political history and, second, commercial strategy. The continuities in bank-industry relations reflect the impact of the economic conditions of industrialisation on German banking and a long-standing recognition of the importance of economic and financial strength to German political aims in Europe and beyond. At the same time banks are commercial actors and are deeply affected by their economic and political expectations. For instance, during the Weimar Republic the banks' conservative attitude towards industrial finance reflected a political distrust of the new Republic and inflationary expectations; the banks could not protect themselves adequately against inflation and hyper-inflation.[3] The relationship between the big banks and heavy industry during the Federal Republic indicates again that the banks give priority to commercial judgements; the banks displayed a new unwillingness to extend credits to a hard-pressed steel industry after 1979 without loan guarantees from government. Perhaps the most striking difference from the Weimar Republic was the attitude of bankers to the state. The bankers of the Federal Republic had confidence that the Bonn government could pursue German aims abroad; also their dependence on and enmeshment in the West's military and economic systems gave them no clear alternative.

Much attention has been given to the radical break in the ideology of state and economy after 1945. Indeed the early years of the Federal Republic are often presented as the interesting story of the new neo-liberal doctrine of the social market economy capturing the Christian Democratic Union/Christian Social Union; of the continuing electoral successes of the CDU/CSU; of the adoption of this ideology by the Social Democratic Party in its Bad Godesberg Programme of 1959; of the latter's subsequent entry into the Federal government in 1966 - in other words, the story of an emerging consensus about the proper relationship between state and economy. The emphasis on the market and on the responsibility of the private sector for economic adjustment, with the state's role as essentially subsidiary and facilitative, seemed to promise a radical break with the concentration and cartelisation of Imperial Germany and with the command economy of the Third Reich. And yet, the ideology of the social market economy breathed new life into traditions of economic behaviour that seemed to have been swamped by the turbulent years of the Weimar Republic, followed by the trauma of the Hitler period. Herbert Feis and Fritz Stern have documented the close connections between the worlds of banking and diplomacy in Imperial Germany: the political dimension of the movement of capital, the use of credit as an instrument of economic warfare, the premium placed on a practical knowledge of finance and industry, the reliance on bankers as suppliers and interpreters of economic knowledge, and the consequent emergence of financiers as 'statesmen in disguise'.[4] The synchronisation of banking and diplomacy was based on a common interest in capital accumulation and the extension of overseas markets.[5] Credit was central to the international competitiveness of the German Economy; international economic competitiveness was the major barometer of Germany's health; hence financiers had a major role to play in German diplomacy. James Spindler has pointed to the liberal traditions of German banking, its loosely regulated and variegated character.[6] In the Federal Republic the social market economy has functioned as an ideological framework for a very complex 'system' of bank-industry relations that has enjoyed considerable freedom from public regulation. This continuity of organisational structure within German capitalism underlies the apparently radical change of ideology: whilst the effectiveness of this structure helps explain the success of the social market economy. Based on old foundations, the Federal Republic has a pattern of tacit cooperation between state, banks and industry. Various actors take decisions independently, but these decisions gain coherence from a natural convergence of interests. Overseas markets and credit remain important components of German politics.

THE HISTORICAL CONTEXT

The strikingly close links between state, bank capital and industry in nineteenth-century Germany owed much to the relative economic backwardness of the country, to the high capital requirements of the most dynamic sectors (coal, iron and steel, electronics, chemicals and heavy engineering), and to the optimism that was inspired by political and economic unification. Industrialisation was not associated with the social and political breakthrough of an independent-minded bourgeoisie.[7] Governments were closely involved in the establishment of private banks; many important firms in the coal, iron and steel industries were under state control; state officials often appeared amongst the founders of private firms, particularly because of their ability to raise capital; the new investment banks took advantage of the new opportunities, mobilising the large amounts of capital needed for new technology and becoming more concerned with the management of firms; whilst company law reform in 1870 recognised the close bank-industry relations that had developed by removing state supervision (*Staatsaufsicht*) and creating the supervisory board (*Aufsichtsrat*) as an organ of control. The supervisory board was a distinctive German innovation through which various interests, notably the big banks, could be represented in the affairs of firms. Although the permanent management board (*Vorstand*) could achieve substantial autonomy, supervisory boards often displayed a will to lead, and in times of crisis were ready to intervene decisively in management. Banks has an even greater identity with a firm when they had been closely involved in its formation through the legal device of *simultane Grundung*. Here the bank put capital into the firm and then sold shares to the public over the counter when the firm was safely off the ground.

The changes in German banking were as radical as those in Germany's economic structure. In the 1850's private bankers were mobilising foreign capital for the great railway boom; by the 1880s the big universal banks were making their breakthrough; and by 1914 banks like the Deutsche Bank had already successfully nurtured multinational firms.[8] In the case of Mannesmann the Deutsche Bank provided a protective umbrella through its early difficult years 1890-1905. (In the latter year the first dividend was paid.) Mannesmann was to be an extraordinarily successful firm and continues to have close links with the Deutsche Bank. The big banks were visibly powerful, as the following figures indicate. In 1896 the banks held 29.4 per cent of seats in supervisory boards; 91 bankers had more than ten posts each. By 1905/6 the six big Berlin banks had 751 seats, the Deutsche Bank alone 221. In 1907 four of the top five German companies (in terms of capital) were banks; of the top 20, twelve were banks (with Deutsche top and the Dresdner Bank joint second with Krupp).[9] The extraordinary missionary zeal within German banking found expression in their statutes (e.g. the Schaaffhausen'sche Bankverein of 1848), in their policy statements (e.g. the Deutsche Bank's early priority to a planned industrial policy focusing on overseas markets), and in individual bankers (e.g. Gerson Bleichroder, a private banker and confidante of Bismarck, Georg Siemens, a director of the Deutsche Bank and member of the Siemens family, and Karl Helfferich, also director of the Deutsche Bank and a great believer in finance capitalism's importance for German diplomacy.[10]

In their early years the banks tended to specialise in particular sectors: the Deutsche Bank in electronics and shipping (with close links to Siemens and Haske and to North German Lloyd), the Dresdner Bank in textiles and chemicals, the Schaffhausen'sche Bankverein in coal (the giant Harpener Bergbaugesellschaft) and iron and steel (Hoesch and Phonix), the Berliner Handelsgesellschaft in electronics (with close links to AEG and the Rathenau family). In 1856 alone the Darmstadter Bank founded seven industrial firms to which it remained committed. The strategic industrial vision of the big banks was best seen in their involvement with the electronics industry, with the potash industry (notably the Darmstadter Bank) and with the new oil industry (the Deutsche Bank's establishment of Deutsche Petroleum in 1904 was emulated in 1905 by the Disconto-Gesellschaft and in 1906 by a Dresdner-Schaffhausen'sche partnership in this field). The Disconto-Gesellschaft and the Schaffhausensche Bankverein played a major role in industrial cartelisation and, in particular, in the formation of the Rhine-Westphalia coal syndicate of 1893. In turn, industrialists had been important in the foundation of banks: railway promoters in the case of the Darmstadter Bank (1853) and Georg Siemens in the case of the Deutsche Bank (1870). Thirteen industrialists sat on the supervisory board of the Berliner Handelsbank, 17 on that of the Schaffhausen'sche Bankverein. Herr Schuster of the Dresdner Bank was prepared to claim in 1908: 'in Germany our banks are largely responsible for the development of the Empire, having fostered and built up its industries.'[11]

The close, informal and confidential links between the big Berlin banks and the German Foreign Office and Kaiser before 1914, the industrial involvements of the banks and the missionary zeal and political acumen of certain bankers has generated a monolithic and oversimplified view of German banking. Limits to bank involvement in industry were established by reference to commercial rationality and responsibility to their own shareholders, as well as by examples of bank failure as a result of overextension of loans to firms. The major concentration of German banking did not take place till 1929-31 when the Disconto-Gesellschaft merged with the Deutsche, and the Darmstadter with the Dresdner. Before 1914 a fair measure of competition was ensured by the number and variety of banks as well as by rivalries between provincial centres and Berlin. Firms tried to develop their own financial resources. For instance, AEG (aided by a consortium of banks) established the Bank fur elektrische Werte in Zurich in 1895; in similar fashion Siemens set up the Schweizerische Gesellschaft fur elektrische Industrie in Basle in 1896.[12] The Siemens family connections to the Deutsche Bank were paralleled by the Rathenau family connections to the Berliner Handelsgesellschaft: Walter Rathenau, a director of the Berliner Handelsgesellshaft, reorganised a large part of its industrial undertakings.[13] The important role of banks like the Schaffhausensche in the supervisory boards of coal, iron and steel firms was counterbalanced by the emergence of 'captains of industry' like August Thyssen and Hugo Stinnes; yet even they emulated the role of bankers. Whilst the industrial power of banks was constrained in these ways, it is still possible to speak of an elite core of bankers who enjoyed close links to the foreign policy establishment, gained high political status from the primacy attached to exports and credit as instruments of policy, presided over a complex web of industrial interests, and were able to inject a broad, 'statesmanlike' perspective into industrial decision-making.

The history of twentieth-century German banking is the story of the resilience of an elite in the face of two disastrous world wars, the financial chaos of the Weimar years, the political compromise of the Nazi period, and the hostility of the Allied occupying powers after 1945. In pursuit of decentralisation of power the Allies sought to impose the American principle of 'state banking', thereby limiting any one bank's operation to one *land*. Yet by 1950 the Deutsche Bank and the Dresdner Bank had re-established central control over almost the whole of their national branch networks; the 1952 law on the Regional Scope of Credit Institutions recognised this fact. Faced by a massive task of reconstruction, recognising the importance of economic success to stabilisation of a new democracy and perceiving threat from the East, German policy-makers turned to, and relied on, an elite with the commercial experience and expertise to mobilise credit effectively and allocate it efficiently.

THE ORGANISATION AND REGULATION OF WEST GERMAN BANKING

The paradox of German banking is provided by the coexistence of 'the Big Three' (indicating a tradition of concentration in commercial banking) with an extraordinary variety of financial institutions (indicating a liberal tradition of finance). Perhaps surprisingly, compared with other West European countries, the level of concentration in German banking is low.[14] In 1980 the Deutsche, Dresdner and Commerzbank accounted for 41 per cent of commercial banking assets but only 10 per cent of total banking assets (Spindler, 1982, Table 2.2). The Federal Republic has a strong non-commercial banking sector, which in 1980 held 76.4 per cent of total bank assets. Twelve central giro banks control 16 per cent of total assets. Most are owned either by an association of savings banks in their region or by the *land*: they serve as clearing houses to the savings banks and, like the Westdeutsche Landesbank Girozentrale in Dusseldorf, have sometimes become major international lenders. Over 600 savings banks account for 22 per cent of total assets; 39 mortgage banks make up for another 14 per cent; some 2300 credit cooperatives control 15 per cent; and sixteen specialised banks like the government-owned Kreditanstalt fur Wiederaufbau (KfW) control 6 per cent of total assets. In short, the banking system is too diverse and loosely textured to enable one to speak of 'bank control over industry' in any unified sense. Perhaps the most striking change since the 1960s has been in the role of the central giro banks and the savings banks. They have substantially increased their industrial shareholdings and, in the manner of 'universal banks'. have begun to act as 'house banks' (*Hausbanken*), especially for local industry.

Before looking more closely at the big banks it is necessary to analyse the loose, regulatory framework that supports such an open and flexible financial system. The task of regulation falls on the Federal Banking Supervisory Office and the Bundesbank. Physically isolated in Berlin, the Banking Supervisory Office has a small staff and only limited powers from the German Banking Act. In line with the German tradition of universal banking, the Act places very few restrictions on 'banking business'. Moreover, it delimits strictly the grounds on which the Supervisory Office can refuse to grant a licence for banking. Although the foreign subsidiaries of German banks have become increasingly important, the Supervisory Office has been unable to obtain comprehensive data about their activities. The Bundesbank is one of the most autonomous and powerful central banks in the world, charged by statute to 'safeguard the currency'. As such it uses a wide range of monetary policy instruments which have important effects on the banks: thus it can direct public sector deposits towards or away from the banks and vary their reserve requirements. Yet the role of the Bundesbank as regulator is secondary to that of acting as a high-level spokesman for the banks in Bonn. Successive presidents of the Bundesbank have come from the banking community: Karl Otto Pohl (1980-) had once been head of public relations for the Federation of German Banks; Karl Klasen (1970-77) came from the Deutsche Bank and returned to its supervisory board.

It will be helpful to say a little more about the six *Grossbanken* (Big Banks), as defined by the Bundesbank. Amongst the top European banks Deutsche Bank was 6th largest in (1981) with assets of $83.8 billion, Dresdner 9th with assets of $57.6 billion, and Commerzbank 17th with assets of $44.6 billion.[15] They are the classic German universal banks, combining deposit banking with acting as 'house-bank' to a large number of firms. As universal banks they undertake various forms of lending; issue new shares and deal in securities; own large numbers of shares themselves; act on behalf of customers who deposit their shareholdings with the bank; have representatives on the supervisory boards of a large number of firms; and engage in leasing and factoring. Of the other three *Grossbanken* two have their base in Bavaria: the Bayerische Vereinsbank (in 1981 19th largest in Europe with assets of $43.4 billion) and the Bayerische Hypotheken-und Wechsel-Bank (21st largest with assets of $39.4 billion). Even more striking is the Bank fur Gemeinwirtschaft (30th with assets of $25.4 billion). It is owned by the trade unions and the cooperative societies, acts as their 'house bank' and is the newest of the big banks. As already indicated, the role of the six *Grossbanken* in universal banking has been challenged by the public sector giro centres, notably the Westdeutsche Landesbank (10th largest in Europe) and the Bayerische Landesbank (24th largest).

BANKS, GOVERNMENT AND FOREIGN ECONOMIC POLICY

The role of German bankers as an exclusive elite is closely related to a firm conviction in government that Germany is export-dependent: that political room for manoeuvre, indeed survival, depends on the effective mobilisation of capital for investment and of credit for trade.[16] According to the Dresdner Bank (1978), exports accounted for 24.8 per cent of total industrial sales in 1978: the percentage for automobiles was 38.4, chemicals 36.7, iron and steel 35.2, and mechanical engineering 43.3. In 1980 the Bundesbank calculated that exports supplied 23 per cent of GNP (from 15 per cent in 1965) and 20 per cent of jobs. The Federal Republic's position as the world's second largest exporter was not only a source of pride. As the Bundesbank repeatedly underlined, the priority to an export drive was essential in a country that had to import 97 per cent of its oil and most other raw materials, and that had to pay an ever more expensive oil bill. Political priority to exports was complementary with the commercial interests of the banks in the health of those firms and industries with which they were closely identified as 'house-banks' as well as in profitable international financing opportunities. It meant also that the international experience and expertise of German bankers had a particular relevance to foreign and economic policies. Their breadth of perspective is combined with a detailed knowledge of the industrial world, both sectoral and intra-firm.

At an institutional level bankers enjoy close and varied contacts to government, notably to the several interministerial committees for coordinating foreign economic policy. Particularly important is the interministerial committee responsible for Hermes, the export credit programme: it considers individual applications for loan guarantees and, by adjusting their terms, seeks to induce the banks towards or away from certain types of activity.[17] Decisions are taken by civil servants from the Ministries of Economics, Finance, Foreign Affairs and Development: but bankers and representatives from export industries participate in an advisory capacity. Bankers play a similar role in the interministerial committee dealing with insurance for direct foreign investments. A central role in German foreign economic policy is occupied by the government-owned Kreditanstalt fur Wiederaufbau.[18] In particular, it joins with the commercial banks in co-financing major German exports, like the export of nuclear reactors to Brazil in 1976. The combination of KfW participation with Hermes guarantees and an addition of capital aid from the KfW can give a major competitive edge to German contracts. The KfW has also substantial assets ($29 billion in 1979), with trade-related and other international commitments of $15.5 billion, substantially outstripping the US Export-Import Bank. Once again, the board of KfW includes major bankers: Hermann Abs was its first general manager; F. Wilhelm Christians of the Deutsche Bank was on its board in 1979. Prominent bankers are also to be found on the advisory councils of Federal Ministries, notably in the Foreign Trade Advisory Council of the Ministry of Economics.

The strength of informal links of bankers to the political elite is clear from their presence in the official parties accompanying Chancellors and Ministers abroad. Individual bankers whose expertise could link together German industry with international finance have come to enjoy close relations with successive Chancellors: Robert Pferdmenges (Bankhaus Sal. Oppenheim), Hermann Abs (Deutsche Bank), Jurgen Ponto (Dresdner Bank) and Wilfried Guth (Deutsche Bank).

The relationship between banks and governments has three main features. First, despite the highly formalised structure of interest representation in three 'peak' associations of bankers, the 'Big Three' have maintained a dominant role in the articulation and aggregation of banking interests. The most important of the professional associations remains the Federation of German Banks, representing the commercial banking sector. It benefits, like the two other professional associations, from the legal requirements that the Federal government must consult them when considering new laws for banking; and that the Federal Banking Supervisory Office must consult them before drawing up principles to determine the adequacy of bank capital and liquidity. In practice, the Big Three, especially the Deutsche Bank, provide the major funding and staff support for the Federation of German Banks; their managing directors sit on its praesidium and chair three of its four central working committees, notably those for credit policy and legal issues.[19]

Second, German banking combines a marked preference for self-regulation with the exercise of restraint on issues of 'high politics'. The best examples of self-regulation are provided by the Central Capital Market Committee (ZKMA), formed by the big banks in 1957, with agreement of the Ministry of Economics, to control and coordinate access to the German capital market; and its Eurobond sub-committee, established in 1968 to arrange queuing of foreign issues in the domestic market. A sub-committee whose six members represent over 90 per cent of the new issue market for DM Eurobonds and include senior officials of the five largest German banks was bound to evoke complaints about a 'self-serving' oligarchy.[20] This preference for a quiet, informal consensus was accompanied by a willingness to be led by government on matters of high, strategic significance. Michael Kreile (1978, p.208) has emphasised that business and financial interests played a subordinate role in the formulation of Ostpolitik by the Social-Liberal coalition (SPD/FDP) after 1969. Nevertheless, Ostpolitik created new commercial opportunities and, most notably, the German banks were prepared to make huge loans to Poland and to assist the construction of a 3300-mile gas pipeline across the Soviet Union. The future course of Ostpolitik was then shaped by this web of interdependence between commercial and political factors.

Third, successive German governments have preferred to rely on utilitarian inducements rather than to intervene directly in order to influence the transactions of German banks.[21] The prime mechanism is the use of government loan guarantees as a 'policy signal' to the banks, topped up in special cases (e.g. nuclear reactor sales to Brazil in 1976) by co-financing from the Kreditanstalt fur Wiederaufbau. These guarantees under the Hermes programme are typically aimed at stimulating German exports or securing supplies of raw materials. As such they show a high degree of sensitivity to the international commercial interests of German banks and are strongly influenced by the latter's estimates of creditworthiness. Where government's perception of national interests and the banks' commercial interests do not neatly coincide the liberal tradition of bank-government relations is reflected in the outcomes. Government is not prepared to impose solutions, whilst the banks are prepared to be tough in defence of their interests. As the foreign policy stakes rise for the government and the financial risks increase for the banks, the banks play up the importance of loan guarantees for their cooperation (e.g. the DM 1.2 billion credit to Poland in 1980). Government seeks to combine guarantees with moral suasion and the implicit threat of withdrawal of support in the future.

BANKS AND INDUSTRY

A major influence on the character of relations between banks and government comes from the close reciprocal links between banks and major corporations in West Germany: as in the case of the Krakatau steel project (1975-76), private corporations and their (*Hausbanken*) function as teams. In 1975 Indonesia's faltering credit rating coincided with liquidity problems of the state-owned Pertamina oil company, the majority shareholder in the huge Krakatau steel project. At stake were massive orders for such prestigious German corporations as Salzgitter, Kloeckter and Siemens. The rescue package announced by the Deutsche Bank in 1976 represented a most intriguing form of collaboration between the Indonesian government, the German Ministry of Economics, major German banks and some German industrial corporations. An all-German banking consortium provided a credit of DM 1.175 billion: DM 450 million was covered by Hermes guarantees, DM 725 million by guarantees from a German industrial consortium. As collateral Pertamina was to ship 2 million tons of crude oil annually for five years to West Germany, the payments of the oil going back to the bank consortium to repay the loan.[22]

The close working communications characteristic of the Krakatau steel rescue draw attention to one of the most controversial issues in the German economy - the industrial power of the banks. Before assessing the extent of this power it is necessary to identify its sources. At the root of this relationship is the overwhelming importance of the banks in providing industrial finance. With recession, notably after 1974, German industry exhibited a clear preference for reliance on internal funds and for a high liquidity position - reflecting a declining propensity to invest and a hedge against uncertainty. Yet external funding has been crucial during periods of expansion, reaching 40.4 per cent in 1968 and 42 per cent in 1976 (after playing a negligible role in the two previous years). Most striking is the composition of external funding. German industry is traditionally highly 'geared', that is the equity of German corporations forms only a low proportion of their total assets. Shares and bonds are of relatively minor importance as means of raising funds, accounting respectively for 6 and 4 per cent during the period 1968-73 and 4.4 and 0.4 per cent in 1976. More important have been bank loans (60 per cent in 1968-73, and 32.7 per cent in 1976), and in particular long-term bank loans (39 per cent in 1968-76) and 21.5 per cent in 1976.[23] This important long-term financing role for industry is made possible by the ability of the German banks to attract household savings into medium and long-term saving deposits and bonds. Tax concessions have played an important role in encouraging this process. Since 1960 savers have increasingly placed savings in higher interest-bearing long-term deposits with the savings bank sector, taking advantage of state savings premiums and tax rebates. Correspondingly, giro centres like the giant Westdeutsche Landesbank Girozentrale have come to play an increasingly important role in long-term industrial finance. The commercial banks have become increasingly critical of the tax privileges enjoyed by this sector.

The German stock market has remained weak, with only 465 companies quoted on Germany's Stock Exchanges in 1977 (compared to 551 in 1963) out of a total of some 2200 public companies (*Aktiengesellschaften*). Most important of all, almost 60 per cent of shares were either owned by or deposited with banks.

Bank shareholdings have three main dimensions: direct shareholdings, a phenomenon inherited from the nineteenth century but greatly extended after the two world wars when outstanding credits were converted into bank-held shares to assist reconstruction; of greater quantitative importance, exercise of proxy rights for shares that they have on deposit from their customers; and *Leihstimmen*, the loan by one or more banks of voting rights to another that specialises in a particular sector or company. A Monopoly Commission report of 1976 revealed that the voting rights of the banks (including proxies) amounted to 26 per cent of the total in the top 100 companies; the 'Big Three' held more than 25 per cent shares (in effect, a power of veto) in 28 of the top 100 companies. In 1979 the Gessler Commission's analysis of direct shareholdings by the banks indicated that almost three-quarters were in the top 50 companies; that over 90 per cent were large shareholdings of 25 per cent or more; and that shareholdings were notably concentrated in construction, brewing and retail distribution. The banks were also important shareholders in investment trusts which themselves have major industrial holdings. The Monopoly commission report noted that the direct shareholdings of the 'Big Three' represented more than 25 per cent of voting rights in 11 of the top 100 companies. Some examples are useful: in 1980 the Dresdner Bank had an involvement of 25 per cent or more in 15 companies, most notably AEG-Telefunken, Hapag-Lloyd, Kaufhof and Metallgesellschaft; the Deutsche Bank's portfolio was highly profitable and included Daimler-Benz (31 per cent), Holzmann (35 per cent), Karstadt (over 30 per cent), Nixdorf (25 per cent) and Metallgesellschaft (some 15 per cent).

Perhaps the most visible sign of bank power in industry has been the presence of bank representatives on the supervisory boards (*Aufsichtsrate*) of companies. In 1975 the banks held 179 (14.9 per cent) of the seats on the supervisory boards on the top 100 companies; only 25 of these companies had no bank representative, and in 31 cases a bank provided the chairman. The Big Three alone accounted for 102 of these seats and 21 of the chairmen. Of the 66 large companies examined by the Gessler Commission, 59 had bank representatives; 51 had more than one bank representative. Of the 74 largest companies (including 8 banks) banks provided the chairman in 32 cases and accounted for 18 per cent of seats. Bank representation was notably strong in chemicals, construction, engineering and metals and was not always associated with the strength of bank shareholdings or proxy voting. Perhaps the most famous example of the accumulation of seats on supervisory boards was provided by Hermann Abs of the Deutsche Bank: he had some 30 seats. Since the so-called 'Lex Abs' of 1965 there is an upper limit of 10 such seats for an individual. Despite this restriction, a banker can build up a formidable array of industrial contacts in this way; and banks can continue to cast their nets wide. Prominent amongst the 54 representatives that the Deutsche Bank had in major industrial companies in 1979 was Wilfried Guth and F. Wilhelm Christians, co-speakers for the Bank's board of directors. Guth was chairman of the supervisory boards of Daimler Benz, Holzmann and Metallgesellschaft; he was a member of the boards for Siemens, Thyssen and Allianz Insurance. Christians chaired the supervisory boards of Mannesmann and RWE and sat on the boards of Karstadt, Bayer and Volkswagen.

The supervisory board was created in 1870 as an organ or representation and control over the permanent management board (*Vorstand*). By the interwar period it was clear that supervisory boards tended to function as administrative organs of companies; that they built up a community of interests with management; and that informally, through special committees of the supervisory board, leading members took a detailed interest in corporate decision-making. Despite a statutory effort in 1965 to strengthen the control function of the supervisory board these tendencies have continued. The representative function of supervisory boards has meant that the external functions are even more important than the internal. Its membership is a mirror of the business relationships of a company: employee representatives in the post-war period, large shareholders, former managers, experts, other industrialists (usually its so-called 'market partners' - customers and suppliers) and, not least, bankers. In this way, 'outsiders' become 'insiders'. Close, continuous commercial contacts faciliate the construction of consortia and the implementation of large collaborative projects. Firms seek bank representation on their supervisory boards as a way of reducing uncertainty and managing interdependence: for banks have a broad sectoral and macro-economic perspective, and, combining their economic and industrial expertise with their ability to mobilise capital, offer an unrivalled consultancy service, particularly at time of corporate crisis. The collapse of Bauknecht in 1981 was testament to the danger of failing to establish such close links to a *Hausbank* that might be able to organise a bank consortium.

Above all, it must not be forgotten that the German commercial banks are 'Universal' banks, combining the services of a merchant bank with those of a deposit bank. The provision of long-term credit for industry is combined with the issuing of shares and floating of debenture loans for firms. As Riesser noted in 1912, the active role of the banks in the capital market remains the cornerstone of the vast structure of relations between banks and industry in Germany. Hence, when faced with a massive problem of post-war reconstruction, German government built upon the inherited industrial strengths of the banks by augmenting their activities (e.g. through the Kreditanstalt fur Wiederaufbau), and by using bankers like Abs and Pferdmenges as economic advisers. Indeed, Abs became the first chairman of KfW. The KfW was established in 1948, essentially as a bankers' bank, to administer the European Recovery Programme loan. By 1980 it had a capital of DM 1 billion, and raised funds by means of loans and bond issues as well as receiving direct grants from the Federal government, notably in relation to the regional programme. Some half of its loan commitments are now for export credits and foreign aid. Most importantly the banks have been the channel for sifting claims to the KfW and making recommendations for low-cost loans. In this ingenious way the strengths of the banks were put to good effect during the 1950s and 1960s.

The banks were also a central part of what Wilhelm Hankel terms 'a multi-tiered system of long-term export finance' in which the Bundesbank provided commercial banks with cheap credit lines for export accounts, the banks established their own consortium in the Export Credit Company (Ausfuhrkredit-Gesellschaft, AKA), the Federal government cooperated through the KfW, and the Hermes programme provided loan guarantees for risky foreign ventures.[24] Much less impact has been made by the German Risk Financing Company (Deutsche Wagnisfinanzierungs-Gesellschaft), a venture capital company that was formed by 27 banks in 1975. The aim was to close a major gap in industrial financing for new innovatory firms. However, this venture capital company was put together under political pressure from the Social Democratic Party and from the Federal Research and Technology Ministry: and much criticism was levelled at its caution, and notably the stringency of its loan conditions. Though the structure of bank support has its weaknesses as well as strengths, the German banks have continued to be channels that can deal comprehensively with the problems of their industrial clients.

The German tradition of universal banking, allied to the conception of the *Hausbank* and the extent of bank participation on supervisory boards, has major consequences for the character of investment decision-making. First, banks take a detailed and long-term view of sectors, analysing profit rates within different sectors as a basis for their lending decisions. They rely heavily on their intelligence departments for assessment both of the 'standing' of a firm in relation to industry, area and national averages and of the relation of a particular loan to bank strategy.[25] Having made inter and intra-sectoral comparisons German banks are prepared to dispense with considerations of short-term profits and early returns in favour of mobilising financial, technical and managerial resources to secure market share and to improve the long-term cost structure of the firm. The solidarity of a *Hausbank* with the firm's management finds it clearest expression in the bank's sense of duty to organise rescues in times of crisis, using at such times its wide range of industrial, financial and governmental contacts as well as its own expertise and numerous services. Not least, when dissatisfied with corporate policy, banks are prepared to take an active role in the power-game within management. In 1983 the head of Gutehoffnungshutte fell victim to the opposition of the Commerzbank and Allianz; whilst in 1984 the Deutsche Bank mobilised bank opposition to the head of Thyssen. Banks maintain a network of favoured industrial managers and their proteges who can be drafted in to a corporation in difficulties (as in the case of the Dresdner Bank and AEG-Telefunken).

A bank like the Deutsche can stand then at the centre of a web of industrial interests, with (in 1981) some 140 representatives on supervisory boards, proxy votes to the value of DM 70 billion, excellent internal organisation, managers (like Guth and Christians) of world stature and earning annually more in dividends from its industrial shares alone than it pays out to its own shareholders. Most important of all is the cumulation of modes of industrial influence by bankers: shareholdings, proxy voting, floating shares, credit business and presence on supervisory boards. Yet the constraints on the industrial power of banks are considerable. Not least, German bankers are cautious, both in the sense of not wanting to evoke political suspicions and opposition that could make their job harder and in the sense of not wanting to take risks in investment financing that could undermine the confidence which is the lifeblood of efficiently functioning financial markets. Faced by new, rapidly changing markets it may prove difficult for the most sophisticated economic and industrial analysis to reduce the element of risk sufficiently to overcome the native caution of the banker. Thus during the early 1980s criticism mounted of the failure of the big banks to give adequate backing to the information technology industry. Bankers were a good deal clearer about the need to disengage from the steel industry by 1979/80, particularly when structural change in the world economy was accompanied by rising interest rates. Deutsche Bank disengaged partially from Hoesch, irritation between Krupp Stahl and its Hausbank, the Dresdner, was followed in 1983/84 by conflict between the Deutsche Bank and Thyssen over the latter's unwillingness to fulfil the terms of the steel plan, thereby making possible a general rationalisation of the industry, whilst the banks emphasised to government that loan guarantees were essential for their future participation in the steel industry.[26]

The banks are certainly capable of putting together consortia to rescue a corporation in crisis (e. g. AEG-Telefunken) or to mount a concerted export promotion (e. g. the nuclear exports deal to Brazil in 1976 and the financing of the Krakatau steel project in 1975-76). Yet they are also in competition for corporate business (witness the highly competitive strategy of the Westdeutsche Landesbank in the 1970s) and for industrial power. Tension and conflict amongst the banks has been notably apparent in the construction industry. Here there are two main rivals: Holzmann, the largest with a turnover (in 1981) of DM 6.3 billion and with a major exporting record; and Hochtief, with a turnover of DM 6.1 billion. Commerzbank is the *Hausbank* of Hochtief; Deutsche Bank the *Hausbank* of Holzmann (with a 35 per cent shareholding and Wilfried Gutt as chairman of the supervisory board). In 1981 the Deutsche Bank was shocked and angered when the Westdeutsche Landesbank made a sudden and very profitable sale of its 25 per cent shareholding in Holzmann to Commerzbank: the latter passed on a large part of this shareholding to Hochtief, which acquired a seat on the supervisory board of Holzmann. The deal was seen by the Deutsche Bank as as attempt to curb the power of Holzmann in the industry by interlocking the two largest companies.

Thirdly, industrialists played an important role in the establishment of German banks (e. g. the Deutsche), and today many of the large industrial corporations own shares in banks and prominent industrialists are to be found on the supervisory boards of banks. Thus in 1979 the supervisory board of the Deutsche Bank included the chairman of Bosch (Hans Merkle), the honorary president of Siemens (Dr Peter Von Siemens) and the managing director of Klockner; the bank's circle of advisers was a list of the most powerful industrialists in Germany. Taking the supervisory boards and circles of advisers of the Big Three together, a majority of their members come from corporations in which the bank has seats on the supervisory boards. There is, therefore, an important element of reciprocity in the relationships between banks and industry in Germany.

SOME ILLUSTRATIVE CASES

An important factor in the behaviour of German banks is their definition of their sphere of influence. Individual banks continue to be influenced in these definitions by long-standing historical identifications with particular countries (e. g. the Deutsche Bank and Turkey) and particular corporations (e. g. Dresdner with AEG-Telefunken and Deutsche with Bayer, Siemens, Daimler-Benz, Mannesmann and Holzmann). A bank may also continue to have a strong historical identification with a particular sector, though this phenomenon is rarer: an example is the Bayerische Hypotheken Bank and the brewing industry (thus it owns more than 25 per cent of the Loewenbrau brewery). In these spheres of influence it is normal banking practice to defer to 'the lead bank', whether by loaning shareholding votes or letting that bank take responsibility for putting together a financial and managerial rescue package. In line not just with the prevailing doctrine of the social market economy but also of a deeper liberal tradition in government - banking relations, governments too tend to defer to the analytical competence of the 'lead bank' for a given country, corporation or perhaps sector.

An example of a bank playing a leading role in sectoral restructuring on behalf of a corporation with which it has long identification is provided by the Deutsche Bank and the rubber industry. On behalf of a major client, Bayer, the Deutsche Bank acted between 1969 and 1972 to prevent control of the industry falling into foreign hands. The Deutsche Bank bought up major shareholdings in the two major firms, Continental Gummi-Werke and Phoenix. By 1972 the bank was providing the chairman of the supervisory boards of both companies. Similarly the Deutsche Bank's history of financial relationships with Indonesia was reflected in her lead role in organising the complex rescue package for the Krakatau steel project, reputedly the largest export deal in German history; and later, after 1979, in the attempt to put together a financial package for Turkey.

In the management of corporate crises the phenomena of banks' spheres of influence and sense of duty to rescue are to be most clearly seen. 'Bank-led' rescues are by now a familiar feature of German industry. They involve a banking consortium organised by the *Hausbank*, and normally government loan guarantees. If the corporation in difficulties is a private empire (e. g. Siemens in 1897; and Krupp in 1967), the bank (or banks) will use the opportunity to transform it into a public company and gain seats on the supervisory board that is then necessary. The two most spectacular 'bank-led' rescues in the history of the Federal Republic have provided intriguing insights into the conduct and outlook of German bankers.

In 1966 Krupp, a household name across Europe as a giant of German heavy industry, announced losses of DM 50 million; in 1967 its debt to the banks amounted to DM 2. 5 billion against the background of a turnover of DM 5 billion; and at the end of 1966 the banks' own Export Credit Company (AKA) precipitated a corporate crisis by refusing further export credit. The crisis negotiations involved Federal Economics Minister, Karl Schiller, Berthold Beitz as general manager of Krupp, Abs of the Deutsche Bank and three other bankers; and concentrated on drafting an agreement (*Vertrag*) designed to safeguard Krupp's role as a major exporter. The Federal government provided loan guarantees of DM 300 million for export orders; the state government of North-Rhine Westphalia offered a loan guarantee of DM 150 million; and the banks extended a further DM 100 million of export credit. In return, Krupp was to be transformed from a private empire into a limited liability company with a supervisory board. The presence of the ubiquitous Abs and of a banker from the Dresdner Bank on the new supervisory board was intended to ensure a careful monitoring of the rescue operation, including the proper and effective use of the government's loan guarantees.

The case of AEG-Telefunken was different because from its inception (it was born as a giant company) it had been closely linked to two banks: first to the Deutsche (which tried to regulate competition between AEG and Siemens), then to the Berliner Handelsgessellschaft (Walter Rathenau joined its management). The Deutsche, Dresdner and Commerz-und Privatbank used AEG's crisis of 1936 to acquire seats on its supervisory board: and after the Second World War the Dresdner Bank emerged as the undisputed *Hausbank*, paralleling the Deutsche Bank's role in the electronics industry *vis-à-vis* Siemens. AEG-Telefunken's crisis was dramatic because it was Germany's second largest, Eurpoe's 4th largest and the world's 12th largest electronics company (in terms of turnover). In the 1960s and 1970s it had failed to shift its production on a sufficient scale to high-value, profitable products in office technology and data processing: expansion concentrated on electronic consumer goods and power-engineering, which accounted for over 50 per cent of turnover. Also, unlike its larger and successful rival Siemens, AEG-Telefunken was slow to engage in overseas production. A series of costly and ill-advised company acquisitions were made; overly ambitious investments were made in nuclear power and computer development; and overseas competition led to falling sales in a range of electronic consumer goods. From 1974 onwards losses were incurred, and in 1979 a financial crisis was unleashed by a loss of DM 968 million.

In the autumn of 1979 the Dresdner Bank, as AEG-Telefunken's *Hausbank*, organised a rescue by means of a large consortium that included 20 banks and insurance companies as well as Daimler Benz. AEG-Telefunken received financial aid of DM 3. 4 billion in the form of replenishment of its equity capital and of additional long-term loans. The price was a restructuring and rationalisation programme. Restructuring meant greater concentration on certain products (notably telecommunications), a doubling of overseas production, closure of unprofitable plants and cooperation with partners. Rationalisation meant a loss of 10 per cent of jobs (some 13, 000) by the end of 1980: the workforce had already been reduced by 25 per cent (some 40, 000 jobs) over the previous decade. The close monitoring of the rescue programme was ensured by the election of Hans Friderichs from the Dresdner Bank as chairman of AEG-Telefunken's supervisory board. Friderichs brought in a new general manager, Heinz Durr: the latter's career was closely linked with the engineering company Robert Bosch (with which the

Dresdner Bank enjoyed long-established links). Bosch was keen on diversification and might play a major part in the restructuring programme. Accordingly, in 1981 AEG, Bosch and Mannesmann announced a new joint venture in telecommunications. The deal was to have the financial support of the Dresdner Bank, the Deutsche Bank, the Westdeutsche Landesbank and the Allianz, who agreed to take equity stakes. In sum, the rescue of AEG-Telefunken in 1979 seemed to display the remarkable capacity of self-organisation in German capitalism, the central role of the banks in insulating government from difficult and complex corporate problems and the commitment to an export-led modernisation policy.

Unfortunately, the problem of restructuring AEG-Telefunken proved obstinate and soured relations between the big banks, notably the Deutsche and the Dresdner. Continuing losses meant that in 1981 the consortium agreed to write off DM 240 million of outstanding loans. By 1982 the problems of this sprawling industrial giant threatened to turn into West Germany's biggest industrial disaster. The new management was unable to free itself from the burdens imposed by a past phase of rapid empire-building based on borrowed funds. After 1979, and despite the rescue programme, this inheritance of enormous financial liabilities was aggravated by record high interest rates. In 1979 the banks had pumped into AEG-Telefunken DM 930 million at DM 150 a share: by August 1982 the value of the shares had dropped to DM 22. The search by the banks and management for strong industrial partners in the more viable areas ran into difficulties. In the summer of 1982 the restructuring programme appeared to collapse when the works council of AEG-Telefunken rejected the proposal that Britain's GEC should acquire a 40 per cent equity stake in the profitable capital goods business (in large part because of Lord Weinstock's reputation for 'ruthless' personnel policy). Chancellor Helmut Schmidt rejected trade union pressure for the Federal government to take an equity stake and stressed the need for a 'private sector' solution. In July 1982 the Federal government limited itself to an export credit guarantee of DM 600 million on condition that the banks provided new loans of DM 275 million.

In the autumn of 1982 the most dramatic event in the post-war history of German industrial corporations occured. Faced by continuing losses and the failure of its restructuring programme, AEG-Telefunken invoked the German legal procedure known as *Vergleich* ('composition'). *Vergleich* enables a corporation to ward off bankruptcy by a court-supervised settlement with its creditors. In a situation in which debts exceed assets a corporation can seek protection from its creditors, relief of its external debt burden and financial room to restructure. An administrator is appointed by the court to supervise the settlement which involves the attempt to persuade creditors to write off up to 60 per cent of the corporation's unsecured debts. The creditors are eventually assembled to vote on a settlement and the court-appointed administrator monitors the settlement for 18 months. When *Vergleich* proceedings began, AEG-Telefunken had debts of at least DM 5 billion. Banks and other creditors faced prospective losses of some DM 2. 6 billion. The *Vergleich* of 1983 underlined the immense financial resources that the Federal government and the banks were prepared to pump into AEG-Telefunken. A corporation whose sales revenue in 1981 had been DM 15 billion was given DM 4. 6 billion of loan write-offs and new finance. The banks offered DM 1. 1 billion of new funds and wrote off DM 1. 8 billion of the DM 3 billion that was owed to them (the latter 'profit' was to be used to cover restructuring costs); whilst the Federal government provided a DM 1. 1 billion loan guarantee and an additional DM 600 million of export credit guarantees. In 1982-83 restructuring in the interest of a slimmed-down corporation gathered pace. Bosch acquired the bulk of the profitable telecommunications business; Bosch-Siemens, the joint venture in household appliances, took over Neff; and the French electronics giant Thomson-Brandt, frustrated in its attempt to acquire Grundig, made a successful bid for Telefunken.

The course of the crisis of AEG-Telefunken indicates the strengths and the limits of German economic organisation. Strongly liberal presuppositions in relations between government and industry was matched by a capacity for self-organisation in the private sector and a willingness of banks and industry to attempt bold solutions to the problem of a major corporation in crisis. Government was effectively insulated from a huge industrial problem, its commitments being limited to loan guarantees. On the other hand, the combination of the crisis at AEG-Telefunken with crises in the steel, shipbuilding and shipping industry cast doubt on the resilience of a German banking system that had strongly developed identifications with particular corporations. The Dresdner Bank faced losses of DM 300 million on unsecured loans of some DM 500 million to AEG-Telefunken, in addition to heavy write-offs on loans to Bauknecht and to Korf. The banks were forced to make massive loan loss provisions: the Deutsche Bank increased its provision from DM 29. 7 million in 1978 to DM 1. 7 billion in 1982; whilst between 1981 and 1982 Commerzbank more than trebled and the Dresdner nearly trebled their provisions. In 1983 the dangers of overexposure for a bank were graphically underlined when the Bundesbank organised a rescue of an important German investment Bank Schroeder, Muenchmeyer, Hengst (SMH). About 20 German banks injected over DM 400 million into SMH. The immediate cause of the crisis was the problems of IBH, the world's third largest construction equipment-maker. SMH's total exposure to IBH, including shareholdings and loans, amounted to about a quarter of its DM 2. 2 billion capital.

CONCLUSION

The continuities in the relationships between government, banks and industry in Germany are most striking. An élite of bankers continue to enjoy a salient position on the borderlines of foreign and economic policies. They enjoy close informal relations with the governmental élite and mediate in the relations between government and industry. Their closest contacts are to an élite of industrial managers whose career prospects are in large part dependent on the managerial assessments of bankers. Indeed one can speak of a mobile élite of industrial managers, as dependent for their careers on the banks and their management network as senior public servants are dependent on the political parties and possession of the right 'party book'.[27] The phenomenon of 'party penetration' in the Federal Republic is not characteristic of government - industry relations: more important is 'bank penetration' of industry.

Yet these continuities exist in a state of tension with the commercial judgements of banks. A sense of responsibility towards established and recognised spheres of corporate influence will tend - particularly during periods of rapid structural change - to clash with the native caution of the banker. Thus in the early 1980s the question arose of whether the commercial judgements of bankers were compatible with macro-economic rationality. From a macro-economic perspective, the question was about the ability and willingness of the banks to develop a strategy of industrial engagement to match that of disengagement in sectors like steel and shipbuilding. The West German economy was confronted with the harsh reality of a qualitative change in the world economy akin to that facing Britain from the 1860s onwards. The challenge was not simply to the doctrine of the social market economy but to the tradition of institutional relationships on which it rested and which predated it.

NOTE OF THANKS

The author would like to thank the Universities of Konstanz and Liverpool for their financial assistance with this research; also James Spindler and Michael Kreile for making their own research available to me - research on which I have freely drawn.

NOTES

1. K. Hilferding, *Das Finanzkapital* (Vienna, 1910).
2. A. Shonfield, *Modern Capitalism* (Oxford: Oxford University Press, 1965).
3. P. Barret Whale, *Joint Stock Banking in Germany* (London: Frank Cass, 1968, and B. Weisbrod, *Schweirindustrie in de Weimarer Republic: Interessenpolitik zwischen Stabilisierung and Krise* (Wuppertal: Peter Hammer Verlag, 1978).
4. H. Feis, *Europe, The World's Banker, 1870-1914* (New York: Augustus Kelley, 1964); F. Stern *Gold and Iron: Bismarck, Bleichroeder and the Building of the German Empire* (New York: Albert Knopf, 1962)
5. F. Fisher, *Kreig der Illusionen* (Dusseldorf, 1969).
6. J. A. Spindler, *International Banking and Foreign Policy: A Study of Their Co-ordination in West Germany and Japan with Inferences for the United States* (Washington D.C.: Brookings Institution, 1982).
7. A. Gerschenkron, *Economic Backwardness in Historical Perspective* (New York: Praeger, 1962).
8. P. Hertner, 'Fallstudien ze deutschen multinationalen Unternehmen vor dem Ersten Weltkrieg', in N. Horn and J. Kocka (eds.), *Recht und Entwicklung der Grossunternehemen im 19 and 20 Jahrhundert* (Gottingen: Vandenhoeck and Ruprecht, 1979).
9. J. Kocka and H. Siegrist, 'Die Hundert grossten deutschen Industrieunternehmen im spaten 19 und 20. Jahrhundert' in Horn and Kocka, ibid. , p. 119.
10. For details see Stern, *op. cit.* ; G. Siemens, *Geschichte des Hauses Siemens* (Munich, 1947-52). 3 vols; J. G. Williamson, *Karl Helfferich, 1872-1924* (New Jersey, Princeton University Press, 1971); and J. Riesser, *Die Deutschen Grossbanken und ihre Konzentration* (Jena: Gustav Fischer, 1912).
11. J. H. Clapham, *The Economic Development of France and Germany, 1815-1914 (London: Cambridge University Press, 1955), p. 390.*
12. Hertner, *op. cit.*
13. P. Bergler, *Walter Rathenau* (Bremen: Schunemann, 1979).
14. B. T. Bayliss and A. A. S. Butt Philip, *Capital Markets and Industrial Investment in Germany and France: Lessons for the UK* (Farnborough: Saxon House, 1980); and The Economists Advisory Group, *The British and German Banking Systems: A Comparative Study* (London: Anglo-German Foundation, 1981).

15. 'The FT 500', *The Financial Times* (21 October 1981).
16. M. Kreile, 'West Germany: The Dynamics of Expansion', in P. Katzenstein (ed.), *Between Power and Plenty* (Cambridge, Mass. : Harvard University Press, 1978).
17. Spindler, *op. cit.*, p. 37.
18. Ibid., pp. 53-60.
19. Ibid., p. 14.
20. Ibid., pp. 14-15; and Kreile, *op. cit.*, p. 212.
21. Spindler, *op. cit.*, passim.
22. Ibid, pp. 68-73.
23. Baylis and Butt Philip, *op. cit.*, pp. 14-17.
24. W. Hankel, *Der Ausweg aus der Krise* (Dusselfdorf: Econ, 1975), pp. 117-18.
25. The Economists Advisory Group, *op. cit.*, pp. 197-9.
26. For further details see: K. H. F. Dyson, 'The Politics of Corporate Crises in West Germany', *West European Politics*, vol. 7, no. 1 (January 1984); and K. H. F. Dyson and S. Wilks (eds.), *Industrial Crises* (Oxford: Martin Robertson, 1983).
27. On this see K. H. F. Dyson, *Party, State and Bureaucracy in West Germany* (Beverly Hills, California: Sage, 1977).

5 State, Finance and Industry in Italy
Paul Furlong

INTRODUCTION: HISTORICAL BACKGROUND

Since 1945 the Italian state has been closely involved in a variety of ways in the process of economic development, and the forms of that involvement owe their origins partly to the political and economic demands of the post-war years and partly to the institutional structures in the economic sphere which survived or had grown up in what is confusingly referred to as the *ventennio fascista* - actually the 21-year period of fascist rule (1922-43). Before going on to consider the changing role of the Italian state in relation to the financial and industrial sectors since the war, we should briefly look at the ways in which a pattern of relationships was established prior to 1945.

As will emerge later, Italian development has been characterised by major imbalances and weaknesses as well as by sectors of perhaps startling vigour and capacity. The modern interpenetration of the state and the financial and industrial sectors, which is intense, cannot be understood without recognising the continuity of all three sectors with earlier historical structures. The failure of the modern state to impose a collective will on finance and industry despite the battery of formal controls and financial instruments available is partly the result of earlier apprehensions about the interpenetration of state and economy combined with political and market pressures for state action. In particular, the institutional conformation now visible in the financial sector is determined to a considerable extent by the successive interactions of traditional liberal free-market banking with the nationalism of the liberal state, the corporatist rhetoric, and inconsistent practice of the fascist regime, and after the war the pluralistic Catholic-conservative pragmatism of the Christian Democrats. It is argued here that neither the state nor market mechanisms have given coherent overall direction to development in Italy; nor can it be said that a reasoned autonomous consensus within the sectors has emerged to compensate for the lack of clear policy orientation towards state objectives or for the lack of priorities imposed by free-market mechanisms. Italy is an intensely pluralistic and fragmented polity characterised by a number of actors possessing veto powers. The short term is much more important in Italian politics than the long term, the scope for strategy is limited, and market mechanisms, such as they are, operate in ways that are neither simple nor linear.

In general historical terms, Italy's industrial development took place within the framework of selective protectionist policies, which were adopted by the Italian state from 1880 onwards in favour of certain sectors of particular importance to the prosperity of the most advanced areas, the north-western regions of Piedmont, Lombardy and Liguria.[1] Those sectors were the textile industry, which was a traditional motor of Italian industrialisation, heavy engineering and the food industry. For our purposes, however, it is important to note two features of this development. First, the involvement of the state was extremely small - the state was neither entrepreneur nor financier; only in very limited areas (such as railways and ship-building) was it a major customer, and in these sectors the Italian market was dominated by foreign companies, mainly British. Rather, a stronger impulse to the process of industrialisation in this period appears to have been foreign trade, and despite the priority given to heavy engineering and iron and steel works in contemporary Italian debates on development, it was as a manufacturer of consumer goods or newer producer goods that Italy developed. As well as this, it would be misleading to ignore the importance in Italian industrial expansion of the remittances from abroad of Italian emigrants, particularly from the depressed Mezzogiorno, the rural south of Italy, which found their way into the advanced northern areas by way of the growing network of small local savings banks and which had a major impact on Italian foreign trade accounts certainly until the 1930s. Second, despite this latter point, the financial support for development came not initially from domestic sources but from foreign venture capital; after the banking crisis of 1893 which resulted in the collapse of the two major indigenous banks, the market was taken over initially by German financiers who promoted the development of the Banca Commerciale Italiano (Comit) and the Credito Italiano. These banks developed their operations in ways similar to the German model; they were 'mixed banks', closely involved in industrial expansion, particularly in the new mechanical sectors, and taking shares in industrial ventures as well as giving loans. At this time, however, the banks were still clearly identifiable as banks rather than as holding companies; even where they had a controlling interest, they tended not to be routinely involved in managing the entrepreneurial and manufacturing operations. This pattern of relationships clearly was brought to an end by the onset of war and the urgent need for Italian industry and finance to change to meet the new military demands and then later the boom - slump conditions of the inter-war years; the weakness of domestic private credit was recognised by the establishment in December 1914 of the state-aided consortium for the support of Industrial Securities, and from this time on the relations between government, finance and industry changed with some rapidity.

By the mid-1930s a series of financial and industrial crises had resulted in the establishment of a battery of state-owned holding companies: Kindleberger describes this general process as 'expediency elevated into principle'.[2] The initial dependence on foreign capital, the restricted nature of the expansion in terms of numbers and location of industrial companies, the generally low level of company profits in the early decades of the twentieth century and the volatile career of some well-known companies all tended to make the Italian saver particularly cautious about the equity market and more prone to prefer highly liquid claims on banks and government bonds. We do not need here to describe in detail the several banking and industrial crises of the 1920s; throughout the period a small number of banks, mainly the larger ones, became progressively more active in the industrial sector, and developed long-term commitments in industrial companies, to such an extent that Cassese argues:

The Italian pre-crises banks were holding companies rather than mixed banks: they had large and stable holdings in a relatively small number of industrial undertakings, which they not only controlled but actually administered.[3]

It does seem however that since the banks continued to take deposits and carry out other banking operations - albeit to a diminished extent - it is stretching a point to claim that because of their increasing intimacy with industry they could no longer be described as 'mixed banks'. At the same time, partly because of the structural dependence of Italian industry on foreign markets but also because of the economic policies pursued by the fascist regime - in particular the notorious 'Quota novanta' revaluation of the lira against sterling in 1925 - the state found itself increasingly, even though reluctantly, compelled to support the major banks which ran into repeated liquidity problems as a result of their close association with troubled industrial companies.

In 1921 the first major state intervention in industry involved the state in the takeover of the Ansaldo engineering firm of Genoa, which was in difficulty from the liquidity problems of its subsidiary bank, the Banca Italiana di Sconto. But this was untypical, for later interventions followed the reverse pattern, with the state taking shares in banks troubled by problems in their manufacturing subsidiaries and associates. In 1922 the war-time consortium was expanded to make a special unit attached to the Treasury called Autonomous Section. In 1926 the unit was expanded further to become the Liquidation Institute with the specific short-term purpose of mopping up the excess liquidity generated by government-inspired salvage operations. After a brief period in which the government attempted to return to a supposed *status quo ante* by withdrawing from the field of industrial finance through the Liquidation Institute, the post 1929 depression finally induced the major restructuring which formed the Italian finance system into what is recognisable as a close ancestor of its present form.[4]

CONSOLIDATION OF THE MIXED ENTERPRISE SYSTEM

The effective priorities in this reorganisation are significant and, in terms of the constellation of interests, understandable. The three major mixed banks - Banca Commerciale Italiano, Credito Italiano, and Banco di Roma - were all heavily dependent on short-term loans from abroad, and throughout 1930 found themselves faced by a relatively sudden withdrawal of these credit lines, just as the domestic private sector began to increase its demand for credit, which the major banks were reluctant to deny. They developed serious liquidity problems which in turn affected the lender of the last resort, the Bank of Italy, since it was similarly reluctant to turn their credit demand away, and for similar reasons - the fear of a collapse of prices on the Stock Market embroiling financial and industrial shares in a major crisis of confidence. It has been estimated that by 1932 outstanding credit from the Central Bank to the three major mixed banks was equivalent to 57 per cent of the currency in circulation, and though nominally short-term the incapacity of the system to repay meant that the loans were renewed repeatedly. The concerns of the authorities and the conditions faced by the financial sector may not appear fundamentally divergent from those of other similar European countries at the beginning of the 1930s, but what did differentiate Italian conditions and responses were the short-term reliance of major banks on foreign credit, the degree of their financial commitment to the industrial sector in terms of equity participation, and the willingness of the fascist regime to support what it regarded as operations in industry which were essential for the national interest and for the political legitimacy of the regime.

The immediate and effective short-term solution to these problems was founded on the sale of all the industrial holdings of Comit and Credito Italiano to two holding companies, Sofindit and SFI, which were controlled by the Bank of Italy. The long-term strategy was to separate all high-risk credits, especially those in industry, from short-term deposit-takers, and the provision of long-term industrial finance was to be the function of new specialised institutions previously lacking in Italian finance. The 'mixed bank' was no longer appropriate for Italian conditions. As a first step towards the development of specialised units, a state-owned institution was set up on 1931 to help fill the gap left by the withdrawal of the big banks from long-term finance, named Istituto Mobiliare Italiano (IMI), this was intended to provide finance, not to act as a holding company. It rapidly became obvious that the state needed some means of directing the future of the industrial companies it had acquired through Sofindit and SFI, and in 1933 the Institute for Industrial Reconstruction (IRI) was established as an amalgamation of Sofindit, SFI and the Liquidation Institute.

The supposed function of IRI at first was actually to liquidate the government's holdings and to administer a return of the companies held to the private sector in as good order as possible. In practice, the weaknesses which had necessitated the state takeovers prevented the rapid return of the companies to the private industrial sector which apart from its historic weaknesses in industrial finance, was still suffering liquidity problems and which saw no prospect of domestic or international demand picking up sufficiently to allow for operations of this kind, even at very favourable prices. Added to this, Italy's need to re-arm for the war in Abyssinia and the fascist policy of autarky made IRI an important instrument in public spending policy. The movement was therefore in the opposite direction from the supposedly envisaged when IRI was first established. IRI was headed by a former Minister of Labour in a 1921 Liberal government, Alberto Beneduce, who, with the support of Donato Menichella, the long-serving managing director, was able to keep the new institution relatively free from control by the fascist hierarchs.[5]

Under Beneduce's control, IRI reorganised its banking and industrial sectors; in 1934 it gained majority control of the three national interest banks, namely Comit, Credito Italiano and Banco di Roma, and by 1937 had established several financial companies as sectoral managers, including STET for the telephone industry, Finmare for shipping interests, and Finsider for steel. In 1937 IRI was deemed a permanent institution, and its formal structure, in terms of the juridical scope of its powers, has altered little since then. A crucial advantage which it has enjoyed from its inception is its capacity to issue long-term bonds which are not only guaranteed by the state but which also carry major fiscal privileges and are therefore equivalent to government bonds. But unlike the public administration proper, IRI counts in law as a private entity, and is subject to the ordinary laws of contract and labour, even though the state is its major shareholder. Nominally, then, IRI and the other public enterprises which were modelled on it are a mixture of public and private, supposedly combining the flexibility of private enterprises with the durability and social perspective of governmental agencies.

At the same time as IRI was spreading its roots, major changes were occurring in the banking sector, the most important of which were introduced by the Banking Law 1936, which is still in force, though some of its principles are increasingly under attack. Under the 1936 Law, the Banca d'Italia was made the sole issuer of national currency (prior to this date, the Banca di Napoli and Banca di Sicilia had also been entitled to issue notes). The Bank was brought under full public control, given status in law as a public body, and was provided with a wide range of legal instruments to enable it to control monetary policy. These instruments, which are still the Bank's major weapon, give it considerable and direct control over reserve requirements, deposit ratios, loan quotas and currency dealings, and it has tended since then to favour these rather than indirect instruments such as interest rates. The Bank also has control over the establishment of banks and the opening of branches, which it seems to have used in such a way as to discourage concentration. At the same time Comit and Credito Italiano were compelled to sell off all their industrial securities and long-term loans to state-owned agencies. A fundamental distinction was made between short-term (ordinary) credit, which is the function of the deposit-taking banks, and long-term credit, which is to be carried out by special credit institutions, the first of which, in time at least, was, of course, IMI.

The rationale behind this arrangement reflects very strongly not so much the need for allocative efficiency, though this is certainly present, as the priority of keeping industry and finance separate. In the short-term this has the function of ensuring that liquidity problems in one sector do not threaten the stability of the other, but it also is intended to avoid concentration; to preserve the big banks from takeover by industrial companies; and, in general, and perhaps paradoxically, to encourage competition. It is not the function of finance to direct firms into socially desirable investment, or indeed into areas to which the financial sector, for non-financial reasons, might have a predilection. The financial sector as such should consider financial factors only - mainly risk and return - and should be indifferent to other considerations. Thus industry and finance operating in a dialectical relationship are supposed to ameliorate efficiency by providing completely separate judgements each in their own terms. It is only in the light of this thinking that one can understand the post-war concern, associated particularly with Saraceno, that the state should provide a subsidy for a rigorously calculated social cost in objectives imposed by it.[6]

The entire arrangement smacks strongly of a perception on the part of the state authorities, then and since the war, that Italian industry and finance tend strongly towards oligopoly, if not towards monopoly, unless a prior authority intervenes. The function of the state is not, therefore, at least in this conception, that of rigorous centralised planning using state agencies. It is rather the use of state agencies to compensate for weaknesses in industry and finance, particularly in the capital market, and later, to direct industry towards socially preferable objectives. The conventional phase, well-worn but certainly applicable to the state operations until 1963, is 'capitalism without capitalists'.

FINANCE IN THE STATE SECTOR AFTER 1945

It is not difficult to understand the ready acceptance of the IRI model and its application to a variety of sectors in the first two decades after the war. The urgent demand for industrial reconstruction and the opportunity of Marshall Aid fell jointly on a state which was itself lacking in solid authority and whose institutional framework, after the collapse of Fascism, was sparse. The option of dismantling IRI was not, it appears, seriously raised, and its continued importance was confirmed by a 1948 law which in effect gave it considerable autonomy and scope in a variety of sectors. In 1947, the central role IRI had in post-war rebuilding had been reinforced by its takeover of major engineering and shipbuilding works in Genoa through a newly-created financial subsidiary, Finmeccanica. At the beginning of the 1950s, the steel industry was given major investment through Finsider, on the grounds that a competitive national steel industry was a precondition of Italy's economic development.

The emphasis on steel has persisted throughout the post-war period, not only resulting in major investments (such as Gioia Tauro) when other countries were beginning to cut back on capacity, but also enhancing the strategic importance of IRI in the national economy.[7] But it should also be observed that the IRI model was open to a wide variety of interpretations and different usages: to private sector liberals, it was a second-best solution to the problem of ensuring finance for industry where the domestic capital market was weak; while to Catholics it was a flexible instrument of governmental policy which avoided the dangers of imposed planning. Rather later, after 1963, the model assumed a central role in centre - left (particularly socialist) intentions of maintaining the growth rates of the 1950s through long-term public sector expansion.

Other state-owned holding companies were established at intervals, with similar structures to IRI's and in some cases overlapping operations. In 1951, a major report by a Junior Minister, Ugo la Malfa, later leader of the Republican Party, called for the rationalisation of state holdings and the establishment of a Ministry of State Participation to direct and control activities and to be responsible to Parliament for the state holdings. This report also demanded regular surveys of the state sector with detailed quantified results, but the report itself constituted the first and only time that anything similar to a census of the area has been done. In 1953 the Ente Nazionale Idrocarburi (ENI) was set up to include AGIP, the state-owned petrol company taken over in 1926, in a holding company aimed at developing a national strategy for energy; and in 1956, the Ministry of State Participations was established, with a special Cabinet Committee to oversee its functions.

One of its first fruits was a law passed in 1958 which envisaged a considerable expansion in particular sectors. In part, these developments were the result of the extreme reluctance of IRI to take on ailing companies even in sectors in which it was already operating. Even though it had been originally established as a vehicle for industrial salvage, after the war IRI, and the public sector managers in general, saw themselves as proponents of dynamic expansionary policy, self-financing, independent and profitable.

Soon after the war, a separate fund was constituted, the *Fondo di finanziamento dell'industria meccanica* (Fim), and it was from this loose agency, together with other state holdings accumulated haphazardly, that the new public sector holdings were built up. Thus while IRI and ENI were trying to push back the frontiers of production and trade with large-scale capital investments in steel, energy, and petrochemicals, another side of the public sector was developing, often in sectors of less than strategic importance. EAGAT (1960), mainly heating and ventilation, and the Ente cinema (1961) were followed by EFIM (1962) which dealt with a variety of manufacturing operations but also aero-engineering; EGAM, a much troubled holding company specifically instituted in the 1958 law, only began operations properly in 1973. After expanding from mining to ore-processing and metallurgy, EGAM soon lost its first chairman, Mario Einaudi, who was forced to resign in June 1975, and after accumulating debts of over 500 miliard lire, EGAM (together with EAGAT, not involved in the same scandal) was dissolved in 1977. Egam's unhappy subsidiaries however were not generally wound up, but with few exceptions were distributed as unwelcome non-paying guests to the remaining holding companies. All of these holding companies were engaged in rationalising and managing industrial companies which had come into the state's hands already for a variety of reasons; future salvage operations were to be dealt with by a new holding company instituted in 1971, GEPI, in which all the other major state-owned companies participated.[8]

It is not the place here to go into the detailed criticisms that have been made of this system (the term is used loosely) in recent years. There are a variety of problems centring on the extent of party political control at various levels and there are other problems associated with the fragmentation of decision-making within the poly-sectoral groups that now make up the major state-owned holding companies (IRI, ENI, EFIM, GEPI). But if we want to consider the forms of finance and relations with the financial sector, these can be readily analysed in a more limited way, even though they clearly have implications for the more directly political institutions.

One of the supposed advantages of the IRI model was that, while it involved the state in supporting productive enterprises, those enterprises were still characterised by large minority and sometimes majority shareholdings in private hands, and this was intended to ensure both that private money was encouraged towards production and away from speculation, and that, in general, market criteria of allocative efficiency predominated. This was reinforced by the deliberate separation of the state from the enterprises and the proliferation of levels of authority between the two: the state's shareholdings are actually in the major *enti di gestione* (IRI, ENI, EFIM, GEPI) and the state owns no shares directly in the sectoral financial companies, such as Finsider or Snam, nor, *a fortiori*, in the subsidiary companies operated by these. But this private participation, which in many cases was never substantial, has diminished as the *partecipazioni statali* have come to look less attractive either in terms of profits or in the terms of real prospects of control. In 1979, Finmare, for example, the financial subsidiary of IRI which controls its shipping operations, was 97.95 per cent owned by IRI.[9]

IRI had begun its career in the 1930s by successfully issuing convertible bonds; these are now only issued rarely, though they appear to be making a minor comeback in some areas. In these circumstances the quotation on the Stock Market of the financial holding companies like Finmare is a mere juridical exercise. Few of the ordinary shares of Finmare, Finmeccanica, Finsider and the other financial subsidiaries ever come onto the market since the IRI is not active in share-dealing, and there are so few shares held in private hands. There are several important consequences of this. First and most obvious, ownership and participation is crystallised in the public sector, without the possibility of private entry or effective market control. Any private interest in the shares of these companies is minor and speculative, and potentially destabilising because of the small proportions of share-holdings involved. Second, the purpose of these financial subsidiaries was to collect and channel long-term capital from the private sector for the individual enterprises: but the development of state-ownership in fact restricts very considerably the capacity of IRI, ENI and EFIM to raise capital from private sources through increases in the share capital of their financial subsidiaries. When such increases are made, it appears that the *enti di gestione* now guarantee to buy up all the new shares and to allow the minority shareholders the option of taking up part of the new issue at a later date (sometimes up to five years later) under the original conditions. The result of new share issues may therefore be extremely expensive for the controlling companies as well as encouraging speculation and instability.

Another method by which the public sector should operate in the pursuit of credit is the issue of bonds, in which the main public sector companies are supposed to have an advantage. In practice, it appears that they find increasing difficulty in raising money direct from savers in this way: in 1969, the value of bonds in circulation issues by the state participation companies was 7.3 per cent of the value of all bonds in circulation; by 1979, this proportion had decreased to 2.1 per cent.[10] In part, this decline is the result of the changing nature of the credit system, in particular the increasing dominance of the market by the Treasury and the special credit institutes, which we discuss later. The greater fiscal advantages of Treasury credit, together with a less than imaginative approach to this sort of financing on the part of the state sector, have in any case resulted in the overall reliance of the state sector on forms of finance which are politically much more restrictive than own-issues bonds.

Of these forms of finance the simplest and most direct is of the type authorised by law no. 825 (1978), which provided state guarantees for IRI bonds dated up to 10 years and worth up to a total of 500 milliard lire (about £300 million sterling at 1978 rates). What was unusual about this was first, that it was a specific authorisation with a formal guarantee for a sum much larger than IRI was normally allowed to issue independently; second, that it was authorised for the specific purpose of consolidating IRI's short-term debt; and third, that for the first three years the interest was to be paid by the Treasury. With operations of this sort, IRI no longer retains the characteristics of a mixed enterprise but looks increasingly like a nationalised enterprise under the relatively close control of the political authorities. Certainly, its function as a stimulus to efficiency in the credit market is difficult to maintain in these conditions.

A further large step down this road was taken in 1980, when with law no. 281 IRI's endowment fund was increased by 2268 milliard - a gift in effect from the state to cover IRI's mounting losses, a large proportion of which was due to political decisions to persist in subsidising unused capacity in long steel products. Part of this gift - 930 milliard - was in the form of Treasury credit notes which were to be used to transfer some of IRI's debt with the banks directly to the Treasury. This procedure had already been used to rectify the financial position of hospitals and local authorities when these had been reformed some years earlier. It barely needs stating that while the operation may be understandable for organisations which are non-profit-making and dependent on governmental policy direction, it is not at all clear how IRI could continue to be regarded as a fully-fledged commercial operator (as it was intended to be) if these methods continue to be used for it.

For more routine purposes, however, the state participation companies preferred for much of the 1970s to use the special credit institutes (SCIs). Despite the fact that IRI and ENI are large enough and on the whole sufficiently good risks to be able to operate independently even on international markets if they wished to, they tended, during the 1970s, as we have seen, to relinquish this autonomy, though there are now signs of greater activism on their part in this sector. Though for the most part the use of SCIs committed them to loans on less favourable terms than they might have been able to achieve with a vigorous and competitive effort on the bond market, the attraction of the special credit institutes initially was that they were the obligatory channel for companies seeking the easy credit terms offered by the government for investment in particular sectors and in particular areas (mainly the Mezzogiorno).

During the period 1969-73 there was a marked increase in investment on the part of IRI and ENI which was encouraged by a relatively easy credit policy on the part of the government, particularly in 1970 and 1971, and which had a clear counter-cyclical effect; this was to a considerable extent financed through the special credit institutes, and went to steel and mechanical engineering sectors in particular, and to the South.[11] After 1973, the worsening international trade conditions and increasing domestic losses (partly the result of earlier ill-considered investment) did not deter either the SCIs directly or the ordinary banks indirectly from lending to the public industrial agencies, though from 1973 to 1977 these loans were apparently going not towards capital investment or asset accumulation but to cover operation losses.

The major change that occurred after 1977 is that from this time on the credit agencies as a whole began to favour smaller and medium-sized enterprises, while the larger companies, whether public or private, are either going into international markets or receiving transfer payments from the state, as we have already discussed. This change is partly the result of changes in banking regulations which we discuss in the next section, partly the result of the greater level of activity of the Treasury in financing the government's debt and, not least, the result of a minor but significant change in attitude on the part of the finance sector, after the collapse of EGAM and the forced rescheduling of large debts owed by hospitals and local authorities on terms which were widely regarded as unfavourable to the banks. Before considering the impact of all these changes on industrial policy, we should now look briefly at the financial sector itself.

CHANGE IN THE FINANCIAL SECTOR

The financial sector in Italy has been subject to considerable structural change since 1968, which has been partly the result of legislation and partly the result of responses to conjunctural factors.[12] The most important pieces of legislation were the industrial restructuring law in 1977 and the Stammati law in 1978. The first of these, the famous law no. 675, was intended to provide Italy for the first time with a national policy for industry as contrasted with an industrial policy which previously had been, in practice, limited to the changing frameworks of policy for the South. The new policy also provided for a streamlined credit system, so that the favoured sectors, such as small and medium-sized firms in new industrial products, but also, quite typically, the steel sector, could be assured of rapid access to capital. The system was intended to operate on lines similar in some ways to the French, in that the special credit institutions would occupy a central role: they would evaluate proposals coming to them from individual public or private companies and would pass on those they wished to support to CIPI, the Interministerial Committee for Industrial Policy. If CIPI approved the investment scheme, the special credit institute could then release the funds to the company. The credit would have a state guarantee, and the company would pay a low rate of interest, with the government making up to the SCI the difference between this discounted rate and the market rate.

In practice the law proved less than successful; the lack of coordination between ministries involved in the state sector, disagreement or lack of communication within CIPI, and failure of CIPI to provide adequate criteria by which proposals could be assessed were the major problems. Radical reform of law no. 675 was under consideration from 1983 onwards, but had not produced results by early 1985.

The Stammati law, on the other hand, had a more immediate and once-for-all effect: named after the Treasury Minister of the time, the decree law no. 43 of 27 February 1978, to which we have already referred indirectly, was intended to bring local authority spending under tighter control by preventing banks from granting loans to local authorities. It also wiped the slate clean by transforming existing loans into securities. This had the effect on the banks of excluding them to a certain extent from the loans market, which by default gave further prominence to the role of SCIs in all types of loans, not only medium and long-term. In practice this appears to be a rare move against the trend towards despecialisation: the growing incapacity of the credit system to match investors' needs with savers' preferences led throughout the 1970s to the decay of the principle of separation enshrined in the 1936 banking law. Not only were the SCIs becoming more active in a wider variety of banking activities, but also the banks were developing more long-term business, as the Bank of Italy, apparently with the aim of encouraging 'merchant bank' - type institutions, allowed banks increasingly to establish their own autonomous special credit sections. This despecialisation, which affected not only the national interest banks but also the major regional and local banks, looks likely to continue despite the Stammati law and will be further encouraged when the Bank of Italy produces its regulations for the proposed 'banche d'affari', the merchant banks whose absence from the Italian financial sector is widely though not always convincingly blamed for many of the inadequacies of the sector.

As well as the Stammati law and law 675, regulations imposed by the Bank of Italy or the Treasury made significant changes to the functioning of the sector. As we have indicated, the financial authorities have preferred until recently to use direct controls rather than interest rates and other market mechanisms. Their willingness to do so, and the effectiveness of their actions, are among the reasons why Italy still appears to be regarded as a good risk by foreign banks despite the volatility of Italy's external trade balance.[13] It is also the case, of course, that whatever regulatory practice might have been, interest rates in Italy have been high relative to Italy's foreign competitors for some time, for the main purpose of financing Italy's growing public sector deficit, though real rates have been broadly comparable with those of its competitors. While the high nominal rates encourage foreign banks to invest in Italy, they encourage Italian firms to look abroad where possible, though this is not something that small and medium-sized firms will have the resources to do.

The most important regulatory mechanisms used to control lending to industry in Italy have been the loan ceiling which operated from 1973 and the *vincolo*, the portfolio constraint operating from 1973 onwards which obliged banks to invest specific proportions of their deposits in government securities and in SCI bonds. The major priority in these and other changes has been not the amelioration of allocative efficiency in risk capital but rather the control of money supply for macro-economic policy objectives. The control of total domestic credit, which has been the central objective, has been mainly sought through restriction on bank credit, and this has proved increasingly difficult and ineffective. First of all, public sector deficit has been consistently above target since 1974 and is now the predominant element in aggregate financial flows. According to OECD figures, total government debt as a percentage of GDP increased from 36.9 per cent in 1970 to 70.3 per cent in 1982, and net borrowing as a percentage of GDP p.a. increased from 5.0 per cent in 1970 to 11.9 per cent in 1982.[14] Overall, the extent of PSBR overruns has been such that an offsetting restriction of private sector financing by equivalent amounts has not been possible in recent years, and the monetary authorities have had to allow TDC to rise well beyond the targets set. Also, the banks when faced with the greater administrative control developed greater sophistication in their financial methods so as to evade the constraints, and the monetary authorities gradually had to increase the scope of their regulations and exact higher penalties. Finally, the incidence of bank credit in total private sector financing diminished sharply in response both to the restrictions and to high government rates, and after a period of very rapid growth of bank intermediation in the early 1970s, recent years have seen a general decline from an admittedly high level in the role of banks in channelling financial flows.[15]

If we consider more directly the result of these events in terms of industrial finance, the incidence of loans on total financial flows fell throughout the 1970s; between 1972 and 1982 the incidence of loans on TDC (on amounts) fell from 37.7 to 26.9 per cent.[16] Since during the same period the proportion of TDC which went to the PSBR rose from 36.3 to 51.0 per cent, the question obviously arises of the extent to which the extraordinary increase in the extended public sector's financial demand has affected the credit available to industry either in amount or in composition. While it is clear that some crowding-out has occurred, analysis of the detailed flows appears to indicate that other factors have contributed to modify the overall effect. First of all, we have already detailed some of the increase in transfer payments from government to industry (mainly public sector) which have had an important effect on investment patterns. In both private and public sector, big corporations showed greater propensity to seek credit abroad - between 1977 to 1981 foreign borrowing as a proportion of corporate external financing increased from 7 per cent to over 20 per cent. In response to this, the authorities changed their policy on financing from reserves. Second, if we consider the direction of financial flows, while the share of TDC which went to the business sector (public and private) fell from 57 per cent at end 1972 to 47.5 per cent end 1982, over the same period the grip of the business sector over the loans market increased from an already dominant position - from 82.7 per cent at end 1972 to 90 per cent at end 1982. Within the business sector of the loans market itself, important changes were taking place, and there are clear indications that while the smaller private firms had increasing recourse to loans from all sources over this period (and incidentally increased their share of deposits also) the large public sector and private firms took far less in loans. There may be several reasons for this. One of them is that over the period in question the share of such large firms in the Italian GDP diminished, while unexpected and unprecedented growth in the number of small to medium-sized firms and in their share of GDP took place. But another important reason is that the loan ceiling introduced in 1973 had a selective element, in that is was specifically designed to allow small loans to be made with relative ease and to encourage banks to lend to those sectors of industry which previously had not had easy access to banking finance. The larger firms got round this to some extent by splitting and diversifying their loan applications to evade the ceiling, and the intermittent exemption of loans in foreign currency also helped this sector. But in general, throughout the 1970s, the composition of bank loans by size of firm changed considerably. At the end of 1975, minor private firms already accounted for 49.9 per cent of all bank loans by amount; by the end of 1982 they accounted for 71.3 per cent - an increase that continued throughout the period when the ceiling was temporarily removed (March 1975 to October 1976) and that persisted after the ceiling exemption for small loans was removed at the beginning of 1981. While the ceiling contributed to the shift in resources, it could not be regarded as the sole cause; and this shift to the smaller firms, it should be observed, took place even though the larger public and private firms were able to get loans at lower than average rates of interest, while the smaller firms had to pay a consistently higher rate. The fact that this differential actually increased in favour of the large debtors over this period appears to indicate that changes on the demand side were a significant factor in the shifts described. In brief, while there certainly are problems in the distribution of venture capital and credit in general to various sectors of the economy, it does not appear that the sustained growth in PSBR of itself has been a major constraint, though its volume and the methods of its financing have certainly had significant consequences for the financial resources sought by the industrial sector. [17]

What we have been discussing so far in this section relates mainly to the determination of credit flows by wider monetary policy. If we consider the provision of credit at a more micro-economic (and micro-political) level, the routine functioning of the financial sector may be more readily understood, and it may be clearer why it is monetary policy that by default exercises most control over the entire field of financial support to industry in terms of institutional objectives.

Banks in Italy are highly politicised, and play a major role in the clientelist operations by which political factions maintain themselves and improve their standing. Indeed, so close is the relationship between the governing parties and some of the banks that the terms of the previous statement might be reversed. In some cases it is clear that the primary objectives in achieving political office is the use of political leverage to obtain positions and resources in the financial sector for the purpose of personal and family self-aggrandisement. These relationships and practices are, to say the least, a significant distortion in the decision-making procedures by which resources are finally allocated. After the major banking scandals of the 1970s and early 1980s (Sindona, Italcasse, Sofid, Ambrosiano, and others), the banking climate became more rigorous and the banks began to appear more commercial in their objectives, but top appointments in major banks are still highly politicised and it is possible to locate the managing directors and chairmen of most of the major banks within specific political alliances associated with individual parties. Therefore, when considering the relationships between the state, the financial sector and industry it is necessary to give some attention to the politicisation of the banks and at least implicitly to the scandals of recent years.[18]

From the sorry story of Italian banking in the 1970s several major themes emerge. First, while most major industrialised countries in the West have sporadic problems with fringe banks, as Britain did in the early 1970s, or with combinations of incompetence and illegality in relatively large institutions, the Italian banking crises appear different because of the extent and frequency of the occurrences of serious incompetence or major illegality. Between 1973 and 1983 there were two major scandals - Sindona and the Banco Ambrosiano - which involved fraudulent bankruptcy for hundreds of milliards of lire and which had serious financial repercussions for institutions of central importance such as the Banco di Roma, the Vatican's IOR, ENI and Carlo Pesenti's IBI. As well as these there were other episodes, only small in relation to the two already mentioned, which involved various local or regional banks and special credit institutes, not always fatally. Second, where evidence of serious fraud does occur elsewhere, as in the Lloyds scandal in Britain, the incidents are not usually associated directly and intimately with conflict within or between political parties, though this certainly does happen on occasions. In the Italian case, the political links are ever-present and are too close to be ignored. Both Michele Sindona and Roberto Calvi, head of Ambrosiano, were very well connected with Vatican financiers and Christian Democrat politicians, and several of the other cases (ENI-Petromin, IRI-Italstat, Cefis-Montedison) have directly concerned the illicit financing of political parties (mainly the DC). Finally, the disclosure and subsequent judicial action on financial scandals in Italy are also highly politicised, with certain magistrates and certain judicial districts known to be associated with different political parties or even with different factions within parties, and able to use their office accordingly. The case of the Bank of Italy and Italcasse which we refer to below is emblematic.

Formal supervision of the entire banking sector rests with the Bank of Italy, which gained control of the Banking Inspectorate immediately after the war. For much of the post-war period the juridical effects of the Bank's investigations were diminished by insistence on the part of the Bank that its officers were bound in their investigations by Article 10 of the Banking Law 1936 which imposes confidentiality on the Bank. It would also be fair to say that the Governor of the Bank for much of this time, Guido Carli, did not show great enthusiasm for this aspect of the Bank's duties, preferring to concentrate on its more general monetary and administrative functions with particular concern for macro-economic policy. Carli was also concerned for Italy's international integration and for the likely effect on Italy's trading partners of unwelcome revelations about the difficulties of Italy's banking institutions, as were other senior figures of the time in finance and industry. Carli also insisted with some justification that ultimate responsibility for these unfortunate characteristics of the Italian financial sector lay in the political sphere and with less support that they were directly attributable to the easy credit policies of successive governments since 1963.

In 1971, the issue of confidentiality was apparently clarified with an exchange of letters between Carli and Carmelo Spagnuolo, the Procurator-General for Rome. Thereafter the Bank's investigatory section was more forthcoming; between May 1971 and January 1979, 443 reports were sent from the Inspectorate to the Magistrates. When Carli retired in May 1975, his successor, Paolo Baffi, showed considerably more concern for this side of the Bank's activities and appointed a like-minded figure, Mario Sarcinelli as Deputy Director-general with responsibility for the Inspectorate. An indication of the difficulties involved in working in this part of the financial sector may be gleaned from the observation that Spagnuolo was later forced to resign for his attempts to protect Michele Sindona. Carli himself was charged briefly and without effect in the Sindona affair with omission of acts of office: a charge brought against him apparently at the instigation of shareholders in Sindona's companies. Sarcinelli was remanded in custody for a brief period and Baffi charged with criminal offences, again without effect, in 1979 in an episode that was widely regarded as a warning to the Bank not to pursue its investigations into the Italcasse-Caltagirone affair.[19] Baffi resigned after a decent interval to be replaced by Carlo Azeglio Ciampi, and Sarcinelli was appointed to a senior position in the Treasury Ministry.

But the Bank's investigations had already revealed a considerable variety of malpractice and misjudgement both in the ordinary banks and in the SCIs. In some cases it found mere incompetence, in others, fraud and serious misuse of public office. Among the widespread practices objected to by the Bank, and which led on occasions to reports to the judicial authorities were: the granting of loans without proper information on the clients or against the technical advice of officials; loans granted in excess of the institutes or banks limits on duration or size; the purchase of securities with improper commissions to third parties (including political organisations); and share dealings carried out by foreign subsidiaries either for the purpose of illegal export of capital or to secure internal control of the institutes and banks. The sector where the greatest problems were found was, perhaps not surprisingly, long-term credit operations.

While the financial sector is dominated overall by the ordinary banks of various kinds, of which there are many, the field of long-term credit is dominated by three main institutions: IMI, which is a state-owned SCI controlled by the Treasury and the Bank of Italy; Mediobanca (in full, Banca di Credito Finanziario) which is controlled by a consortium made up of the three national interest banks; and Italcasse (in full, Instituto Centrale Delle Casse di Risparmio e dei Monti di Pegno) which is state-controlled and which exists to act as a central clearing-house for the deposits collected by the numerous small local banks. As well as these, there are a large number of national and regional institutes with particular roles and under various ownerships (usually at least partly public), such as ISVEIMER for the South of Italy, the Cassa Depositi e Prestiti which provides loans to local authorities from the very popular post office savings accounts, and Efibanca, the Interbank Investment Corporation. The SCIs have in practice considerable independence from the government of the day. Their credit policies vary not only with government monetary policy but also with the short-term factional needs and long-term strategic designs of the various parties.

In so far as there is a general pattern to the conduct of the SCIs, the system as a whole is not one which fits easily into any of the commonly accepted political categories: the prevailing ethos in the financial sector in the post-war period has been Catholic-corporatist, and the practice often frankly clientelist. Against this, rearguard actions are fought intermittently by, on the one hand, technocratic socialist groups who have achieved footholds in the public sector; and on the other hand, by those financial institutions (mainly in the private sector) which are committed, at least in principle, to free-market principles. In this group may be placed the Bank of Italy and the financial companies associated with the leaders of Confindustria (IFI, Mediobanca, SME). The 'old liberal' group is hampered by the weakness of its political base, but with the accession

of Ciriaco de Mita to the Secretaryship of the DC in 1981 the DC itself
has been divided along ideological lines, since De Mita has been pursuing
(not with great success) a lay conservative policy which the traditional
liberals find not uncongenial.

Partly as a result of this, but also because of the economic changes
already referred to, there have been significant shifts in the management
of the SCIs, which are now the sites of repeated skirmishes over senior
appointments and matters of policy. IMI, the first of the venture capital
houses, declared profits of 301 milliard lire for 1984 (about £130 million
sterling) and net assets of 2231 milliard.[20] After some activism in the
late 1950s and early 1960s, including the financing of the FIAT - Soviet
venture of Togliattigrad, its career was uninspiring and little noticed, when
under Giorgio Cappon, one of the so-called 'technomafia', it seemed little
more than an accomodating banker for enterprises favoured by the DC.
However, Cappon became involved in attempts by DC politicians to gain
further political control over the part-public chemicals industry
conglomerate Montedison, and in 1979 Cappon was forced to resign under
charges of unauthorised loans to Montedison's competitor, the privately-
owned SIR. This venture left IMI with losses of 530 milliard lire. At
the behest of the then Treasury Ministry, a DC technocrat Filippo Pandolfi,
the chairmanship was taken by a banker of an altogether different school,
Luigi Arcuti, who had previously been managing director of one of the
largest and most aggressive of the local banks, the San Paolo di Torino.
Under Arcuti, IMI finally began to act more as a politically independent
merchant bank, allying itself with the progressive chairman of Olivetti
and Buitoni, Carlo de Benedetti.

The main rival to IMI - indeed, for many years the most important
SCI without exception - is Mediobanca.[21] This was headed for a
considerable time by Enrico Cuccia, one of the most influential financiers
of the post-war and a personage usually associated with the liberal
and Republican parties. The three national interest banks who between
them own 58 per cent of Mediobanca are nominally controlled by IRI,
but this control, typically, only shows itself in its senior appointments.
When Cuccia finally retired to a consultative position in Mediobanca
(from which he continued to try to direct operations) his post was taken
by a former deputy director of IRI, Fausto Calabria, like Cappon, one
of the technomafia, involved in the Italstat scandal, and close to the
Fanfaniano faction of the DC. Thus, while IMI was distancing itself from
Roman politics, Mediobanca appeared to be moving in the opposite
direction, though the efforts of Cuccia to see Mediobanca privatised before

his full retirement might indicate otherwise.

It is one of the many paradoxes of Italian finance that Mediobanca though formally controlled by public sector banks should operate as a bulwark of the oligopolistic private firms. The influence of Cuccia did not apparently result from the size of the financial holdings of his institute, though these were certainly significant; what is more significant is the range of companies, both public and private, in which Mediobanca held an effective interest. In Italy controlling shareholders often expect to have an absolute majority of all shares directly in hand and are traditionally reluctant to allow significant minority shareholdings. This phenomenon, which helps explain the weakness of the Italian Stock Market, is the result of a perhaps excessive concern about unfriendly takeovers, though it also follows a widespread tendency to undercapitalise.

As with the public sector financial holding companies, many of the largest private firms are quoted on the Stock Market in Milan for formal purposes only, and little substantial dealing is ever done in their shares. At the end of January 1985, the Italian equity market was valued at about 58 thousand milliard lire (about £24 billion sterling at January 1985 values), of which approximately 60 per cent could be regarded as unavailable for dealing and unlikely to become available in the foreseeable future. Mediobanca, an exception to this pattern of bulk share-holding, has been able to get is nominees onto otherwise impregnable company boards through merchant bank operations.

It is clear that the control exercised by IRI over Mediobanca has been extremely limited, which should not be surprising, since coordination among the three banks is hampered by the factionalism and weak lines of authority common to the entire state participation system. Because of the breadth of its holdings, and its stake in most of the major private companies including Fiat (2.15 per cent), Olivetti 2.87 per cent), Fondiaria (9.85 per cent), Pirelli (11.10 per cent), Mediobanca is in a unique position to mediate between companies and to influence financial operations in a way that gives it a high degree of independence from its nominal controllers. Mediobanca has been involved in many of the major deals of the post-war period, including the ultimately unsuccessful merger of Pirelli with Dunlop, the sale of a substantial minority shareholding in Fiat to Libyan government interests, the merger of Montecatini with Edison, and the purchase of the ailing Rizzoli publishing company by Fiat. Cuccia has also been credited with a major role in the collapses of Sindona's Banca Privata and Calvi's Ambrosiano, not least by the main protagonists themselves.[22]

Thus for most of the post-war period the two largest SCIs, both in the public sector and both nominally having venture capital functions, were on opposite sides of the great divide in Italian finance, which separated the Christian Democrat public sector from the traditional liberal private sector, and in neither case were they able fully to function effectively as providers of risk-capital for all sectors of the economy. While IMI bent to the tortuous factional pressures of party political demands, Mediobanca being relatively immune from such pressures proved a strong support for the large family-owned private manufacturing firms of Northern Italy, in alliance with the liberal-oriented Bank of Italy, particularly under Guido Carli. The structure of Italian industry, however, is such that this *de facto* division of labour leaves a significant proportion disadvantaged. In practice, this has resulted in a proliferation of smaller SCIs brought into being for specific limited purposes, often regional in structure, subject to the *lottizzazione* endemic in Italian politics, and not always assured of the funds, the expertise or the influence to work efficiently - we have already referred to ISVEIMER, one of the largest in this archipelago, but there are others also for Sardinia (CIS), Sicily (IRFIS), public works (CREDIOP), small artisan firms (ARTIGIANCASSA), small and medium-sized firms at regional level (MEDIOCREDITI REGIONALI), and so on. The haphazard and uncoordinated creation of a plethora of SCIs which vary widely in objectives and resources and which have different degrees of public ownership and control is not the optimal method of ensuring efficient allocation of funds; they are subject in practice neither to central and regional planning authorities, nor, because of their party political control, to recognisable free-market mechanisms. Undoubtedly, they do provide access to loans for industrial companies who might otherwise be deprived of finance, but their relationships with the industrial sector and with the state fit in practice into no coherent overall pattern and obey no nationally agreed consensus. In this perspective the Italian system might be one based on negotiation between finance and industry, but the negotiation should be understood in its own way.

CONCLUSION: IMPACT OF STATE INTERVENTION

The core of the relationship between state, finance, and industry in Italy lies in the institutions straddling these sectors, which were founded in the 1930s to resolve particular problems and which have survived and developed beyond the crises of that time. Antonio Gramsci wrote in prison that the establishment of IRI in 1933 was not the realisation of an effective step forward but the acknowledgement of a weakness.[23] As an attempt to preserve major industries and protect the financial structure, IRI's first operations were on the whole a success, even if the policies were based on industrial salvage: this was not welfare capitalism, rather welfare for capitalists. ENI, on the other hand, the junior of the two, acted more as an aggressive entrepreneurial public capitalist, though its general aims were not greatly dissimilar. In both cases, the state participation schemes sought national autonomy in a major sector - steel for IRI, petrol for ENI. This imposed different strategies for the different products: IRI tended from the outset to strive to replace steel imports with Italian manufactured steel, while ENI's horizons had to be international since its primary target under Mattei was to release Italy from dependence on the major multinational oil companies through the establishment of a national oil company dealing directly with producer countries. This tended to exclude other domestic capitalists from the Italian petrol sector as far as possible.

This pursuit of national autonomy continued into the post-war period. Then, during the period of the 'economic miracle' and beyond, IRI and ENI, though virtually uncoordinated, made a major contribution to sustained investment levels, particularly in the South, and particularly in the steel industry.

Throughout the 1950s and until 1969, the public sector companies made up approximately 8.5 per cent a year of the total fixed investment, and approximately 15 per cent of fixed investment in industry, and the rate of growth in fixed investment in the public sector was superior to that in the private sector in every year from 1956 to 1964.[24] But as well as these operations, both IRI and ENI aimed at breaking the dominance of single companies in other sectors - in IRI's case, its interests in car manufacturing had this explicit aim, and were largely unsuccessful, at least as far as Alfa-Romeo is concerned. In car manufacturing, IRI has remained subordinate to the overwhelming Fiat presence; in chemicals, far from breaking the concentrated control of the market to allow greater competition, the public sector has colluded, through Enichimica and Montedison, in maintaining the oligopolistic character of this primary industry; in banking, IRI and the public sector SCIs can be an important stabilising and counter-cyclical influence, but the effect relies on the strength of the virtual state guarantee behind them, not on the specific policies or operations, which have not been controlled by the state, whatever the formal relationship.

During the period of 'capitalism without capitalists' the state participation companies and the public SCIs operated with a considerable degree of autonomy by virtue of their self-financing capacity; but after 1963 the advent of the centre-left governments introduced a period which we might call, without overstretching the terms, 'socialists without socialism'. In the first period a confident and expansive managerial class attempted to make up for the deficiencies of market mechanism in Italy through the use of the public sector holding companies, which though owned and nominally controlled by the state were intended to substitute for the weakness of the capital market and the rigidities of private ownership by their access to financial resources and the flexibility of their portfolio policies. In the second period, after the failure of the public sector firms to break down the traditional obstacles to indigenously-motivated capital formation in Italy, attention shifted to the state itself as the spur to continued development. This required not so much reform of the state participation companies but rather the provision of a network of state planning procedures within which they were to operate: it was the turn of the technocrats to attempt to break down the rigidities within the bureaucracy, to reform the apparatus of the state as a major part of the economic responses to the problems of the late 1960s and the 1970s. Though there were some successes, notably the massive increase to state investment between 1969 and 1973 at a time when the private sector was in a period of retrenchment, on the whole the costs and the problems weighed heavily.

Practical control of the gangling giants proved extremely difficult; neither Parliament nor the Ministry of State Participation ever had sufficient information to begin to exercise their statutory functions, nor did they show the political will to prise it out of the reluctant holding companies. The various plans of the period (Saraceno 1964, Giolitti 1970, in particular) were delayed in implementation and lacked the full support of the governmental parties. The Interministerial Cabinet Committee for Planning, CIPE, which took over from the Committee for State Participation in 1967, was no more successful than its predecessor in fitting the public sector holding companies into the planning mechanism, and problems of overlapping responsibility occurred with other Interministerial Committees when they were formed, mainly the Committee for Industrial Policy (after 1977) and the Committee for Credit and Finance. In the context of the muddled lines of authority, it is not surprising that even in the planning optimism of the 1960s and the early 1970s the control over the public sector was sporadic and opportunistic: senior appointments in the financial subsidiaries were guaranteed to be occasions for factional disputes, major repayments by the state seemed to require authorisation by the Ministry, but investment programmes apparently required no prior formal authorisation in that quarter. In southern policy, the Cortese amendment to the 1957 law on the South required IRI and ENI to spend 60 per cent of all their new investment in the South; investment in the South did increase significantly in the 1960s, but this was for a variety of reasons and the formal obligations were met only by the inclusion in the accounts of an investment category *'non-localizzabile'* - investment which could not be located in a specific area and which was therefore discounted.[25] Implicit recognition of the weakness of this legislation lies in the 'double subsidy' element which emerged in southern policy and has expanded to cover national industrial policy after 1977. The public sector holding companies have endowment funds from the state which have been 'topped up' with increasing frequency in recent years, and as well as this they have access, like any other industrial company, to the subsidised credit made available for certain kinds of investment. It should also be observed that in some cases the state is also the end-customer for the work carried out and IRI both agent and contractor: in the autostrada programme, a usual practice was for the agency to be given to Italstat, the IRI financial subsidiary for the sector, which would draw up the plans in the appropriate manner, and the contract would be given on tender to Italstrade, Italstat's construction subsidiary. In such cases control of state spending becomes extremely difficult.

With the failure of the planning experiences (perhaps because planning was never actually implemented), and after the crises of the 1974 - 76 period, the attention shifted again, this time to modes of financing and revenue-raising. The periods for the confident schemes of politicians-turned-entrepreneurs and of planners-turned-politicians were over, and the turn of the accountant had come. But this did not mean that financial constraints previously discounted now became predominant. On the contrary, if planning procedures had been a justification for more finance from 1963 to 1977, after 1977 the political constraints stood more clearly revealed. The need to support employment particularly in the South, the difficulties of achieving operating surpluses, the distorting effects of recent financing methods all became more apparent. As we have discussed, a policy conflict over industrial policy occurred within the DC itself between the traditionalists and those who sought radical reform of the public sector, including if necessary privatisation. In 1978 Giuseppe Petrilli, chairman of IRI since 1960 and a close collaborator of Amintore Fanfani, came to the end of his contract and was not reconfirmed in office, partly because of concern over charges of corruption. Fanfani found Petrilli a safe seat in the Senate to enable him to avoid prosecution, and there followed a period of considerable uncertainty over senior positions in IRI, which appeared to be resolved in 1982 with the appointment as chairman of Romano Prodi, a former Minister of Industry and also a member of the DC, but from a different wing of the party.

In 1983, Franco Reviglio, a Socialist and former Minister of Finance, took over as head of ENI. In keeping with the new concern over the sources of finance for state industry, both Prodi and Reviglio adopted strategies aiming on the one hand at retrenchment in industrial policy, and on the other at securing the maximum freedom of movement for their holding companies. Both chairmen sought to privatise areas of their respective companies which they held to be non-essential to their primary purposes, and both demanded significant job losses in the areas that were to remain - in the case of IRI, this was apparently held by Prodi to mean those major sectors which privately-owned companies were unable to function because of particular conditions or because of the strategic demands of the economy, such as steel (Finsider), transport networks (Italstat and Alitalia), the major banks, and information services (Stet). But there are major obstacles to achieving these objectives. Both Prodi and Reviglio had to seek financial support from the state to enable them to consolidate and reorganise.

In September 1984 Prodi sought 47,000 milliard lire and Reviglio 37,000 milliard, including 15,000 milliard from the state, and the remainder from privatisation and from productivity increases including job losses, to enable their companies to go from large operating deficits in 1982 and 1983 to profitability in 1986. Even this would leave IRI with consolidated debts of about 35,000 milliard lire. But despite their recognition of the seriousness of the problem, neither Parliament nor Ministers for differing reasons have shown much sympathy for the efforts of the two chairman to achieve managerial independence, and typical problems that have occurred have been the blocking of Prodi's attempt to sell SME, the food sector finance company, to Buitoni, and the difficulties over the appointments to senior management positions, including the continuation in office of Ettore Bernabei, former boss of RAI-TV, managing director of Italstat from 1974; Bernabei was a collaborator of Petrilli and Fanfani and was charged in December 1984 with involvement in the recycling of the illicit finances to the DC which continued even after Petrilli had left IRI. Neither Prodi nor Reviglio could claim to be masters in their own houses, and they and their successors have no obvious or easy solution available to the *lottizzazione*, the sharing-out of public offices by politicians on the basis of existing balances of power.

It would be grossly misleading to suggest that the post-war experience of state relations with finance and industry have been a chapter of unmitigated problems. On the contrary, the experience of the first 25 years gave grounds for optimism and ambition at the beginning of the 1970s, even though some of the difficulties in coordination and financing were already apparent. If the triumphalism of 1970 was not realistic, neither was the catastrophism of 1980. After 1977, there were clear indications of realistic recognition of the problems inherent in the relationship, problems which derive not only from the clientelistic and short-term approach imposed by certain kinds of political influence but also from the continuation of the economic weaknesses, imbalances and external vulnerability which engendered the development of the state sector in the first place. In 1978, the Report on Banking Systems Abroad drawn up for the Wilson Commission commented tersely,

> The rigidity of the Italian financial system is aggravated by the weak financial position of the corporate sector which has accumulated a mass of virtually non-recoverable debts and is seriously undercapitalised. The financial problems of a large number of publicly-owned companies are causing particular concern. Although a major reform of the system is required for the financial restructuring of industry, a satisfactory solution does not appear to be in sight.[26]

Accurate as it is, this should not be interpreted to mean that the industrial sector is about to collapse and to threaten to bring down the financial sector also. As we have seen, after 1977 the state began to assume the role of 'hidden banker' to the public sector, replacing an overstretched financial sector with its own resources and making it unlikely that the non-recoverable debts would ever be called in in such a way as to threaten the stability of the system. But despite the efforts of IRI's and ENI's new managers to achieve competitiveness and to remove labour rigidities the problem identified by Saraceno remains: Italy seems still to need its public sector but has not yet achieved a stable long-term solution to its management. In so far as they carry out strategic or socially desirable ends the state participation groups are dependent on the state to act as financier of last resort - indeed, sometimes the only financier, since the private finance system is extremely limited. But the state shows no great propensity to identify its priorities in any rational way, nor does it allow the state participation companies to identify and to act on their own priorities in a responsible manner. This problem is now greater because of the dependence on the state for finance for ordinary capital as well as for extra-ordinary, so that the division of responsibilities envisaged by Saraceno cannot function in practice. The consequences for the entire Italian political economy are far-reaching.

NOTES

1. On the scope and pace of the early development, see Caracciolo, A. (ed.), *La Formazione dell'Italia Industriale* (Bari: Laterza, 1969); also Cafagna, L., Italy 1830-1914', in Cipolla, C.M. (ed.)., *The Fontana Economic History of Europe*, vol. 4, pt. 1, *The Emergence of Industrial Societies* (Glasgow: Fontana/Collins, 1973, pp. 279-328.
2. Kindleberger, C.P., 'Banking and Industry Between the Two Wars: an international comparison', in *Journal of European Economic History*, vol. 13, no. 2 (Fall 1984), pp. 7-28.
3. Cassese, S., 'The Long Life of the Financial Institutions Set Up in the Thirties', in *Journal of European Economic History*, vol. 13, no. 2 (Fall 1984), p. 288.
4. In Ciocca, P.L. and Toniolo, G., 'Industry and Finance in Italy, 1918-1940', in *Journal of European Economic History*, vol. 13, no. 2 (Fall 1984), p. 131.
5. Beneduce's principles were of profound importance in the establishment and development of IRI, and his relationship with Mussolini was close. Despite his liberal antecedents, Beneduce was widely believed to have socialist leanings, and indeed two of his daughters gloried in the names Vittoria Proletaria and Idea Socialista (the latter married Enrico Cuccia, post-war head of Mediobanca).
6. See Ajmone Marsan, V., 'The State-holding System and Italian Financial Development', in Baumol, W.J. (ed.), *Public and Private Enterprises in a Mixed Economy* (London: Macmillan, 1980).
7. On the steel sector, see Eisenhammer, J., 'The Politics of the State Steel Industry in Italy', in Quartermaine, L. (ed.) with Pollard, J., *Italy Today: patterns of life and politics* (Exeter: University of Exeter Press, 1985).
8. The development of the public sector in the 1960s, though not so much its later problems, were the focus of considerable interest. See for instance, Holland, S. (ed.), *The State as Entrepreneur* (London:Weidenfeld/Nicolson, 1972); Posner, M.V. and Woolf, S.J., *Italian Public Enterprise* (London: Duckworth, 1967); Shonfield, M., *Modern Capitalism* (Oxford: Oxford University Press, 1965); Vernon, R. (ed.), *Big Business and the State* (London: Macmillan, 1974).
9. Figures quoted in Cesarini, F., 'La situazione finanziaria', in Gerelli E. and Bognetti, G., *La Crisi delle partecipazioni statali: motivi e prospettive*

(Milan: Franco Angeli Editore, 1981), p. 57.

10. See Banca d'Italia, *Relazione* (1972) and *Relazione* (1979, Appendici.

11. For detailed description of official investment figures, see Gatti, B., 'La politica industriale', in Gerelli, E. and Bognetti, G. (1981) on whose estimation this part of the analysis and interpretation are based.

12. On changes in the financial sector generally, see Monti, M., Cesarini, F. and Scognamiglio, C., 'Report on the Italian Credit and Financial System'. special issue of *Banca Nazionale Del Lavoro Quarterly Review* (June 1983), particularly Appendix and Tables pp. 174-257. On changes in financial flows and their effects on finance to industry, see *The Italian Economy: Monetary Trends*, nos. 14 (August 1979), 19 (December 1981) and 24 (August 1983).

13. See on this issue Savona, P. and Tullio, G., 'Italy's International Reserves and their Determinants in the 1970s - an assessment of the country risk', *Banca Nazionale Del Lavoro Quarterly Review*, no. 141 (March 1982).

14. For discussion of the major factors underlying this problem, see Furlong, P.F., 'Political Underdevelopment and Economic Recession in Italy', in Cox, A. (ed.), *Politics Policy and the European Recession* (London: Macmillan, 1982); and Furlong, P.F., 'Italy', in Ridley, F.F. (ed.), *Policies and Politics in Western Europe* (Beckenham: Croom Helm, 1984).

15. See Monti *et al* (1983), pp. 221-50.

16. For data used in this section of the analysis, see *The Italian Economy: Monetary Trends*, no. 24 (August 1983); see also Saini, K.G., 'Economic Policy Management in Italy', in *Review of Economic Conditions in Italy* (1984), no. 3.

17. On the question of 'crowding out', see Carone, G., 'State Transfers in Italy', in *Mezzogiorno d'Europa*, no. 1, January/March 1984.

18. It is not possible here to describe in detail the political scandals of this period in the sectors of finance and industry. Surveys of the problem may be found in Galli, G., *L'Italia sotterranea - storia politica e scandali* (Bari: Laterza, 1983; for the connection with the political system, see Scalfari, E. and Turani, G., *Razza Padrone: Storia della borghesia di stato* (Milan: Feltrinelli, 1974); and Tamburrano, G., *L'iceberg democristiano* (Milan: Sugarco Edizioni, 1975). A clear account of the Calvi episode may be found in Cornwell, R., *God's Banker - an account of the life and death of Roberto Calvi* (London: Victor Gollancz, 1983).

19. See Gatti, S. *et al.*, 'Librobianco sulla Banca d'Italia', in *L'Espresso* 15 April 1979.

20. On IMI's 1985 holdings, see Malaspina, T., 'Il banchiere senza partito', in *L'Esprsso*, 7 July 1985.

21. See Turani, G., 'L'ultimo intrigo', in *L'Espresso*, 2 December 1984.

22. See for example Magri, E., 'Intervista a Mechele Sindona', in *L'Europea*, vol., no 28, 11 July 1975.

23. In Gramsci, A., *Quaderni del Carcere* vol. 3 (a cura di Gerratana, V., Torino, Einaudi, 1975), pp. 1749-50.

24. Figures from Gatti, B. (1981), pp. 122-5.

25. On the southern policy and finance for industry, see Lo Cicero, M., 'Development Finance: Market and Planning', in *Mezzogiorno d'Europa*,

no. 1 (January/March 1984); also Martinelli, F., 'Public Policy and Industrial Development in Southern Italy: anatomy of a dependent industry', in *International Journal of Urban and Regional Research*, vol. 9, no. 1 (1985).

26. In Vittas, D., *et al.*, *Banking Systems Abroad: the role of the large deposit banks in the financial systems of Germany, France, Italy, the Netherlands, Switzerland, Sweden, Japan and the United States* (London: Interbank Research Organisation, 1978), p. 137.

6 The State Regulation and Deregulation of Financial Institutions and Services in the United States
John E. Owens

Regulation of financial institutions has always been a highly controversial area of public policy in the United States, as the pressures for central organising mechanisms - whether in New York or Washington - have conflicted with the country's dominant political-cultural traditions of private enterprise and localism. The result has been a pervasive ambivalence in this most important area of economic policy and a history of government regulation all too often born out of successive crises. Largely as a result of policies adopted in the 1930s, financial institutions and services in the United States are amongst the most highly regulated in the world, and amongst the most punctiliously regulated industries in the country. Yet, both the regulators and the regulated industries have never been very comfortable with such a pervasive framework of restrictions and have frequently sought to dismantle parts of it. Presently, Americans are witnessing the most successful attempts to date to remove these regulatory restrictions.

The first part of this chapter traces the development of regulatory policy from the 1930s until the present. The second part explores the different and often conflicting rationales for regulatory policies and explains why policies have been adopted and implemented. Finally, an assessment is provided of the impact of regulation and deregulation on the stability and safety of the American financial system and the availability of credit and financial services to different geographical areas and to the small business and housing sectors.

THE ORIGIN AND DEVELOPMENT OF AMERICAN REGULATORY POLICIES

The United States did not have anything resembling a Central Bank until the Federal Reserve Act was passed in 1913. From the early days of the American Republic, such a notion had been viewed with suspicion.

Alexander Hamilton's National Bank of the United States was established by Congress in 1791 as a means of helping secure the young Republic's credit. The Bank, however, was bitterly contested by a coalition of interests (most prominently, the farmers) who either opposed banks in general or feared the central government pre-empting the rights of the individual states;[1] and in 1811, these interests were successful in preventing its charter being renewed. State-chartered financial institutions flourished during this period, but as organisations for handling the Federal government's business they were poor substitutes for a national bank, especially during the war of 1812; and they often failed to redeem their own notes. Five years later, Congress approved a 20-year charter for the second Bank of the United States, but when renewal of this Bank's charter was sought in 1832, President Jackson vetoed the Bill and removed the Federal government's deposits.

Contemporary federal regulation of financial institutions in the United States originated in the 1860s. In order to finance the economic and financial disruption of the American Civil War, and to cope with the chaos of state-chartered banks issuing different notes at varying discounts, another attempt was made to nationalise government control. In 1863, Congress approved the National Currency Act which, as amended by the National Bank Act 1864, authorised a new Office of the Comptroller of the Currency (OCC) in the Treasury Department to issue charters for national banks. The hope was that the new system of national banks would provide the US Treasury with some (albeit crude) means of controlling credit by establishing a ceiling on the quantity of money, safer conditions for note-holders and depositors, a large market for government securities, and mechanisms by which bank notes could be apportioned amongst the states and territories according to their populations, resources and business needs. Contemporary federal regulation of banking originates from this legislation.

In the last quarter of the nineteenth century, it became clear to both eastern finance and industry and to their opponents that neither the existence of a national banking system regulated and controlled by the Federal government nor the financial organising power of J.P.Morgan was sufficient to prevent severe financial panics in 1873, 1893 and 1907-9 or the widespread social and political unrest which followed. The problem was that the national system was a system in name only. The national banks had common characteristics and centralised supervision, but the control exercised by the national government was primarily indirect and incidental. From the 1890s onwards, the political debate focused on two crucially interrelated problems. First, the financial system's ability to allocate credit efficiently about the country. Under current arrangements, the system was grossly inelastic in as much as the quantity of money in circulation could not be regulated to accommodate either increased or reduced seasonal demand.[2] The second problem concerned whether control over the system should rest in Washington or New York. As matters stood at the turn of the century, the main source of financial power remained with a few large banks in New York,[3] much to the cost of agricultural areas of the South and West.

By the beginning of Woodrow Wilson's presidency in 1913, no economic issue was so pressing as banking and currency reform. The existing private arrangements plainly did not serve the needs of business and industry, and Congress was determined to have a government-controlled institution. Legislation was approved within the space of just one year, but the Federal Reserve System it created was closely modelled on the existing privately controlled National Reserve Association.[4] Its purpose was to promote currency elasticity, mobility of banking reserves, and more equitable distribution of reserves and credit. The establishment of the Federal Reserve did not, however, dilute the OCC's authority, but rather superimposed a second regulatory structure on the existing national banking and state banking systems and created a second Federal bank regulatory agency. The effect of this reform was to considerably strengthen Federal control. National banks were required to become members of the system; state banks were to be encouraged to become members and accept Federal supervision by the creation of a new agency.

It was the New Deal reforms introduced as thousands of financial institutions failed in the Depression[5] which established the broad outlines of contemporary Federal regulatory policy. Throughout the 1920s, there were frequent demands for greater Federal control, particularly over branching and bank involvement in the securities business. It was not until after the Wall Street Crash and the subsequent collapse of the financial system that reform became a priority on Congress's agenda. Most bankers interpreted the failures as discrete events, the punishment for violations of basic economic laws. Even when President Hoover begged them to take urgent concerted private action through the creation of a National Credit Corporation, these same individualistic views persisted, with the consequence that public confidence could not be restored.[6] In 1931 alone 2298 banks failed with deposit liabilities of $1.6 billion. As the crisis deepened some leading bankers came round to the view − also shared by the incoming Roosevelt administration

— that since only the government could bail them out, government should reform the system.

The Reconstruction Finance Corporation was authorised in 1933 to make short-term finance available to the banks [7] in order to ensure that communities retained their banking facilities.[8] In Congress, however, various committees were studying the causes of the Crash which many believed to be the basic cause of the subsequent financial crisis. Their hearings soon uncovered dubious and sometimes scandalous banking practices which has evidently contributed to the bank's liquidity problems. Investigation and criticism focused on bank investment practices, particularly the use of bank credit to finance the purchase of securities; conflicts of interest; speculative abuse; and personal enrichment. The hearings were conducted in a highly-charged atmosphere. Their effect was to place the financial community on the defensive, and to strengthen considerably the hand of those in Congress advocating tighter regulation of the system.

Three months after Roosevelt's inauguration in 1933 and just eight hours after the Bill's first reading, Congress approved the Glass-Steagall Act.[9] Its central thrust was to encourage the development of a safer financial system by separating investment banking business from commercial banking. Since it was also widely believed that excessive interest rate competition for deposits had contributed to the waves of bank failures - because deposits had been drained from the rest of the country into the main financial centres - interest rate ceilings were imposed by the Banking Acts 1933 and 1935. Banks were explicitly prohibited from paying interest on demand deposits, and restricted in the interest they could pay on time and savings deposits by ceilings imposed by the Federal Reserve through Regulation Q. Because so many banks had failed for lack of sufficient capital, the minimum capitalisation for national banks was doubled from $25.000 to $50,000, thus making it far more difficult for new banks to be chartered.

Safer banking, however, was to be achieved not only through the imposition of important new restrictions on banks' activities, but also by significantly enhancing the Federal regulatory structure. Indeed, in many respects the core element of the 1933 Act was the establishment of a deposit insurance scheme under the auspices of another new regulatory agency, the Federal Deposit Insurance Corporation (FDIC). To reformers in Congress, Federal deposit insurance was a means of restoring public confidence in the banking system while at the same time increasing Federal authority.[10] Bank deposits would be insured by the

Federal government up to certain limits. Membership for national banks was made mandatory. For state banks, membership was optional but deposit insurance was such an attractive proposition when state schemes were not viable that many joined, accepting when they did the FDIC's supervision of their operations. Indeed, the FDIC succeeded to a far greater extent than either the national banking or the Federal Reserve systems in extending Federal regulatory authority over state chartered banks.[11] By this means, Federal authorities would also gain considerable influence over state chartering and other regulatory policies.

In a further effort to strengthen Federal regulation of the financial system, the position of the Federal Reserve was also enhanced. The Banking Act 1935 transferred powers which had hitherto been exercised by the Federal Reserve Bank of New York to a new Board of Governors of the Federal Reserve System in Washington. This body could approve or reject presidential and vice-presidential nominations for the regional Federal Reserve banks, alter banks' reserve requirements, and for the first time exercise control over open-market operations. However, because of the necessity of political compromise and bargaining to pass the legislation, even after the Act was implemented, the United States still did not have the type of Central Bank advocated by the Roosevelt administration and many congressional and banking leaders. Control over the money supply still rested essentially with private bankers. Moreover, the more radical proposals - national branch banking, nationalisation of the banks (perfectly feasible at the time, given the crisis conditions), socialisation of the credit function - promoted as attempts to ensure tighter governmental regulation of the credit system were rejected. The 1935 law overturned the Glass-Steagall Act by requiring that only the larger state banks become members of the Federal Reserve System; 6000 smaller insured state banks representing-on-seventh of the total bank assets were allowed to take up only partial membership.[12]

Just as the Depression had wrought havoc on the banking system, so savings and loan associations, cooperative banks, homestead associations and insurance companies, as investors in home mortgages, experienced liquidity problems as savers demanded cash, and mortgagees defaulted on their loans. Federal policy-makers responded to these problems in more or less the same way as they did to the banking crisis. As a temporary measure, loans were also made available to these institutions from the RFC. In order to improve their long-term viability, Congress authorised the creation of a Federal Home Loan Bank System with twelve regional FHLBs in 1932.[13] Its purpose was to support the home loan and building construction markets by providing discounting and lending facilities similar to those which commercial banks enjoyed through the Federal Reserve. At the urging of the newly-elected Roosevelt Administration, and with something approaching 40 per cent of existing home mortgage debt in default and mortgage foreclosures running at 1000 a day in June 1933, [14] Congress approved the Home Owners' Loan Act in 1933. Section 5 of the Act granted the FHLB Board authority to charter and supervise Federal savings and loan associations. Federal control over the savings and loans was further consolidated through a provision in the National Housing Act 1934 which created a separate share insurance scheme operated by a Federal Savings and Loan Insurance Corporation (FSLIC) under the direct control of the FHLBB which state chartered associations were eligible to join. [15]

The reforms of the 1930 not only established the basis on which Congress and the federal agencies could regulate and supervise most of the country's financial institutions, they also legitimised - indeed, institutionalised - a highly segmented system in which different types of financial institutions specialised in the provision of particular types of credit and accepted funds from fairly specific sources. Commercial banks received the deposits of corporate business and concentrated on providing them with credit (which non-bank institutions could not). Non-bank institutions − savings and loans, mutual savings banks and credit unions[16] − derived most of their funds from personal savings and made various types of consumer loans. Commercial banks were encouraged to limit their activities primarily to the provision of short-term credit for business, and specifically prohibited or discouraged from entering the investment bank, insurance and mortgage markets. Savings and loans and to a lesser extent mutual savings banks were encouraged to serve the mortgage market and credit unions to serve the market for small consumer loans. The net effect of this regulatory system was a cartelised financial system: institutions within each industry - banking, savings and loans, mutual savings banks, insurance, investment banking - were effectively prevented from competing too much with one another in their own product markets, or against other firms in other markets. In these ways, it was assumed that institutional safety and soundness would be assured.

AMERICAN REGULATORY POLICIES AND DEREGULATORY PRESSURES AFTER 1945

In the long term, as any observer of OPEC will know, cartels become unstable. Market conditions change and because the profits to be made within cartels are high, outsiders soon design and offer competitive substitutes. When the cartel is threatened, its members have basically two choices: either they can reform their organisation, perhaps dismantle it so as to allow more competition; or they can try to incorporate outsiders into their system of regulation, so as to control them. The history of credit institution regulation after the 1930s reveals both these processes at work. In the next section, they are discussed within three difference contexts: government regulation of price, product lines and geographic expansion. In financial institutions regulatory policy, price regulation is concerned with interest rate ceilings on deposit and loans; product line regulation with the functions and services institutions may perform; and geographic regulation with where institutions may establish facilities to conduct their business. [17]

Price Regulation

The regulatory system established in the 1930s restricted price competition between financial intitutions by prohibiting the payment of interest on demand deposits and by setting ceilings on interest rates which could be paid on savings and time deposits (Regulation Q). In the 1960s and 1970s important new developments occurred in American credit and capital markets which encouraged widespread circumvention of the price restrictions established in the 1930s. Successive efforts by Federal regulatory authorities to reinstate the restrictions failed.

Beginning the the late 1950s corporations began to respond to rising interests rates by shifting their short-term funds from bank demand deposits (on which interest could not be paid) into Treasury bills, commercial paper and other short-term investments. These shifts of funds had a fairly dramatic effect upon the large money-centre banks in New York and Chicago, since these institutions depended on these corporate deposits for a large part of their funds. If they were to compete successfully with the securities markets for the cash balances of corporations (indeed, if they were to survive), the money-centre banks needed to develop new money market instruments to attract funds. Federal bank regulators succumbed to the realities of the new market conditions in 1960 and allowed the banks to offer negotiable certificates of deposit (CDs). The impact of their action on commercial banks was immediate and, as a result, since the 1960s commercial banks have derived most of their loan funds from CDs rather than from deposits. The loosening of price restrictions, however, caused severe 'disintermediation' problems for thrift institutions who relied on a steady supply of savings deposits to finance home mortgage loans.[18] In order to assure a continued flow of funds to housing, Federal regulators responded by enforcing ceilings on bank savings and time deposits (Regulation Q) and then in 1966, by extending rate regulation to savings and loans and by formalising a rate differential which allowed thrifts to pay higher rates on some deposits. Effectively, the original justification for rate restrictions was jettisoned in favour of a new rationale which required the allocation of credit to housing.

The regulatory action taken in 1966 failed,however, to solve the problems caused by rising and increasingly volatile interests rates. Savers looked increasingly to the unregulated sectors of the financial system in the money markets for higher and higher rates of return. Eventually as these money market opportunities increased, the Fed was obliged to suspend rate ceilings on large CDs in 1970.[19]. However, for those savers who could not raise such large amounts, the depository cartel was extended even as market interest rates increased with further inflation and as new unregulated firms entered the competition for funds. In 1973, mutual savings banks in Massachusetts began offering NOW accounts - effectively, interest-bearing checking accounts. Congress responded initially by restricting the offering of NOWs to Massachusetts and New Hampshire, but then extended it to New England in 1976, and New York and New Jersey in 1979.

By 1979, a new crisis to the depository cartel had emerged in the form of the money market mutual funds (MMMFs) offered by investment companies. MMMFs are in everything but name demand deposits which pay money market interest rates. Once again, the traditional depository institutions, and particularly the savings and loans experienced disintermediation, as MMMFs caused massive withdrawals of funds from banks and thrifts. For the first time since the 1930s, there was a serious possibility that large numbers of depository institutions would fail. Clearly, the restrictions of interest rates could not be maintained.

Congress responded by passing the Depository Institutions Deregulation and Monetary Control Act 1980 (DIDMCA). This legislation authorised depository institutions throughout the country to offer NOW accounts, thus effectively abolishing the prohibition against paying interest on checking accounts (demand deposits) and the banks' monopoly on these accounts which had been in force since 1933;[20] and established a Depository Institutions Deregulation Committee (DIDC) with a mandate to phase out interest rate ceilings on time and savings deposits. When it became clear that the thrifts were being seriously disadvantaged by the deregulation of interest rates, Congress subsequently included in the Garn-St Germain Depository Institutions Amendments Act 1982 a provision instructing the DIDC to develop a thrift account which would be substantially equivalent to money market funds as an investment instrument. The account known as the money market deposit account (MMDA) was not made subject to interest rate ceilings and was authorised in December 1982. These new instruments were immediately successful in attracting new funds to the thrifts since they were also more accessible and covered by federal deposit insurance. Other accounts, such as All Saver Certificates and Super NOWs, were later developed and ultimately, the DIDC abolished interest rate restrictions on most deposits over $2500.[21]

Product Line Regulation

Traditionally, the product line of national banks were restricted by the National Banking Act to activities 'necessary to carry out the business of banking'. However, commercial banks have periodically sought to expand their activities into non-banking areas which they claimed were part of banking. For example, in 1916, Congress allowed national banks to sell insurance but only in communities of less than 5000 people. In 1927, the McFadden Act granted national banks the authority to buy and sell marketable securities. Following the collapse of the banking system after the Wall Street Crash, the Glass-Steagal Act 1933 reversed this policy and stipulated a strict separation between commercial and investment banking, although it did not prohibit banks from underwriting and dealing in US, state or local governments obligations. Congress reinforced this policy when it approved the Bank Holding Act 1956. Since the 1960s, however, the banks have again mounted strenuous efforts to expand their product lines, particularly into securities, real estate and insurance. In the 1960s, they found a sympathetic response from the OCC which, under the leadership of Comptroller James Saxon, proceeded to interpret the terms of the National Banking Act in a very liberal and expansionary fashion. Most of the OCC's rulings were, however, subsequently nullified by the courts, following petitions from industries threatened by bank incursions, or states unwilling to have their own regulatory policies threatened by Federal action.

Partly to avoid further suits brought against them or the OCC, the larger banks began in the late 1960s to exploit a loophole in the Bank Holding Company Act 1956 which allowed holding companies which owned just one bank to escape important restrictions on product diversification.

By the end of 1970, one-third of all commercial bank deposits in the US were controlled by bank holding companies. Henceforth, this would be the most important way banks would try to expand their product lines. Congress, however, quickly moved to reinstate its policy of separating banking from non-banking businesses by requiring the Federal Reserve to restrict holding companies to activities 'closely related to banking' and by May 1982 the Board had approved only 25 activities; 21 of which national banks were already permitted.[22] Following extensive litigation over the Fed's rulings, in the Garn-St Germain Act, Congress specifically prohibited bank holding companies from engaging in the insurance business.

Recently, Federal regulation of product line diversification has been subject to new pressures from the ingenuity of the holding companies in finding regulatory loopholes. According to the 1970 amendments, a bank is an organisation which makes commercial loans and accepts demand deposits. Non-banking companies, such as Sears and Roebuck (a large retailing company) and Merrill Lynch (a large securities firm), Shearson/American Express (a travel company) and The Dreyfus Corporation (an investment adviser and mutual fund sponsor) - firms congressional policy has intended to prohibit from entering the banking business - have successfully exploited the 1970 Act's definition of divesting themselves of either of the required banking activities (although still offering their customers NOW accounts), thereby enabling them to purchase chartered commercial banks as non-bank banks. The effect has been to threaten once again congressional policy requiring separation of banking and non-banking business, and in the case of Merrill Lynch, circumventing the restrictions contained in the Glass-Steagall Act.[23]

Individual states have also tried to force the pace of deregulation in this area. Using a particularly ingenious route which allows outsiders to benefit from their efforts to liberalise restrictions on banks' activities, South Dakota, for instance, has encouraged out-of-state banks (e.g. Citibank) to establish state-chartered banking subsidiaries which can sell insurance (supposed to be denied them by the Garn-St Germain Act) but only to out-of-state residents. Indeed, apart from this special device, some 29 states also permit their banks to engage in some type of insurance brokerage, and 15 in some type of travel agency services.[24]

The services offered by non-bank thrift institutions were also restricted by the reforms of the 1930s and by the laws of most states which prohibited them from offering transaction deposits (e.g. checking or demand deposits), consumer loans, and services to business which were not related to their traditional specialisation in real estate. In order to make interest rate deregulation more palatable to the thrifts, Congress agreed in the DIDMCA and the Garn-St Germain Act to broaden their asset and liability powers to include authority to offer transaction deposits, consumer loans, and services to industry quite unrelated to real estate. Indeed, following passage of the 1982 amendments, there are now no banking services these institutions cannot provide, and the are able to hold up to 40 per cent of their portfolios in non-mortgage assets. Savings and loan holding companies, moreover, unlike bank holding companies, are not restricted in the activities their affiliates may undertake.[25] Non-depository financial institutions have also been making incursions into the traditional business activities of depository institutions. Mention has already been made of the non-bank bank phenomenon by which companies such as Merrill Lynch and The Dreyfus Corporation have been able to enter the banking business. For a number of years, however, a number of large industrial and retailing companies such as General Motors, the Ford Motor Company, General Electric and Control Data have been actively engaged in banking activities often through captive finance companies which do not only extend credit on their own products. Sears and Roebuck have run a 'financial supermarket' for some years since they are the country's largest retailer and also own an insurance company, a savings and loan association, a national real estate firm, and a securities firm.[26] Other companies such as Prudential Bache and Merrill Lynch have moved substantially in the same direction.

What is clear, therefore, is that the traditional American financial system composed of familiar institutions operating within narrowly defined areas and offering fairly limited financial services has been transformed into one which are far more diverse and where the distinctions between different types of institutions is no longer clear. Table 6.1 documents the extent of this transformation since 1960.

Proposals made by the Reagan administration in its proposed Financial Institution Holding Company Deregulation Act would have enhanced this process even further, by allowing all depository institutions to expand through holding companies into the insurance, property development and brokerage, and investment banking businesses. Congress did not approve this legislation. Indeed, no consensus presently exists on the future direction of policy and the two chambers of Congress are controlled by different parties. During the 98th Congress, the House Banking, Finance and Urban Affairs Committee approved a Bill which would have specifically prohibited banks from entering the securities business, would have required all savings and loans to hold 65 per cent of their assets in home mortgages, and would have closed both the non-bank bank and South Dakota loopholes. The House Energy and Commerce Committee proposed an even more restrictive bill. However, a Bill which passed the Senate would have permitted banks to underwrite some types of bonds and have given savings and loans more powers, although it would have also closed the non-bank bank loophole.[27]

Geographic Regulation

Government not only regulates the products financial institutions may offer their customers, but also where they can expanded their operations geographically. State branching restrictions are one obvious limitation on expansion. The Federal government, however, also restricts the expansion of financial institutions through holding companies, chain banking and mergers as well as through their international operations.[28]

Branching is the most common form of geographic expansion by financial institutions, Since 1960, the number of insured banks operating branches has increased from about one-sixth to about one-half. The main regulatory restrictions on branching stem from the McFadden Act 1927. Although this legislation allowed national banks to operate branches for the first time, it restricted the operation of branches to the banks' home cities and to the same branching privileges enjoyed by state chartered banks. For these reasons, the Act is generally regarded as restricting rather than encouraging branching. Following the financial crisis, in the Banking Act 1933, Congress granted national banks the same branching powers as state banks, by removing the home city restrictions. Effectively, the policy established by these two Acts set state boundaries as the ultimate limits for the geographic expansion of banks while relinquishing to the individual states control over intra-state branching. This policy was continued in the Douglas amendment contained in the Bank Holding Company Act 1956 which continued the prohibition on inter-state banking and required a holding company with Bank subsidiaries in one state to gain the permission of other states in which it wanted to operate bank subsidiaries.

Despite the intentions of congressional policy since 1933, the trend has been towards removing geographic restrictions. As in other areas, however, the process has been *ad hoc*. Nevertheless, banks have been successful in exploiting the considerable legal uncertainty in this area to achieve geographic expansion through loan production offices, money market mutual funds, deposit brokers, non-bank banks, electronic banking

Table 6.1: The deregulation of products, 1960–84

Products	Commercial Banks		Savings & loans		Insurance companies		Retail companies		Security dealers	
	1960	1984	1960	1984	1960	1984	1960	1984	1960	1984
Checking	★	★		★		★		★		★
Savings	★	★	★	★		★		★		★
Time deposits	★	★	★	★		★		★		★
Instalment loans	★	★		★		★		★		★
Business loans	★	★	★	★		★		★		★
Mortgage loans	★	★	★	★		★		★		★
Credit cards		★		★		★	★	★		★
Insurance					★	★		★		★
Stocks, bonds, } brokerage, underwriting }		★		★		★		★	★	★
Mutual funds				★		★		★		★
Real estate				★		★		★		★

Source: Federal Reserve Bank of Atlanta Economic Review, April 1984.

networks, franchising, and other channels. State and Federal regulators, moreover, have actually encouraged this process. Since 1933, and particularly since the 1960s, states have progressively loosened their restrictions on intra-state branching. Currently, only eight states prohibit branching altogether (i.e. unit banking), 21 allow limited branching, and 21 (and the District of Columbia) permit state-wide branching. Figure 6.1 shows the geographical distribution of these regimes by state.

Since 1980, several states have also relaxed their restrictions on inter-state banking by allowing out-of-state bank holding companies to conduct banking operations within their borders. By August 1984, 27 states had approved statutes permitting entry by out-of-state institutions. Legislatures in Maine, New York, Alaska and South Dakota had passed laws permitting bank holding companies from anywhere else in the United States to operate subsidiaries in their states, although New York's law requires reciprocity with other states involved. Nine other states (Connecticut, Florida, Georgia, Kentucky, Massachusetts, North Carolina, Rhode Island, South Carolina and Utah) also allow entry by out-of-state institutions but only from within their region. Fourteen other states also allow entry by out-of-state institutions to some extent and in certain circumstances.[29]

Federal regulators have also encouraged the movement towards inter-state banking. In 1978, the International Banking Act 'grandfathered foreign

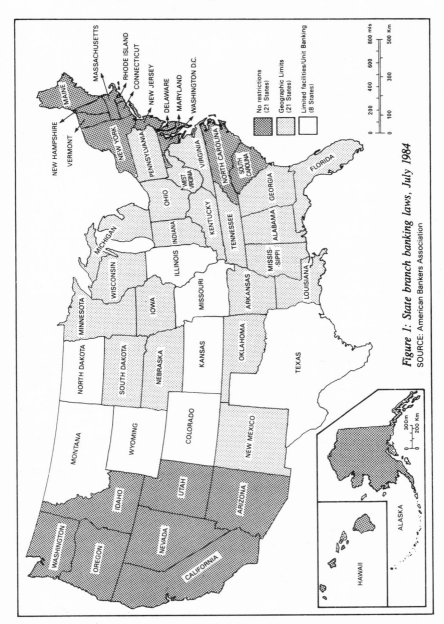

Figure 1: State branch banking laws, July 1984
SOURCE: American Bankers Association

Table 6.2: Assets held by various financial institutions as percentages of total private assets, 1947–83

	1947	1950	1955	1960	1965	1970	1975	1980	1983	Change in percentage shares 1947–83	Change in percentage shares 1970–83
Commercial banking	56.2	51.1	43.9	38.2	36.8	38.0	38.8	35.8	33.3	−22.9	−4.7
US banks	55.6	50.5	43.2	37.5	36.1	36.8	36.5	32.1	30.3	−25.3	−6.5
Domestic affiliates	—	—	—	—	—	0.2	0.6	0.8	0.9	+0.9	+0.7
Savings & loans	4.7	5.7	8.6	11.8	13.7	13.0	15.5	16.0	15.7	+9.0	+2.7
Mutual savings banks	8.0	7.7	7.4	6.9	6.4	5.9	5.6	4.4	3.7	−4.3	−2.2
Credit unions	0.2	0.3	0.7	1.1	1.2	1.4	1.7	1.8	1.9	+1.7	+0.5
Life insurance	20.7	21.4	20.6	19.4	16.6	15.1	13.0	12.0	12.0	−8.7	−3.6
Other insurance	3.3	4.0	4.5	4.4	3.9	3.8	3.6	4.5	4.3	+1.0	+0.5
Private pension funds	1.7	2.4	4.3	6.4	7.9	8.3	8.7	10.6	11.5	+9.8	+3.2
State & local government retirement funds	1.3	1.7	2.5	3.3	3.7	4.5	4.9	5.1	6.0	+4.7	+1.5

	1947	1950	1955	1960	1965	1970	1975	1980	1983	Change in percentage shares	
										1947–83	1970–83
Finance companies	2.2	3.2	4.3	4.6	4.8	4.8	4.6	5.1	4.9	+2.7	+0.1
Real estate invesment trusts	—	—	—	—	—	0.3	0.7	0.1	0.1	+0.1	−0.2
Investment companies	0.6	1.1	1.8	2.8	3.8	3.5	2.0	1.6	2.5	+1.0	−1.0
Money market mutual funds	—	—	—	—	—	—	0.2	1.9	3.1	+3.1	+3.1
Security brokers & dealers	1.1	1.4	1.4	1.1	1.1	1.2	0.9	0.9	0.9	−0.2	−0.3

Source: Board of Governors of the Federal Reserve System, Flow of Funds and Savings Section.

banks' ownership of American banks in more than one state by permitting branching by Edge Act corporations. More recently, the Garn-St Germain Act 1982 specifically authorised inter-state acquisitions of troubled institutions, notably the 1981 acquisition of two out-of-state institutions by the California-based Citizen Savings (since transformed into First Nationwide Savings) and Citicorp's acquisition of Fidelity Savings and Loan of San Francisco immediately before the 1982 legislation was approved. Since the 1982 Act was passed, there have been other out-of-state aquisitions, including two more proposed thrift acquisitions (in Chicago and Miami) by Citicorp. Indeed, by 1983, 10 large bank holding companies were operating subsidiaries (usually finance or mortgage banking companies) with 2084 out-of-state offices in 40 states. Bank of America had 375 such offices in 40 states, Citicorp, 444 offices in 39 states, including national banks in New York, Delaware and South Dakota.[30]

Institutions have also been able to use the non-bank bank loophole to evade prohibitions against inter-state banking. As a result, a number of securities, insurance and commercial firms have acquired non-bank banks and a number of commercial banks have filed applications to acquire non-bank banks in order to establish inter-state networks. Following adverse judicial decisions, the Federal Reserve approved Bankers Trust of New York's application to establish a non-bank bank in Florida in 1984. By the end of 1984, there were nearly 350 such applications, mostly filed with the OCC. Now that Congress has failed to pass legislation to close this loophole, presumably the conflict will move to the courts.

In contrast to national banks, federally chartered savings and loans and mutual savings banks are not currently subject to any Federal restrictions on intra or inter-state branching. Until 1980, the FHLBB generally followed state laws. Since then, the FHLBB has allowed state-wide branching regardless of state laws. As a result, since 1970 the number of savings and loans has decreased by about 30 per cent while the number of branches has increased by over 100 per cent. In 1981, the FHLBB went even further by allowing mergers between savings and loans across state lines, where an institution was in difficulties. Congress endorsed this policy in all respects in the Garn-St Germain Act 1982, which permitted out-of-state non-bank thrift institutions to acquire other failing institutions.

What is clear from the foregoing discussion is that the American financial and regulatory systems have been transformed over the last 40 years, and particularly over the last decade. In contrast to the much smaller and much more structured financial system of 40 years ago, an enormous and highly complex financial system is is place. Indeed, in 1985 it is by no means clear which firms should be regarded as part of the financial system. What has stimulated this change has been a rapid expansion of financial assets which has intensified the competition between financial institutions. Table 6.2 documents this enormous increase in debt, together with the relative importance of the different types of financial institutions over the post-war period. In 1983, the total assets of financial and non-financial institutions were 17 times larger than in 1947. In the competition to finance this burgeoning debt, moreover, the fortunes of the respective financial institutions have fared differently over time, in turn placing pressure on the framework of rules which regulate it. Today, the broad contours of Federal policy are rather different, even from those of ten years ago, although the basic structure of regulation and regulatory institutions remains.[31] In the next section, the discussion turns to why the United States has developed such an extensive regulatory system for financial institutions; and why, in recent years, important elements of the regulatory policy established in the 1930s and maintained as recently as the 1960s have now been abandoned in favour of 'free-'market solutions.

EXPLAINING THE RISE OF DEREGULATION AND THE CONTINUITY OF REGULATION

In the literature on American regulatory policy, writers commonly draw a distinction between 'old style' regulation, dating from the Progressive and New Deal eras, which was and is justified on the ground that it helps ensure the operation of a 'free' market; and 'new style' regulation, typically identified with the environmentalist and consumer movements of the 1960s and 1970s, which is redistributive and justified on social grounds. The regulation of financial institutions and services is typically included in the first category. As the discussion in this section will demonstrate, however, regulatory policy in this area has not always been designed to achieve exclusively 'economic' objectives but also important social and political goals. Indeed, this phenomenon probably explains the lack of certainty of direction in many of the policies presently being pursued. Here, eight different often conflicting rationales for policy are discussed.

1. Expanding The Financial Power of Government

Even before the full development of capitalism, governments regulated financial institutions and services as a means of enhancing their capacity to generate taxation revenue. In the United States, this motivation may be discerned in the early efforts of the states to regulate financial institutions, in the creation of the First and Second Banks, the passage of the National Bank Acts during the Civil War, and most importantly in the establishment of the Federal Reserve System in 1913 and the regulatory regime of the 1930s. More recently, this was an important reason underpinning a provision of the DIDMCA of 1980, whereby all chartered depository institutions are now required to deposit non-interest bearing reserves at the Fed. The money of American financial institutions, like that of institutions in other countries is 'taxed' by requiring that all depository institutions hold vault cash or reserves with the Federal Reserve, neither of which bear interest. In the United States, the Federal Reserve is also granted authority to purchase and rediscount assets in exchange for its own interest-bearing liabilities. All but 3 per cent of the profits from these transactions goes into the US Treasury.

2. Controlling the Macro-Economy

Economists usually cite two further justifications. Both arise from the distinctive nature of financial institutions' products - money. First is the fact that the principal liabilities of financial institutions comprise the principal components of the money supply. In order to exercise control over the money supply which has an effect upon the whole economy and in the United States is required by the US Constitution, government must be involved with the operations of financial institutions. The second justification is that an efficient economy requires an efficient payments system. Financial institutions obviously play a critical role in this respect. Since, however, they cannot guarantee such efficiency and the Federal government at least since the New Deal has accepted responsibility for overall macro-economic performance, policy-makers must actively promote the efficient transfer of funds from savers to investors.[32]

Clearly, however, the provision of an efficient payments system and Central Bank control over the money supply do not require a structure of entry restrictions, price controls, geographic and product line limitations, or even reserve requirements.[33] Much of the *economic* justification for financial institution regulation is, therefore, concerned with reducing externalities which inhibit an efficient payments system, easy convertibility of deposits into currency, and encourage loss of confidence in financial institutions. If government did not regulate the financial system, economists argue, externalities would be too expensive.

3. Ensuring an Efficient Payments System

Since the payments system will work most efficiently if everyone uses it, regulations which encourage the use of cheques and other media for transferring funds may be justified on efficiency grounds alone; although there are also good social reasons for encouraging as many people as possible to use the system. An important reason for the establishment of the Federal Reserve System, for example, was to foster the development of an efficient national clearing system. Similarly, over the last 20 or so years, regulators have sought to encourage the use of electronic funds transfer systems. Both these developments have been perceived as facilitating greater use of financial services by as many people as possible. Since, however, some regulations restrict entry, expansion and institutions' product lines, other justifications are also important.[34]

4. Ensuring Financial Solvency - Safety versus Competition

For a financial system to work efficiently, liquidity is paramount. Financial institutions must be able to convert demand deposits (under whatever name) into hard currency, even in periods of crisis. Banks, for instance, operate with only limited amounts of equity capital and hold reserves equal to only a limited fraction of their deposit liabilities. They can, therefore, easily become insolvent by losing money on their operations or through losses on assets; or they may be unable to meet unexpectedly large demands for cash. A whole host of detailed regulations for financial institutions are justified in terms of their ensuring convertibility and preventing institutions from failing.[35]

The experience of the 1920s and 1930s demonstrated that the failure of one institution could lead to runs. Between 1930 and 1933, some 9096 banks were suspended in the United States, representing over 11 per cent of the operating banks and holding about 4 per cent of the country's deposits. Establishing the Federal Reserve as a lender of last resort was one not very successful solution adopted by Federal regulators in the 1930s to remedy institutions' liquidity problems. Another is contained in a wide range of regulations which attempt to prohibit institutions from taking substantial risks by, for example, selling and underwriting corporate securities. However, the policy which has been most important to maintaining public confidence in the American financial system is deposit insurance, offered by the FDIC, the FSLIC, the National Credit Union Administration and some states. Regardless of the solution, maintaining financial solvency and public confidence in the system has probably been the prime motivating force in most regulatory policy for financial institutions since the 1930s, if not before.

5. Maximising Competition

The single-minded dedication of policy-makers in the 1930s to preventing institutional failures was so intense that considerably less regard was given to the anti-competitive nature of many of the reforms which were enacted. Indeed, quite the contrary. The general perception was that the crisis had been fostered by 'excessive competition' and 'over-banking'. Accordingly, regulators then and since have taken deliberate decisions to limit competition between and within industries. The earlier discussion of the regulation of interest rates and financial institutions' product lines provides numerous examples of regulatory actions designed to serve this purpose. The policy of eliminating interest rate competition between banks, for example, was based on the belief that competition for deposits could raise bank costs, reduce profits, and increase the chance of bankruptcy during periods of economic recession. Similarly, chartering and branching restrictions, limitations on non-banks' loan and investment privileges, and the permissible activities which banks and bank holding companies may engage in are all examples of regulations introduced in the 1930s and since, which have effectively limited competition as deliberate public policy. Only quite recently have policy-makers attempted to balance the objectives of maximising competition more equally against the need to maintain financial solvency and safety.[36]

6. Preventing Concentration and Centralisation of Financial and Political Power

Much more important than competition as a rationale for regulatory policy in this policy field has been an almost pervasive fear of concentration and centralisation of economic, financial and political. Students of American government and politics will not be very surprised by this. Concern over the concentration of economic and political power has been an important theme running through American history. In the politics of financial institutions, this theme has been very strong from the early days of the Republic - in congressional opposition to the First Bank and Jackson's veto of the Second Bank's charter. In the nineteenth and early twentieth centuries, it was reflected in opposition to the National Bank Acts, the financial and political power exercised by J.P.Morgan and the money trusts and the passage of the Federal Reserve Act.[37] Opposition to the McFadden Act 1927, the banking reforms of the 1930s and the Bank Holding Company Act and amendments of 1856 and 1970 also reflected this concern. Despite economic, social, political and technological pressures towards nationalisation of American economy and society and the recently perceived need to increase competition, the regulatory framework for financial institutions remains a dual one in the sense that regulation and supervision is shared between national and state authorities. States' rights and decentralised economic control, moreover, remain potent political forces [38] with many articulate and well-placed representatives in Congress, particularly in the House, to express their views.[39]

7. Protecting the Small Depositor

Since the 1930s, as part of the need to inspire public confidence, regulators have also been concerned to protect depositors who have relatively small funds and who might not be very sophisticated in their investment behaviour. These are concerns which were reflected in the establishment of the deposit insurance schemes and are regularly invoked when Congress considers increasing the insurance coverage. The rationale for this is related to the rationales 3, 4 and 6 discussed above. Should small depositors not have confidence in the payments system, they will abstain from using financial services. More importantly, however, the policy is designed to prevent people from losing their life's savings because a financial institution fails.[40]

8. Allocating Credit to Meet Certain Social Goals

In a society and economy so wedded to the operation of the market, it is perhaps surprising to find the allocation of credit to serve certain social purposes amongst the rationales for regulatory policy affecting financial institutions. Yet, since the 1930s, the US Congress has maintained a fairly consistent commitment to a policy of ensuring adequate supplies of credit to private housing, as part of a broader policy of encouraging home ownership. Through the establishment of the Federal Home Loan Bank System in 1932 and the passage of the Federal Home Owners' Loan and National Housing Acts of 1933 and 1934, Federal regulators promoted the savings and loan associations as the major suppliers of home mortgages. In 1966, Congress extended Regulation Q ceilings to savings and loans and sanctioned continuation of their interest rate advantage over commercial banks as a means of ensuring that adequate funds flowed into mortgages. In 1975 and 1977, Congress passed the Home Mortgage Disclosure and Community Reinvestment Acts as further attempts to encourage institutions in older urban (poorer) areas to invest in local housing and economic development.[41] Federal tax policy has also consistently favoured institutions who invest more than a certain percentage of their assets in mortgages.

Clearly no one rationale can possibly explain the broad range of policies towards financial institutions in the United States. Even the combinations of reasons for particular policies will vary from policy to policy. What is most striking about the previous discussion, however, is the wealth of often conflicting economic, social and political reasons why America - in the true home of 'free' enterprise - has in its regulatory policies towards financial institutions departed from a pure market financial system.

Probably the most significant factor explaining the broad changes in regulatory policy has been the emergence of crises in the financial system. Thus, the impetus to create the national banking system was provided by the strains imposed on the national currency by the Civil War. Similarly, the financial panic of 1907 led immediately to the passage of the Aldrich - Vreeland Act and ultimately to the establishment of the Federal Reserve System six years later. The important reforms of the 1930s were direct responses to the widespread bank failures between 1930 and 1933. Recently, the DIDMCA and Garn-St Germain Acts were essentially responses to the collapse of the interest rate policies of the 1930s, brought on by rising and increasingly volatile interest rates in the 1970s and early 1980s.

Technological development has also provided a catalyst for changes in market conditions which have in turn led to changes in regulatory policy. For instance, an important reason why branch banking became such an important political issue in the 1920s and 1930s was the arrival of mass ownership of motor cars and better road systems. These developments made it easier than previously for banks to operate a large number of geographically dispersed offices together in one unified entity. Most recently, advances in the transmission, processing and storage of information using new computer and telecommunications technology have played a crucial part in the *de facto* and *de jure* deregulation of contemporary financial institutions and services. These changes have now made it possible and cheap for firms operating within a computer network outside the traditional financial sector to issue their customers with plastic cards with which they can withdraw funds from their accounts at financial institutions or sell particular assets such as money market shares, bonds, stock, or even real estate, and then transfer funds to other people's accounts.[42] The effect has been to make it much more difficult for regulators to police the financial system.

The mere existence of crisis, or disruption in the markets, or technological change cannot explain why government regulation is resorted to, or why a particular form of regulation was preferred.

Perceptions of problems need to be translated into political action. In order to explain the conduct and nature of regulatory policy within this area, a number of writers have focused on the well-financed and well-organised lobby campaigns various financial interests have waged to argue that financial institutions legislation has been largely determined by those interests.[43] Some writers have also identified 'sub-governments' within this policy field and argued that regulatory agencies have been captured by the industries they are supposed to regulate.[44] Using a rather different perspective, two financial writers, Eisenbeis and Kane, have drawn on earlier economic theories of regulation to identify what they call 'a regulatory dialectic' between the regulators and the regulated. According to this view, banks find a way to circumvent a particular regulation; authorities then define a new rule prohibiting the circumvention; subsequently, banks find a way round the new rule, and so on and so forth.[45] Finally, Lindblom has argued that in order for business to get what it wants from government it does not have to bribe, dupe or pressure officials since businessmen occupy a privileged position within a market economy and are entrusted with making vital decisions which affect everybody's economic and social well-being. Should government not comply with the political wishes of business, he argues, government and society incur severe costs.[46]

Each of these explanations basically endorses the notion that business in market societies or market forces are the primary determinants of policy-making. Within the financial institutions regulatory area, numerous examples of policy-makers' scope of action being circumscribed by market conditions and private interests may be cited. Congress has frequently found itself in the impossible situation of trying to undo what the banks had already done, whether the concern was price competition, or geographic or product line expansion.[47] Because of this, a considerable amount of deregulation has been forced upon public decision-makers. In the vanguard of this deregulatory movement have been the country's largest banks and bank holding companies, particularly Citicorp, the world's largest banking conglomerate. Over the last 25 or so years, Citicorp has consistently sought to undermine the regulatory structure established in the 1930s. Citibank invented the negotiable CD in 1961, was a leader in the one-bank holding company movement in the late 1960s, developed the consumer floating rate debenture in 1974, the rising rate thrift note in 1977, exploited the non-bank bank loophole in South Dakota, and by playing one state against another has operations in 40 states and the District of Columbia. Citicorp has been actively pursuing and achieving *de facto* inter-state banking through the courts and the state legislatures.

This picture of market dominance, however, requires considerable qualification. First, the American financial system is not monolithic. As the earlier discussion has demonstrated, it is composed of many economic and political actors each trying to promote their own market positions, partly by opposing regulations which hinder their own expansion, and partly by supporting regulation which hinders their opponents' expansion. This reality is reflected in the continual jostling between and within industries which takes place whenever legislative questions affecting them are laid before Congress.[48]

A second objection relates to the conduct of policy-makers. Regulators are not political vacuums to be filled by the rival claims of different industries. One has only to note the fairly distinctive policy perspectives of those President Reagan has appointed to top positions in the regulatory agencies to indicate the decision-making autonomy and political entrepreneurship pursued by policy-makers. Congressmen and Senators are similarly encouraged to develop and promote ideas of their own through a variety of legislative, policy and electoral incentives.[49] Indeed, the earlier discussion of the conflicting rationales for policy provides ample evidence of the success and autonomy of regulators in getting their values and priorities, as well as those of the industries, included in public policy.

Thirdly, the extent to which either the regulators or the regulated will be successful in their policy efforts will greatly depend on the prevailing 'public philosophy'. Although the United States has a very individualistic - or 'liberal' - political culture[50] as well as a market economy, there has been considerable, and often bitter, political conflict about the proper relationship between economy and polity. The 'public philosophies' of certain periods of American history have been characterised by limited government intervention in economy and society, whilst others - notably the period of the New Deal and the 1960s and 1970s - have witnessed very active government intervention.[51] Regulatory policy affecting financial institutions and services has to a great extent reflected these changes in ideological fashions. The passage of the Federal Reserve Act 1913 and the reforms of 1930s embraced the central tenets of social ('corporate') liberalism embodied in progressivism and the New Deal,[52] just as the Interest Rate Control Act 1966 and the amendments to the Bank Holding Company Act 1970 reflected the public philosophy of the 1960s which remained basically sympathetic to government regulatory solutions.[53] Recently, the deregulatory movement which pre-dates the

Reagan Administration has reflected a rather different public philosophy which is deeply antithetical to government regulation of financial institutions and services, except in limited circumstances, and emphasises the importance of monetary policy to economic stability.[54]

Fourthly, any satisfactory explanation of the regulatory policy-making process in the United States must take account of the complex institutional relationships which are involved and the different political perspectives which are typically associated with different institutions. Congressional legislation or agency regulation can only reflect in a very loose way general perceptions about the role of government at certain moments in time. The precise provisions of regulation are also the results of compromises and bargaining between institutions as well as amongst parties, interests and ideologies.[55] Federal - state relations almost always provide an important dynamic, especially where regulatory policy is concerned with product line diversification and geographic expansion. If the voices of the states are not heard in the agencies, their grievances are sure to be aired in Congress. The fragmentation of the Federal government into different parts has also had an important influence on policy. The academic literature on American government and politics indicates how the presidency and Congress, the regulatory agencies and Congress, the House and the Senate, different congressional committees and committee leaders develop different perceptions of policy problems.[56] The Banking, Finance and Urban Affairs in the House tends to develop a perspective which is rather different from that of the Bank, Finance and Housing in the Senate. The House generally has been more sympathetic to the thrifts and small banks and the Senate more sympathetic to the large money-centre banks. The recent emergence of the House Committee on Energy and Commerce as an active participant in this policy area will most likely strengthen the hand of the House against the Senate, and in consequence, further the interests of those opposed to the money-centre banks.[57]

Finally, it is important to emphasise the respective relationships between the relative market positions of different industries within the financial sector and competing political coalitions, including political parties. At the level of congressional decision-making, Kingdon and others have shown how House members selectively perceive events and information received from different sources, rejecting that they do not like and accepting that they do.[58] At the macro level, Ferguson, for example, has documented the declining political fortunes of a dominant political coalition in the early twentieth century which included the interests of J.P.Morgan, the railroads, investment banking and the mainstream of the

Republican Party; and the subsequent emergence of a new dominant coalition, associated with the New Deal and the Democratic Party, comprising of fast-growing industries such as the savings and loans, smaller regional banks and investment houses, as well as a small number of older and larger New York and California banks such as Chase National Bank and Bank of America, all of whom were seeking to weaken the interests of J.P.Morgan's control over the major capital markets.[59] Both these focuses go a long way to explaining past and present changes in regulatory policy within this area. In the 1960s and early 1970s, for instance, with the Democrats seemingly entrenched as a permanent majority party, regulatory policies tended to support the positions of the thrifts and small banks.[60] Then as now, it has been the large money-centre banks, offering technologically innovative financial services, who are at the forefront of the deregulatory movement and are now prominent in the Reagan coalition.[61] It is the thrifts and the small banks and the Democrats who are now finding difficulty in reconciling their traditional objectives with deregulation, and seeking to retain regulation in order to guarantee market stability and access. Within this approach, however, it is as well to reiterate the earlier point that policy-making within this area has been primarily *ad hoc*, and not the outcome of some grand scheme designed and implemented in the 1930s or some other period.[62] There has always been a good deal of backing and filling in the construction of policy, not least in the present 'era of deregulation'. It will be recalled from the earlier discussion that to date deregulation has been mainly confined to the removal of interest rate controls, and even here, it has been accompanied by some new types of regulation.[63] Deregulation of geographic and product line restrictions has been much more limited. There considerations should also be borne in mind in considering the discussion of the impact of policies.

THE IMPACT OF REGULATION AND DEREGULATION ON THE AMERICAN ECONOMY

The discussion of the impact of policy in this section has three primary focuses: the extent to which regulation has maintained the stability of the American financial system or, concomitantly, the extent to which deregulation has threatened this stability; the impact of regulation and deregulation on the geographic distribution and allocation of financial resources; and the availability of credit to different sectors of the economy, particularly small business and housing.

The Impact on Financial Solvency and Safety

The previous discussion has demonstrated that the overriding concern of regulators since the 1930s has been to ensure the stability and safety of the financial system. Few would doubt the success of the regulatory regime established in the 1930s in meeting this objective. For over 50 years, there has been no equivalent collapse of the financial system. The number of failures per year has been extremely low, far removed from the frequencies experienced in the 1920s and 1930s. Government regulators, moreover, have been able to deal with the failures and near failures which have occurred with reasonable ease and with little impact on the operation of the banking system, even where the largest banks have been concerned. A direct result of this successful record has been that that vital commodity in the world of finance - confidence - has been high.

To what extent this record of success has been achieved because of, or in spite of, the high level of regulation it not only a highly controversial question, but one extremely difficult to answer. Virtually all commentators agree that government restrictions on financial institutions and services since the 1930s have restricted competition. Most commentators concede the value of deposit insurance and close examination and supervision in maintaining the stability of the system. Other aspects of regulatory policy - deposit rate ceilings, restrictions on geographic and product line expansion, industry structure, and balance-sheet constraints - frequently generate little agreement.

Certainly, there is more evidence of great instability and fragility in the American financial system today than at any other time since the 1930s. Whereas no more than 17 banks failed in any one year between 1943 and 1981 (an average of 6 failures each year), Table 6.3 indicates that 42 insured banks failed in 1982 and 48 in 1983 - the highest levels since the 1930s. In 1984, at 79, the failures approached levels last reached in 1937. As a result, the cost of bank failures to the FDIC in 1983 was 69 per cent of the Corporation's income from insurance premiums, compared with a mean of just 9 per cent annually between 1934 and 1980. These, however, are only the banks which have actually failed. By March 1985, the FDIC had identified a further 890 banks (almost 4.5 per cent of all banks) as 'problem' banks, more than one-third higher than in 1983 and more than twice the previous record in 1976.[64] In a report to Congress in April 1983, moreover, the FDIC suggested that its authority to borrow from the US Treasury be increased to reflect its current exposure and 'provide a safety valve in the case of a banking crisis'.[65] Perhaps most serious for the future stability of the financial system and the economy is the fact that for the first time failures or near failures have included some very large banks, most recently the Continental Illinois Bank, the 8th largest bank in the country. Continental Illinois's difficulties threatened to induce a bank run because of the large number of transactions involved. The bank provided correspondent banking services for 2000 small banks throughout the Mid-West with millions of dollars in deposits. Similarly, inter-bank transactions between Continental Illinois and other large banks amounted to many millions of dollars. Closing this large bank, therefore, would have frozen a significant portion of the liquid funds held by other banks with Continental Illinois and started bank runs on other correspondent banks. These were the circumstances which persuaded the FDIC, in July 1984, to invest $4.5 billion of government money, thus effectively nationalising the bank. The consequences of letting such a large bank fail, in terms of the availability of credit, were simply frightening. As a result of the failure of the Penn Square Bank in 1982, the OCC is currently planning to examine economic trends in different industries to determine their profitability with a view to establishing evaluative criteria for bank examiners when they analyse individual bank loans. More recently, the prestigious business magazine *Business Week* has documented the extent of bad domestic loans held by the large money-centre banks and has concluded that 'the strongest recovery in post-war history rests on the financial equivalent of the San Andreas Fault'.[66]

It is difficult to state categorically that this evidence of increasing instability and fragility in the financial system is exclusively, or even primarily, the result of deregulation. One would have to take into account other factors, such as the international debt crisis, particularly loans to Poland, Latin America and Third World countries; market conditions outside the US, particularly the increased volatility of international capital movements; high and fluctuating interest rates; and bad domestic loans, particularly in the energy, agriculture, forest products, and real estate sectors symptomatic of general economic conditions in the US.[67] Nevertheless, the analysis will attempt to assess the effects of some of the changes in regulatory policy which have encouraged greater risk-taking and, thereby, threatened the fragility of the financial system.

Certainly, there are good arguments to suggest that deregulation of interest rates has increased the threat of financial involvency. Although the validity of the argument has since been disputed, one of the main reasons interest rate ceilings were imposed in 1933 was to prevent banks from engaging in 'ruinous' competition which it was believed brought

Table 6.3: Number of insured financial institutions in financial trouble, 1979–85

	No. of problem banks	No. of failed/ merged banks (universe approx. 14000)		No. of failed/ merged banks (universe approx. 3000)	
1934–39		402		13	
1940–49		116		27	
1950–59		46		4	
1960–69		57		43	
1970	250	8		10	
1971	240	6		7	
1972	192	3		3	
1973	154	6		5	
1974	183	4	81	2	43
1975	349	14		2	
1976	379	17		6	
1977	368	6		3	
1978	342	7		2	
1979	287	10		3	
1980	217	10		35	
1981	223	10		81	
1982	369	42	206	252	
1983	642	48		101	
1984	848	17		42	
1985 (March)	890	17			

Notes: Excludes voluntary mergers.
Sources: FDIC and FSLIC.

about the widespread bank failures of the 1920s and 1930s. Without ceilings, it was argued, banks would continue raising deposit rates in order to attract funds and then try to cover the increased cost of funds by investing in risky assets promising high returns. Recently, these same fears have resurfaced only to be disputed again by proponents of deregulation.

Now that Congress has deregulated deposit rates, institutions are free to bid up rates for loan funds without price restrictions, with the result that the cost of money has increased.[68] In order to meet these new costs, institutions are encouraged to make risky loans and investments which promise high return, in the knowledge that should their institutions fail most of their deposits (currently up to $100,000 per deposit) will be fully insured.[69] Because they depend for a good part of their income on interest payments, and because their operating costs are higher,[70] it seems that a number of small banks will continue to fail, although widespread failures do not appear likely. However, much more important to the stability and fragility of the banking system is what happens to the money-centre banks.[71] The recent failure of the Continental Illinois Bank provides some evidence of the kind of risks deregulation has encouraged banks to take. Although many have argued that Continental's liquidity crisis was not the result of deregulation, but bad management and declining oil prices, there is considerable evidence to suggest that it was in large part the result of the bank's heavy dependence on large money market and foreign deposits which, in turn, were a consequence of the removal of Regulation Q ceilings on large negotiable CDs in 1970.[72] Because Continental Illinois's funding was so highly dependent on the market rather than on a large consumer deposit base, a bank run was highly probable.

Removing deposit rate ceilings not only allowed banks with highly productive lending and investment opportunities to increase their share of total deposits, it also allowed banks with highly risky lending and investment opportunities to increase their share of deposits. Indeed, even banks which are basically insolvent because their existing loans have little chance of being repaid may be able to escape the attention of regulators,[73] remain in operation and pursue highly risky investment strategies in the hope of receiving returns high enough to compensate for their previous losses. Should they fail, moreover, the past behaviour of the regulatory agencies inspires confidence that uninsured deposits will also be underwritten by the Federal government. To date and with the notable exception of the failed Penn Square National Bank in 1982 large bank failures have been resolved with no losses for uninsured depositors in the interests of preventing bank runs.[74] The likely effect of this policy is to encourage depositors of more than $100,000 to place their funds in money centre and larger regional banks, channelling money away from local markets, in the knowledge that should the (large) bank in which they deposit their funds fail it will be rescued by the regulators.[75]

A direct effect of deregulation of interest rates, it may be argued, therefore, has been to increase the total potential liability of the FDIC's deposit funds.[76] More than this, however, the removal of interest rate ceilings has created a new distortion in risk-taking behaviour, by making it considerably easier for risky institutions, which are currently undercharged for deposit insurance to attract funds away from safe institutions, which are currently overcharged for deposit insurance.[77] Indeed, Congress showed its concern for these problems when it included a provision in the Garn - St Germain Act requiring the FDIC and FSLIC to submit reports and recommendations to Congress. The recent desire of regulators to raise minimum primary capital for large banks with assets over $1 billion also a similar awareness of these problems.

In another sense, deregulation of interest rates has also increased the threat of financial instability by undermining the Federal Reserve's role as lender of last resort. Since the 1970s, institutions which want or need to make risky loans and investments need not wait either for their own geographically limited deposit bases to grow,[78] or go to the Federal Reserve for loans at the discount window which require satisfactory collateral. They can obtain their funds from the brokered deposit market knowing, moreover, that should their institution fail these brokered funds will be insured by the FDIC or the FSLIC at a bargain rate.[79]

If anything, the threat of financial instability has been greater within the thrift industry, although the ramifications for the economy are not so great as when the large banks are concerned. Immediately after the process of deregulating interest rates began in 1981 and 1982, thrift institutions experienced their worst difficulties since the Depression of the 1930s. Table 3 shows that during 1981, 1982 and 1983, 352 insured savings and loan associations - one in six of the country - were either merged or liquidated. This is because of the growing number of insolvent or nearly insolvent institutions still operating. In 1982, for example, 2025 insured savings and loan associations representing 61 per cent of the industry's total assets had ratios of net worth to total liabilities equal to or less than 5 per cent; 201 of these institutions had ratios of zero or less (i.e. they were insolvent). By the end of 1984, the industry's situation showed further deterioration: 2090 insured savings and loans representing 66 per cent of all insured institutions had net worth ratios equal to or less than 5 per cent, and 434 of these were financially insolvent.[80] It has been estimated that thrift insolvencies could cost the FSLIC $2.2 billion in 1984 ($1 billion more than in 1983), out of reserves of $6 billion.

Whether the deregulation of interest rates was the primary cause of the thrifts' failures is difficult to assess. Certainly, however, the increased competition for funds, which deregulation encouraged, made matters worse by encouraging massive outflows of funds. Some of these problems were alleviated by the DIDC's development of new savings instruments for thrifts; by the DIDMCA and the Garn - St Germain Act allowing thrifts to broaden their asset powers; and most importantly, by providing thrifts in financial difficulties with $466 million in capital assistance to increase their net worth. These and other changes in the services which thrifts can offer their customers have certainly helped make them much more attractive to households wishing to do all their financial business with one institution, particularly when it is one where deposits are insured by the federal government through either the FDIC or the FSLIC. Nevertheless, many savings and loans (and savings banks) found they could not survive in the new highly competitive climate and threatened closing down. Despite returning to profitability in 1983 and growing at nearly twice the rate of the commercial banks between December 1982 and June 1984,[81] (primarily because of lower interest rates), some 35 per cent of the 3183 insured savings and loans and 23 per cent of the 294 insured savings banks - were still reporting losses during 1983.[82] Moreover, in 1984, the FHLB had to rescue the large Financial Corporation of America savings and loan holding company in California with a loan of $2 million.

These continued failures, particularly as in the case of Financial Corporation where they involve large firms, taken together with the policy of broadening thrifts' asset bases raise some important questions about the supposed benefits of deregulation. Although the justification for broadening their powers is to reduce their vulnerability to disintermediation, federal taxation policy still encourages them to maintain most of their assets in home mortgages.[83] Secondly, like the banks, savings and loans have been required to depend more on non-deposit funds in the money and capital markets, where the cost and volatility of funds will be greater. These new conditions greatly encourage savings and loan managers to make risky investments often in areas with which they have no previous experience,[84] especially if they are unable to persuade borrowers to accept ARMs.[85] The near failure of Financial Corporation points to both the incentives for institutions to make risky investments and the possibilities of failure.

Expansion of the product lines of holding companies also raises important questions about the future viability of these organisations. Savings and loan holding companies, for example, have been authorised to engage in a wide range of activities, including real estate development, credit, life and health insurance. The Reagan administration's Financial Institutions Deregulation Act proposed to extend similar powers to bank holding companies. Although no systematic research has been conducted which is directly relevant to the operating risk associated with product line expansion (diversification) by banking organisations, there is some limited evidence from past expansion by bank holding companies which shows that without exception bank holding company subsidiaries in mortgage banking, consumer finance and leasing (three of the most popular activities allowed these companies by the amendments to the Bank Holding Company Act 1970) perform worse than independent firms in the same sector.[86] Banks' difficulties with real estate investment trusts (REITs) in the mid-1970s and contemporary problems with loans to foreign governments, oil exploration ventures, and bond companies seem to indicate the need for tighter rather than weaker government controls over what banks can do. Indeed, economic logic also points to this conclusion. Because many firms have pursued expansion in order to withstand future competitive threats, not meet increased market demand, and because they have no previous experience, they risk their profitability and failure. The 'market discipline' approach seems a very dangerous and foolhardy approach to policy.

Regulation and deregulation of financial institutions also raises important questions about the allocation of credit within the American economy. The remaining discussion of policy impact focuses particularly on the geographic allocation of credit, and on two important subsectors - small business and housing.

The Impact on the Geographic Allocation of Credit

To a great extent, the American economy is still a collection of local economies. Most household and small businesses in the United States still rely on local credit institutions for their services.[87] Consequently, the effect of deregulation in enhancing the nationalisation of capital and credit markets becomes very important.

When interest rates were restricted by regulation,[88] local banks and thrift institutions were able to attract relatively cheap deposits. Often these institutions passed the low cost of these funds on to borrowers in the form of lower loan charges and services provided at below cost. Once restrictions were removed from interest rates and funds became more expensive, smaller institutions who had hitherto been content with investing their funds locally (probably with lower returns) were encouraged to take their funds out of their local areas and invest them through national markets,[89] where they could be channelled to investment opportunities offering the highest returns.

Proponents of financial deregulation regard the emergence of national rather than local or regional credit and capital markets as fostering more efficient national allocation of economic resources. This argument, however, raises at least two problems. First, it begs the question whether credit was not being allocated efficiently before deregulation. After all, the existence of the Federal funds market, inter-bank loans, correspondent banking and CD's would seem to indicate that credit was already being allocated fairly well around the country. Developments in communications and electronics technology have further encouraged greater efficiency in credit allocation.[90] If, moreover, there is a credit allocation problem, it surely relates to American banks (like their British counterparts but unlike Japanese banks) generally lending over short periods and only to companies which promise a quick return.[91]

The second problem concerns the social costs of deregulation. Although no data are available to measure such trends,[92] the increasingly national orientation of capital and credit markets seems certain to further marginalise many areas of the country and thus further encourage the development of a dual economy. Institutions in booming areas such as Texas, Arizona and California will find little difficulty in finding attractive investment opportunities in their local communities but institutions located in poorer urban and rural areas will be further encouraged by national market rates to export their funds to the richer areas. The effect on the older industrial 'frost-belt' areas, which are trying to rejuvenate their economies is potentially disastrous. Once capital flows out of a community because older industries are declining and before newer industries have established themselves, it becomes far more difficult to generate funds for reinvestment for new industries and employment and maintain social services at existing levels. Almost inevitably those areas which continually decline will demand government investment of capital, or further strengthening of such legislation as the Community Reinvestment and Home Mortgage Disclosure Acts, which in the former case requires banks to invest some of their funds deposited from an area in the local community in order to prevent the flight of capital.

Even for those communities which successfully attract investment and experience economic booms, there can be no guarantee that their newly found prosperity will continue in this newly volatile investment climate.[93] They too could soon be demanding similar government initiatives, either to finance the newly-required social and economic infrastructure or, in a later period, to cope with their own problems of industrial decline.

It seems unrealistic to argue that in the new competitive climate, once economic resources are allocated more efficiently through national markets, institutions coming into a local community from outside will be less likely to drain funds from it than they were under a regulated regime since differences between returns on investment from area to area will be reduced.[94] Equally, it is unrealistic in the present climate to imply that credit subsidies to certain sectors and certain social groups will be forthcoming from government once competitive pressures have forced the existence of these grants out into the open.[95] Moreover, private sector initiatives for community development have not been very successful.[96]

These concerns have been voiced over the last few years in Congress and by presidential candidates Walter Mondale and Gary Hart in 1984, and have been reflected in debates over industrial policy and community reinvestment, and in such proposals as the establishment of a capital markets commission made by Congressman Timothy Wirth (Democrat, of Colorado).[97]

The Impact on Small Business

A concern related to the impact of changes in regulatory policy on geographic allocation of credit is its effect on small business.[98] Employment in small firms in the US has grown faster than in large firms and is expected to continue to grow.[99] It is, therefore, a vital sector of the American economy.

The available evidence suggests that deregulation of interest rates has not necessarily benefited small business as anticipated by proponents. Small firms tend to be captive consumers who prefer to pay fixed rather than variable interests rates on their bank loans, primarily as the price for personal and reliable banking services.[100] Moreover, there is recent evidence which suggests that while established small businesses have been able to obtain credit,[101] very young firms have experienced much more difficulty, particularly in obtaining longer-term and unsecured credit. Firms which reported declining sales or rapid growth also experienced difficulties.[102] Indeed, because of the new uncertainty in the cost of funds following the deregulation of interest rates, the ability of small banks to make long-term fixed rate loans has been severely curtailed,[103] although the new authority allowing savings and loans to make commercial loans has made a very small difference.[104] Interest rate deregulation has also led to banks charging small business for their services, when previously they were nominally free.[105]

Similarly, the extent to which small business might benefit from relaxation of geographic restrictions on banking appear to be very limited. According to surveys conducted by the National Federation of Independent Business, small business consistently receives more of what it values most in unit banking states where banks tend to be more numerous and smaller,[106] although no clear relationship has been demonstrated between small businesses reporting credit needs not met and banking structure, bank size or market.[107] Moreover, the loan applications of relatively new firms (under five years old) are more frequently rejected by larger banks than by smaller banks.[108] Chiefly because they feared that a reduction in the number of small banks and an increasing number of large branch banks would lead to a deterioration in bank's services to small businesses, organisations such as NFIB has opposed any relaxation of branching restrictions.[109] This argument, however, is refuted by those in favour of deregulation who point to the expansion of many large banks and other commercial investors into small business loan markets over the past few years.[110] No definitive evidence has been presented to resolve this dispute. Clearly, however, the appearance of non-bank banks, most of which are chartered to take deposits but may not make commercial loans, lends credence to the view that removing regulatory restrictions will lead to the export of capital from those local communities where this new type of institution has been established.[111]

The Effect on Housing

The point was made earlier that an important justification for a number of regulatory policies established in the 1930s was to promote home ownership by ensuring a plentiful supply of housing credit. This objective was to be achieved by encouraging the savings and loans as special purpose lenders confirmed by regulation and taxation to home mortgage lending at low interest rates. This system worked very well until the 1960s,[112] when inflation and rising interest rates made mortgage funds increasingly vulnerable to disintermediation and shortages. In 1966, Congress deliberately chose (albeit after bitter wrangling) to use the Regulation Q ceilings which had been originally introduced in 1933 to limit bank competition for funds, as a means of allocating credit to housing. Effectively, savers with deposits under $100,000 would be required to subsidise the cost of mortgage loans.[113] Since 1980, this subsidy has gradually been removed by the DIDC and savings and loans have been allowed to broaden their investment portfolios and offer ARMs. Mortgage funds were thus threatened by rising and increasingly volatile prices, and the prospect of their main suppliers reducing their commitments to the market.

Immediately after Congress authorised the DIDC to remove rate ceilings, the volume of new home mortgages declined significantly, from $120 billion in 1979 to just $56.6 billion in 1982, as savings and loans experienced massive outflows of funds (Table 6.3). By 1983, however, home mortgage lending was almost back to its 1978 level.[114] What has occurred since the late 1970s is that mortgage funds are now being supplied through different instruments and to some extent through different financial institutions. Table 6.4 shows that until the late 1970s, savings and loans and mutual savings banks together accounted for about half of the new mortgages made directly to house buyers in any one year. In 1980, however, these two types of financial institutions accounted for only 29 per cent of such lending; in 1981, for only 21 per cent; and in 1982,

Table 6.4: Net financing of home mortgages by lender, 1950–83

Year	Total (Bill $)	Total	Commercial banks	Savings and loan Assocs. Direct	Savings and loan Assocs. Including ownership of pools	Mutual Savings Banks	Life Insc. Cos.	US govt. & agencies	Mortgage pools Total	Mortgage pools Except SLA Owned	Mortgage pools Other
1950	7.6	100	20.19	26.46	26.46	12.55	31.57	3.87	—	—	5.36
1955	12.6	100	14.12	39.75	39.75	18.70	19.95	1.95	—	—	5.53
1960	11.1	100	0.38	52.78	52.78	15.42	11.69	7.94	—	—	11.79
1965	17.1	100	18.58	41.20	41.20	17.67	6.21	2.34	0.66	0.66	13.34
1970	15.0	100	5.77	45.34	47.55	7.21	(5.91)	29.94	8.10	5.89	9.55
1975	42.0	100	5.00	50.71	58.08	1.90	(3.33)	15.71	17.38	10.01	12.63
1976	63.9	100	14.40	55.09	57.61	4.85	(2.35)	(0.31)	18.62	16.10	9.70
1977	94.0	100	20.11	49.79	52.67	5.21	(1.49)	3.19	16.70	13.82	6.49
1978	112.2	100	21.48	40.20	43.36	4.37	(0.27)	9.71	11.05	7.89	13.46
1979	120.0	100	16.67	32.92	36.22	2.33	1.50	9.58	18.17	14.87	18.83
1980	96.7	100	11.27	27.40	34.46	1.14	1.86	10.65	19.34	12.28	28.34
1981	75.9	100	12.78	21.21	29.02	0.40	(0.92)	9.75	18.58	10.77	38.20
1982	56.6	100	11.13	(46.29)	8.81	(3.18)	(0.88)	20.85	87.10	32.00	31.27
1983	111.4	100	8.53	21.18	45.80	3.86	(1.08)	8.89	58.35	33.73	0.27

Note: Figures in parentheses are negative. For institutions other than SLAs, figures report only direct mortgage investments.
Sources: 1950–70: Board of Governors of the Federal Reserve System, *Flow of Funds Accounts, 1949–1978* (December 1979), pp. 55–7.
1975–83: Ibid., *Flow of Funds Accounts, Fourth Quarter 1983*, (February 1984), pp. 36–7.

they actually decreased their direct lending, before returning to a level of 25 per cent in 1983. The extent of the change in the sources of mortgage funds for these data actually overstate the decline in lending. What has been happening is that thrifts have partly replaced their direct mortgage lending to home buyers with indirect secondary market mortgage lending, through purchases of participations in mortgage pools organised by themselves or others. As Table 6.3 indicates, by 1983, the increase in mortgage pool investments by thrifts had more than offset the decline in direct mortgage loans, so that in that year their actual share of total mortgage investment has returned to near the level of 1978. It seems likely, therefore, that the decline in mortgage lending by thrifts from 1978 to 1982, although substantial and prolonged, primarily reflected problems these institutions were experiencing in adjusting themselves to the new deregulated financial climate, rather than any long-term reduction in their commitment to housing.

Moreover, despite the liberalisation of their asset powers, allowing them to invest up to 40 per cent of their portfolios in non-mortgage assets, there are good reasons to think that thrifts will continue to concentrate most of their lending in this area. Tradition, the taxation system, good returns in mortgages, the high costs of starting up in new lending areas, the risks of accepting credits traditional lenders in these new areas reject are all important factors militating against such expansion.[115]

Finally, because of the good returns on mortgages as investments, there is good reason to think that should thrifts reduce their home mortgage commitments, other institutions will step in to make provision. Almost inevitably, however, this will require prospective mortgages to 'shop around' more than they have been used to in the past; and this may affect mortgage availability for lower and middle-income families. As for the cost of mortgages, the available evidence suggests no relationship between higher mortgage rates and interest rate deregulation.[116]

CONCLUSION

This chapter has sought to outline, provide explanations for and analyse the impact of the major developments in the American financial system and government policies which regulate it over recent years. The analysis of the impact of deregulation showed that the total amount and price of mortgage credit appears not to have been affected by the changes in policy. However, this final part of the chapter raised some particularly important questions about the stability and fragility of the financial system, and about the availability of credit in certain geographic areas and to new small businesses. Although government regulation cannot be the only, let alone most significant, factor in the everyday decision-making of lenders and borrowers, the evidence of increasing fragility begs a very important question: given the unique role that financial institutions play in the economy, should policy-makers have pursued deregulation at a time when the US economy has been performing below capacity?

'Free' − marketeers advocating deregulation emphasise the need in the contemporary economic climate to put financial resources to the most profitable use. The evidence does not suggest, however, that existing allocative mechanisms in American credit and capital markets were inefficient, except as far as new small entrepreneurial businesses are concerned (and there, the problem has probably more to do with American banks' lending practices). Even if these markets were not operating at maximum efficiency, there is little reason to be confident that deregulation and the resulting nationalisation of markets will alleviate the problems for those sectors. On the contrary, there is evidence that markets have instead become internationalised as lending by US banks abroad has far outstripped overall bank loan growth.[117] One important consequence of this and other recent developments is an increasingly volatile financial system, both in the United States and internationally. Deregulation of financial institutions and services in the United States has certainly enhanced financial volatility.

A further concern is that deregulation has noticeably encouraged an increase in risk-taking by lenders, including amongst the very largest money-centre banks who would be expected to evaluate risky loans and investments better. Deregulating interest rates certainly made loan funds more expensive at the same time as business's ability to pay for loans decreased. Indeed, the emergence of new short-term credit instruments surely induced borrowers to borrow too much, too short, for too long. Moreover, as Kaufman has recently suggested, all this financial innovation is not necessarily economically beneficial since it tends to divert the attention of both lenders and borrowers away from the important business of saving and investing. Improving the marketability of financial assets does not necessarily improve their credit quality.[118]

All these factors point to strengthening rather than weakening regulation of financial institutions. In 1982, the Comptroller of the Currency reported to Congress that:

Penn Square Bank failed because it made an extraordinary number of poorly conceived, poorly administered loans that violated the basic principles of safe and sound banking. The loans were made in total disregard of both the bank's own internal policies and procedures and the OCC's supervisory directives. In a flourishing economy, many of these loans would have been marginal at best.

It is difficult to understand how, beyond an ideological commitment to the 'free' market and deregulation, the Comptroller could then conclude that although there should be changes in the frequency of bank examinations and in the collection and public disclosure of information, 'Penn Square justifies neither increased regulation nor a reduced pace of deregulation' because 'the failure was an aberration arising from unique circumstances'.[119] Two years later, similar comments were made when the larger Continental Illinois Bank nearly failed in 1984.[120] Indeed, they are also reminiscent of the 1930s.

The ramifications of this fragility for American business are momentous. At best, banks will become so constrained by their bad loans that they will be prevented from lending even to healthy companies, which in turn will adversely affect economic growth. Even worse, if the banks become unwilling or are unable to finance weaker companies during recessions, then those recessions will most likely be longer and deeper. On past experience, those weaker companies will not only include declining firms but also new small entrepreneurs on which the future economy will depend for jobs. Unfortunately, neither Congress, the executive, or the regulatory agencies have been successful in providing solutions to these problems. All too often, policy-makers (particularly those who are elected) want to avoid the political cross-pressures from financial institutions and different groups of regulators which financial issues attract. When they do address these issues, typically they find their scope of action substantially circumscribed by events outside their control; particularly financial crises, and technological or market change.

ACKNOWLEDGEMENTS

I would like to thank the numerous individuals in the Federal regulatory agencies, Executive Departments, Congress and the Industry Trade Associations who provided me with information, and without whom this chapter could not have been written. Thanks also go to the Dean of the Faculty of Social Science and Business Studies at Polytechnic of Central London and to the United States Information Service for research grants which partly funded my fieldwork in Washington, D.C. I have also benefited from the comments of John Hibbing, David McKay and Michael Moran.

NOTES

1. Even as late as the 1850s, banks were actually prohibited in the states of Texas, Arkansas, Iowa, California and Oregon. In another three states, they were severely restricted, and in two other states, they were permitted only as state monopolies. Bray Hammond, *Banks and Politics in America from the Revolution to the Civil War* (Princeton: Princeton University Press, 1957, pp. 605, 617.

2. This problem is discussed in Irwin Unger, *The Greenback Era. A Social and Political History of American Finance 1865-79* (Princeton University Press, 1964) p. 115.

3. The Pujo Subcommittee of the House Banking and Currency Committee on 'Money Trust' reported in 1912 that just five banking firms on Wall Street held some 341 directorships in 112 corporations with an aggregate capitalisation of $22 billion. US Congress, House Subcommittee of the Committee on Banking and Currency, *Money Trust Investigation: Investigation of Financial and Monetary Conditions in the United States*, 62nd Congress, 2nd session, (February 1913). For the political background to the national banking legislation, see Robert P. Sharkey *Money, Class and Party: An economic Study of Civil War and Reconstruction* (Baltimore: The Johns Hopkins Press, 1959); Unger *The Greenback Era*; and Edward C. Kirkland, *Industry Comes of Age. Business, Labor and Public Policy 1860-1897* (New York: Holt, Rinehart/Winston, 1961).

4. The final version had been stripped of many of the more stringent interventionist provisions insisted upon by progressive Democrats and southern populists in the House of Representatives. For instance, the Board of Governors of the Federal Reserve was deprived of direct authority to set the discount rates of the 12 reserve banks and permitted only to veto changes in existing rates; the required gold reserves underwriting the Fed's notes were increased; and there was to be an advisory committee to the Federal Reserve Board, composed of commercial bankers. See Arthur S. Link, *Woodrow Wilson and the Progressive Era* (New York: Harper Row, 1954), Howard M. Reed 'Bankers and the Origins of the Federal Reserve Act: 1908-1913', *Intermountain Economic Review*, vol. 5, no. 1 (1974), pp. 72-84; Gabriel Kolko, *The Triumph of Conservatism. A Reinterpretation of American History, 1900-1916* (Chicago: Quadrangle Books, 1967), Chs. 6, 9.

5. By 1935, the number of commercial banks in operation had been reduced to about half the figure for 1921.

6. Albert U. Romasco, *The Poverty of Abundance* (New York: Oxford University Press, 1965) pp.82-96. Responding to a contemporary claim, J.M. Keynes wrote: 'A Bankers' Conspiracy! The idea is absurd! I only wish there were one! ... A 'sound' banker, alas! is not one who, when he is ruined, is ruined in a conventional and orthodox way'. Quoted in Arthur M. Schlesinger, *The Crisis of the Old Order, 1919-1933* (London: Heineman, 1957) p. 491.

7. Six months before the RFC began these activities in October 1933, J.P. Morgan had been suggesting authorising the Federal government through the Reconstruction Finance Corporation to deposit money without security

in all banks in need of help: See Arthur M. Schlesinger, *The Age of Roosevelt. The Crisis of the Old Order 1919-1933* (London: Heinemann, 1957), p. 495.

8. By 1935, when it announced it would cease buying bank stock, the RFC held over $1 billion in preferred stock, capital notes and debentures, and loans secured by preferred stock in 6468 banks.

9. The chairman of the House Banking and Currency Committee 'read aloud the only available copy of the bill ... Debate was limited to forty minutes'. Arthur M. Schlesinger, *The Age of Roosevelt. The Coming of the New Deal* (London: Heineman, 1960), p. 7.

10. Deposit insurance was, however, highly unpopular amongst bankers because it appeared to subsidise banks with risky managements by making sound institutions pay, through their insurance premiums, for weaker ones. The American Bankers' Association characterised it as 'unsound, unscientific, unjust and dangerous'. See Susan Estabrook Kennedy, *The Banking Crisis of 1933* Lexington, Kentucky: University Press of Kentucky 1973), p. 216; Schlesinger, *The Coming of the New Deal*, p. 429.

11. From its initial formation, the Federal Reserve System encountered difficulties in attracting state bank members; and most of the banks which failed in the 1920s and early 1930s were state-chartered. In 1930, 15,364 of the country's 24,273 banks were state-chartered and not supervised by a Federal agency.

12. Ellis W. Hawley, *The New Deal and the Problem of Monopoly. A Study in Economic Ambivalence* (Princeton: Princeton University Press, 1966, pp. 312-14; Broadus Mitchell, *Depression Decade. From New Era through New Deal, 1929-1941* (New York: Holt, Rinehard/Winston, 1961), pp. 169-71.

13. This legislation was strongly opposed by the commercial and mortgage bankers.

14. Josephine Hedges Ewalt, *A Business Reborn. The Savings and Loan Story, 1930-1960* Chicago: American Savings and Loan Institute Press 1962), p. 37. At this time, the savings and loan industry was much less significant than it has since become. Its assets in 1930 were $8.8 billion, compared to bank assets of $38 billion. Initially, industry leaders were reluctant to endorse Federal chartering on the grounds that it would be antithetical to the local character of the industry. Previously, all savings and loans had been chartered by the individual states and subject to varied regulations. Federal policy-makers were persuaded to authorise Federal charters in 1933 by the absence of any associations in at least one-third of the counties in the US, the rapid withdrawal of other institutions from mortgage lending, and the improbability of the new FHLB System alone being able to play an effective role in maintaining a comprehensive housing finance system. Savings and loan leaders were ultimately persuaded to accept federal chartering by a combination of fear of further direct government provision of home mortgages, and high expectations that they would be able to expanding their businesses. The 1933 Act also created the Home Owners' Loan Corporation which after the first three years of its life had refinanced something like one out of every five mortgages in the country with a total

value of $2.75 billion. So important was this assistance that Schlesinger concludes that 'probably no single measure consolidated so much middle-class support for the Administration'. Schlesinger, *The Coming of the New Deal*, p. 289. Savings and loan leaders were, however, successful in persuading Congress to accept amendments to the original legislation which would (a) help existing mortgage institutions retain their good mortgages and not have been appropriated wholesale by the HOLC, and (b) require liquidation of the corporation once the emergency had passed. Generally, see Ewalt, *A Business Reborn*, pp. 39-42, 73-79.

15. Title II of the National Housing Act also provided insurance for mortgage lenders against risk of financial loss on approved mortgages. The effect of this was to encourage lenders to grant mortgages with low downpayments and long maturities - a marked change from previous practice. The purpose of this title together with Title III (Which created the Federal National Mortgage Association - 'Fannie Mae') was to facilitate the use of short-term money market funds (especially in the commercial banks) into longer-term mortgages. FNMA performed a similar function in providing a nationwide secondary market facility for mortgages. Both these measures were opposed by the savings and loan industry.

16. Credit unions are by far the small industry considered here. Like the savings and loans, Federal charters were made available following the passage of the Federal Credit Union Act 1934. State credit unions had become increasingly popular during the Depression as an alternative source of consumer finance to the high interest rates usually demanded by finance companies. Credit unions were not, however, provided with a share insurance scheme, a central bank facility or an independent regulatory agency until the early 1970s.

17. State and Federal chartering of institutions is also an important means by which the financial system is regulated. For reasons of space, no discussion has been included in this chapter. Since the 1960s, however, the number of new commercial banks which have been chartered each year has increased from a mean of 172, to 239 in the 1970s, and 336 in the 1980s.

18. 'Disintermediation' refers to financial institutions especially 'thrift' institutions losing deposits as a result of rises in market interest rates above interest rate ceilings. This process encouraged the transfer of funds from institutions providing savings instruments directly to market instruments.

Interest rates on loans have also been regulated by state usury laws. Since the late 1970s, however, Congress had approved laws (permanent and temporary) which effectively pre-empt these state laws, on the premise that ceilings were much lower than market rates. Individual states have also legislated to liberalise their usury ceilings. Space does not permit further discussion of these policies.

19. Between 1945 and 1960, personal savings in savings and loans had increased 750 per cent compared to just 124 per cent in commercial banks. Between 1965 and 1970, however, the banks took 42 per cent of personal savings compared to 26 per cent for savings and loans. US Board of Governors, Federal Reserve System, *Flow of Funds Accounts*.

20. The failure of the Penn Central Railroad in 1970, however, caused public

concern amongst investors about the commercial paper market. Unable to sell their commercial paper, large corporations had to rely more on bank lending. Partly to ensure that banks had sufficient loan funds, the Fed exempted CDs over $100,000 from rate ceilings. Other evidence of pressures on rate ceilings comes from the commercial paper market. From late 1968 onwards, one-bank holding companies (not subject to the restrictions of the Bank Holding Company Act) also entered the commercial paper market to finance their activities in order to circumvent Regulation Q ceilings and Regulation D reserve requirements. In September 1970, the Fed also amended these regulations to include commercial paper sales by bank holding companies and their subsidiaries. In so doing, the Fed effectively priced banking organisations out of this market.

21. To a great extent *de facto* deregulation of interest rate restrictions had already occurred. Since the late 1970s savings and loans have been offering bill-paying services and immediate and easy access to savings account balances through remote service units. Credit unions devised share draft accounts about the same time. Money market funds offered withdrawal orders or 'pay-through' drafts to their customers. All of these cheque substitutes paid interest. In an attempt to hold their market shares against such competition, banks developed automatic transfer services and zero-balance checking with the approval of their regulatory authorities. These instruments allowed an individual depositor to arrange for the automatic withdrawal of funds from savings accounts and the transfer of such funds to demand deposit cheque accounts. Thus, by the end of the 1970s, this aspect of the interest rate cartel had been broken. Banks no longer had a monopoly on cheque accounts, and there was widespread payment of interest on cheque account balances. The US Court of Appeal for the District of Columbia in *ABA v. Connell* (1979) briefly reinstated the cartel by invalidating some of the instruments of non-bank institutions. Congress, however, endorsed the *de facto* changes in the DIDMCA of 1980.

22. At the time of writing, savings and time deposits are still partially subject to Regulation Q ceilings. Demand deposits, moreover, may not bear explicit interest. However, if transaction balances are held in NOW accounts or Super-NOW accounts, they may pay interest: up to the Regulation Q savings deposit ceiling for NOWs; and with no limit on Super-NOWs (although reserves are required for these accounts). Since businesses must still rely on demand deposits - because of restrictions on the number of transactions made on MMDAs and specific prohibitions on their use of NOWs and Super NOWs - they cannot receive interest on their cheque accounts.

23. Activities which have been rejected include underwriting life, property or casualty insurance; real estate brokerage; land development; operating a savings and loan (with some exceptions in Rhode Island, California and New Hampshire); and travel agencies, *Federal Reserve Bank of Atlanta Economic Review* (April 1983).

24. Statement of Superintendent Walter C. Madsen on Behalf of the Conference of State Bank Supervisors before the Committee on Banking, Finance and Urban Affairs, US House, *The Financial Institutions Equity Act of 1984*, 7 July 1984, pp. 5-7.

25. However, the activities of a multi-thrift holding company need to be a 'proper incident' to the operation of a thrift (cf. the 'closely related' requirement for banks in the Bank Holding Company Act). The FHLBB has aggressively sought to broaden the range of non-banking services that thrifts may offer, primarily through service corporation subsidiaries. These subsidiaries may develop and manage real estate, broker most forms of insurance, issue credit cards and extend credit through those cards, prepare tax returns for individuals and non-profit organisations, and provide certain fiduciary services. In 1982, the FHLBB also permitted such firms to engage in securities brokering.

26. Earlier geographic expansion is documented in Cleveland A. Christophe, *Competition in Financial Services* (First National City Bank, New York, 1974).

27. The Federal Reserve Board made two attempts to close the non-bank bank loophole by attempting to define NOW account deposits as demand deposits and by expanding the definition of a commercial loan. Both these rulings were struck down by the Tenth Circuit Court of Appeals in 1984 in *First Bancorporation v. Board of Governors of the Federal Reserve System*. The Fed then proceeded to rule in March 1984 that the non-bank bank loophole was legal but supported congressional legislation to close it. In April 1983, the OCC declared a partial moratorium on the chartering of non-bank banks to give Congress time to address the issue. Since Congress did not take action, the OCC has proceeded with the granting of non-bank bank charters. See US Congress, Senate Committee on Banking, Housing and Urban Affairs, Hearings, *Moratorium Legislation and Financial Institutions Deregulation*, 98th Congress 1st session (July - September 1983).

28. Bank mergers are regulated by the Bank Merger Act 1960, as amended in 1966. The terms of this law are quite rigorous. A bank's regulatory agency (the OCC, the Federal Reserve or the FDIC) must decide whether a merger might substantially lessen competition and consult with the Justice Department which, following approval of the merger by the agency, has 30 days in which to file a suit on the grounds that the merger violates the anti-trust laws. The effect of these restrictions has been to make mergers between large banks almost impossible, with the result that they have sought expansion through holding companies.

29. Information kindly supplied by the Conference of State Bank Supervisors.

30. Conference of State Bank Supervisors, *The Dynamic American Banking System - An Analysis of Geographic Structural Constraints* (April 1983), pp. 7-8.

31. New regulatory agencies have been recently created. As well as the DIDC, which has been discussed earlier, Congress created the Federal Financial Institutions Examinations Council in 1978 consisting of the Comptroller of the Currency, the Chairmen of the FDIC, the Federal Reserve Board and the FHLBB, and the Administrator of the National Credit Union Administration.

32. Paul Horvitz, 'The Impact of Regulation of Financial Institutions on Competition, and the Allocation of Resources', in US Congress, Joint Economic Committee, *Special Study on Economic Change*. vol. 5:

Government Regulation: Achieving Social and Economic Balance, 96th Congress, 2nd session 8 December 1980); George J. Benston, 'Federal Regulation of Banking: Analysis and Policy Recommendations' *Journal of Bank Research*, vol. 14, no. 4 (Winter 1983. pp. 217-44; and E. Gerald Corrigan, 'Are Banks Special?', *Annual Report, 1982* (Minneapolis: Federal Reserve Bank of Minneapolis, 1983), pp. 1-18.

33. For an argument against reserve requirements, see Benston, 'Federal Regulation of Banking', p. 219.

34. For instance, Peltzman has argued that restrictions on new banks' charters has resultd in higher prices and a reduction in the availability of banking services to the public. He found that entry regulation reduced new bank charters by at least 50 per cent during the period 1936-72. Sam Peltzman, 'Bank Entry Regulation', *National Banking Review* vol. III, no. 2 (1965). Rose has shown recently that this cost may be borne disproportionately by those living in rural areas and those in slowly growing banking markets. Peter S. Rose, 'Entry Into US Banking Markets: Dimensions and Implications of the Charter Process', *(The Antitrust Bulletin*, vol. 25, no. 1 (Spring 1980, pp. 195-213. However, a recent study has shown that relatively new banks (between 4 and 7 years old) are particularly prone to failure. See John Bovenzi and Lynn Nejezchleb 'Bank Failures: Why are There so Many?', *Economic Outlook*, vol. 2 no. 8 (August 1984), p. 22.

35. See US Comptroller General, Report, *An economic Overview of Bank Solvency Regulation* General Accounting Office, PAD-81-25 (13 February 1981), Chs. 2, 3.

36. However, provisions of the Bank Merger Act 1960, as amended in 1966, and the Bank Holding Company Act are specifically designed to foster competition by invoking the threat of anti-trust suits.

37. Hammond, *Banks and Politics in America*; Richard H. Timberlake, *The Origins of Central Banking in the United States* (Cambridge, Mass.: Harvard University Press, 1978), pp.192-4; Robert Craig West, *Banking Reform and the Federal Reserve* (Ithaca: Cornell University Press, 1977); Hawley, *The New Deal and the Problem of Monopoly*

38. These arguments are frequently articulated at the national level by such organisations as the Conference of State Bank Supervisors and the Independent Bankers' Associations. See Conference of State Bank Supervisors, *The Dynamic American Banking System*. They are contested by those in favour of deregulation. See Benston, 'The Regulation of Financial Services', pp. 4-5. Membership of the Independent Bankers' Association provides a useful indication of the political strength of small banks across the country. The percentage of the total number of banks in each state who were members of the IBAA (or its ally the Western Independent Bankers' Association) in 1970 were: Minnesota, 77.1 per cent; California 77.0 per cent; South Carolina, 66.7 per cent; Georgia, 65.8 per cent; Mississippi, 64.8 per cent; Kansas, 60.7 per cent; Michigan, 58.9 per cent; Missouri, 53.2 per cent, Wisconsin, 53.0 per cent; Alabama, 50.1 per cent. See John E. Owens, *The House Banking and Currency Committee and American Credit Institutions. A Study in Committee-Interest Group Relations, 1964-1974*. Unpublished Ph.D dissertation, University

of Essex, 1982, p. 188.

39. The current chairman of the House Banking, Finance and Urban Affairs Committee, Congressman St Germain (Democrat, Rhode Island) would fit this description, as would former chairman Wright Patman (Democrat, Texas). On St Germain, see Jacqueline Calmes, 'Banking Chairman: Secretive but Successful', *Congressional Quarterly Weekly Report* (8 September 1984); on Patman, see John E. Owens, 'Extreme Advocacy in the Pre-Reform House: Wright Patman and the House Banking and Currency Committee', *British Journal of Political Science*, vol. 15, no. 2 (April 1985), pp.187-205. On the strength of political support for thrift institutions and small banks in the House see Owens, *The House Banking and Currency Committee*; Salmon, *The Money Committee* p. 107; and Comments of Jane D'Arista, *Eighth Annual Public Policy Week. The Political Economy of Regulatory Reform* (Mayflower Hotel, Washington, D.C.: American Enterprise Institute for Public Policy Research (4 December 1984).

40. Following the passage of the Interest Control Act in 1966, however, small savers were effectively discriminated against by Regulation Q ceilings.

41. For reasons of space, other regulatory statutes, (such as the Truth in Lending Acts 1968; the Consumer Leasing Act 1976; The Real Estate Settlement Procedures Act 1974; the Electronic Fund Transfer Act 1978; the Civil Rights Act 1968; the Equal Credit Opportunity Act 1974; the Fair Housing Act 1968; the Fair Credit Reporting Act 1970; the Fair Debt Collection Practices Act 1977; the Right to Financial Privacy Act 1978; the Federal Trade Commission Improvement Act 1975) concerned with consumer and civil rights protection cannot discussed here. For details, see Kenneth Spong, *Banking Regulation. Its Purposes, Implementation, and Effects* (Kansas City: Division of Bank Supervision and Structure, Federal Reserve Bank of Kansas City, 1984), ch. 6.

42. A useful measure of the increasing use of telecommunication networks in the provisions of credit institution services is the number of ATMs (automated teller machines) in use. In the space of two years (1979 to 1981) the number of machines doubled from 12,400 to 27,200. See Dwight B. Crane, Ralph C. Kimball and William T. Gregor, *The Effects of Banking Deregulation* (Washington, D.C.: Association of Reserve City Bankers, July 1983), p. 30.

The increased range and complexity of financial services has also been matched by increased consumer sophistication. Since the 1970s, individual consumers have increasingly turned to the US government securities market and the money markets for better returns on their liquid savings. For example, as recently as 1978, traditional banking (cheque accounts, NOW accounts, and time and savings accounts) accounted for 73.3 per cent of total deposits, and 'new' money market rate instruments (money market funds and 3- and 6-month Treasury bills, and savings bonds) amounted to 5.5 per cent. By 1982, however, with the addition of 6 month money market certificates, two and a half years SSCs, unit investment trusts, the 'new' money market funds amounted to 34.5 per cent of the total, with traditional banking instruments falling to 38.2 per cent. The trend has continued since.

Large corporations increasingly began to use cash management techniques in the 1970s to minimise idle deposits, and also began to employ commercial paper as an alternative source of funds to bank loans, because of the large difference between the prime rate and the commercial paper rate in the late 1970s. As a result, between 1970 and 1980, the ratio of non-financial company commercial paper to bank commercial and industrial loans increased from 8.7 per cent to 24.3 per cent.

43. See, for example, Lester Salamon, *The Money Committees* (New York: Grossman, 1975); Christopher Elias, *The Dollar Barons* (New York: Macmillan, 1973); G. William Domhoff, *The Powers That Be. Processes of Ruling Class Domination in America* (New York: Vintage, 1978); Morton Mintz and Jerry S. Cohen *America, Inc* (New York: Dell, 1971), Ch. 6.
44. Kolko, *The Triumph of Conservatism*; Marver H. Bernstein, *Regulating Business by Independent Commission* (Princeton: Princeton University Press, 1955); George J. Stigler, 'The Theory of Economic Regulation', *Bell Journal of Economics and Management Science*, vol. 2, no. 1 (Spring 1971).
45. Robert A. Eisenbeis, 'Regulation, Financial Innovation, and the Payments Mechanisms', in Federal Reserve Bank of Chicago, *Proceedings of a Conference on Bank Structure and Competition* (Chicago: 1976); Robert A. Eisenbeing, 'Regulation and Financial Innovation: Implications for Financial Structure and Competition amongst Depository and Non-Depository Institutions', *Issue in Bank Regulation*, vol. 164, no. 2 (Winter 1981); Edward J. Kane, 'Accelerating Inflation, Technological Innovation and the Decreasing Effectiveness of Banking Regulation', *Journal of Finance*, vol. 36, no. 2 (May 1981), pp. 355-67.
46. Charles E. Lindblom, *Politics and Markets, The World's Political-Economic Systems* (New York, Basic Books 1977), pp. 170-2, 175.
47. For discussion of this pattern of policy-making in the 1960s and early 1970s, see Owens, *The House Banking and Currency Committee*, Chs. 5-7.
48. For an example of this fragmentation applied to the analysis of financial institutions' campaign contributions, see John E. Owens, 'The Impact of Campaign Contributions on Legislative Outcomes in Congress. Evidence from a House Committee', *Political Studies* (forthcoming).
49. Recent review of the best of this literature include Robert L. Peabody, 'Research on Congress: The 1970s and Beyond', *Congress and the Presidency* vol. 9, no. 1 (Spring 1982), pp. 1-15; Charles O. Jones, 'New Directions in US Congressional Research', *Legislative Studies Quarterly*, vol. 6, no. 3 (August 1981), pp. 455-68.
50. Louis Hartz, *The Liberal Tradition in America. An Interpretation of American Political Thought Since the Revolution* (New York: Harcourt, Brace/Jovanavich, 1955).
51. By 'public philosophy', I mean 'an outlook on public affairs which is accepted within a nation by a wide coalition and which serves to give definition to problems and direction to government policies dealing with them'. The definition is taken from Samuel H. Beer, 'In Search of a New Public Philosophy', in Anthony King (ed.), *The New American Political System* (Washington, D.C.: American Enterprise Institute for Public Policy Research, 1978), p. 5.

52. See, for example, Beer 'In Search of a New Public Philosophy'; Alan Wolfe, *America's Impasse. The Rise and Fall of the Politics of Growth* (New York: Pantheon Books, 1981; James Weinstein, *The Corporate Ideal in the Liberal State: 1900-1918* (Boston: Beacon Press 1968); Ellis W. Hawley, 'The New Deal and the Vision of Interests as Social Partners: The Corporate Ideal As Liberal Philosophy', mimeo (University of Iowa, March 1983).

53. See, for example, David Vogel, 'The Power of Business in America: A Reappraisal', *British Journal of Political Science* vol. 13, no. 1 (1983), pp. 19-43; Graham K. Wilson, *Interest Groups in the United States* (Oxford: Clarendon Press, 1981, Ch. 4.

54. Banking economists such as George Benston have certainly played an important part in the evolution of this new public philosophy. Since the 1960s, a considerable body of revisionist literature has appeared in learned journals on banking and finance. American economists are, moreover, probably more inclined than their British counterparts to voice their views through the mass media.

55. For example, interest rate ceilings on time and savings deposits (Regulation Q) were included in the Banking Act 1933 primarily to offset the cost of premiums which they would have to pay to join the deposit insurance schemes. For a discussion of the considerable manoeuvring which surrounded financial institutions legislation in the 1960s and early 1970s see Owens, *The House Banking and Currency Committee*, Chs. 6 and 7.

56. The classic statement of the differences in presidential and congressional constituencies is James MacGregor Burns, *The Deadlock of Democracy* (Englewood Cliffs: Prentice Hall, 1963). On bicameral differences, see e.g. Richard F. Fenno, *The United States Senate. A Bicameral Perspective* (Washington, D.C.: American Enterprise Institute for Public Policy Research, 1982). On the House and Senate Banking Committees, see John F. Bibby, 'The Congressional Committee. The Politics of the Senate Committee on Banking, Housing and Urban Affairs', in John F. Bibby and Roger H. Davidson, *On Capitol Hill. Studies in the Legislative Process*, 2nd edition (Hinsdale, Illinois: The Dryden Press, 1971), pp. 183-206; and Owens, *The House Banking and Currency Committee*, Ch. 2. See also John T. Rose, 'Aggregate Concentration in Banking and Political Leverage: A Note' *Industrial Organization Review*, vol. 6, no. 1978; cf. Neil T. Skaggs and Cheryl L. Wasserkrug, 'Banking Sector Influence on the Relationship of Congress to the Federal Reserve System', *Public Choice*, vol. 41 (1983), pp. 295-306. For argument against banker influence in regulatory decision-making, see Stephen A. Rhoades and Roger D. Rutz, 'Economic Power and Political Influence: An Empirical Analysis of Bank Regulatory Decisions', *Atlantic Economic Journal*, vol. 11, no. 2 (1983), pp. 79-86. On the importance of policy entrepreneurs exploiting crises, see James Q. Wilson, 'The Politics of Regulation', in James Q. Wilson (ed.), *The Politics of Regulation* (New York: Basic Books, 1980), p. 370. Congressman Wright Patman, former chairman of the House Banking and Currency Committee, was an excellent practitioner of policy entrepreneurship. See Owens, 'Extreme Advocacy Leadership'.

57. Those in favour of banking deregulation considered this event a major setback. Carter Golembe, 'Memo: Banking Legislation in 1984 ... What Happened' (Washington, D.C.: Golembe Associates, vol. 1984-87), p. 2. On this phenomenon in the energy field, see Bruce I. Oppenheimer, 'Policy Effects of US House Reform: Decentralisation and the Capacity to Resolve Energy Issues' *Legislative Studies Quarterly*, vol. 5, no. 1 (February 1980), pp. 5-30.

58. John W. Kingdon, *Congressmen's Voting Decisions*, 2nd edition (New York: Harper/Row, 1981).

59. Ferguson has shown, for example, that banking reform in the 1930s enjoyed the support of many growth-minded businessmen of the south and west who, like many bankers from these regions, resented the tight-money policies of the New York establishment, moreover, there were important divisions between those in labour- and capital-intensive industries, and those with nationalist and internationalist perspectives. Thomas Ferguson, 'From Normalcy to New Deal: Industrial Structure, Party Competition, and American Public Policy in the Great Depression', *International Organisation*, vol. 38, no. 1 (Winter 1984), pp. 41-94, especially pp. 80-5, 88-92. See also Schlesinger, *The Coming of the New Deal*, p. 415; and Elizabeth Saunders, 'The Politics and Economics of the American Regulatory State, 1910-1940', Paper presented to the American Regulatory State, 1910-1940', Paper presented to the Annual Meeting of the American Political Science Association (30 August-2 September 1984).

60. Owens, *The House Banking and Currency Committee*, Chs. 6, 7.

61. On the Reagan coalition, see Thomas Ferguson and Joel Rogers, 'The Reagan Victory: Corporate Coalitions in the 1980 Campaign', and Alan Stone, 'State and Market: Economic Regulation and the Great Productivity Debate', in Thomas Ferguson and Joel Rogers (eds.), *The Hidden Election. Politics and Economics in the 1980 Presidential Election Campaign* (New York: Pantheon Books, 1981).

62. When Congress, the Executive, or some other body has attempted wholesale restructuring of financial institutions policy, they have failed. Witness, for example, the failure of the Hunt Commission's proposals; the House Committee's FINE proposals; and most recently, the Reagan administration's Financial Institutions Deregulation Bill in 1984. On the pragmatic and experimental nature of the New Deal reforms, see Hawley, *The New Deal and the Problem of Monopoly* and Schlesinger, *The Coming of the New Deal*.

63. For example, while the DIDMCA called for the removal of deposit rate ceilings, it is also authorised the Federal Reserve to impose reserve requirements on a large number of depository institutions over which it did not exercise jurisdiction.

64. Annual Reports of the FDIC (1982 and 1983). Additional information from the Division of Research and Strategic Planning at the FCIC.

65. Federal Deposit Insurance Corporation, *Deposit Insurance in a Changing Environment* (15 April 1983), P.V 9.

66. 'Behind the Banking Turmoil', *Business Week*, 29 October 1984, p. 100.
67. 'Behind the Banking Turmoil', pp. 100-3. A recent FDIC study shows that the pattern of bank failures is consistent with a 'boom to bust' theory, i.e. that whereas bank managers in regions historically susceptible to cyclical fluctuations learnt to adopt more conservative lending policies which allowed them to survive, their counterparts in regions which either experienced extended economic booms or generally more stable economic conditions were less concerned about survival and more concerned about growth and consequently adopted more liberal lending policies. Bovenzi and Nejezchleb, 'Bank Failures', pp. 18-19.
68. It has been estimated that the higher cost of bank funds resulting from deregulation has probably raised the general level of interest rates about one and a half percentage points. Karen W. Arenson, 'Why High Interest Rates Are Here To Stay', *New York Times*, 9 October 1983, p.F. 29; see also Kenneth H. Bacon, 'Flexible Interest Rates May Add to Stability', *The Wall Street Journal*, 7 November 1983.
69. Something like 75 per cent of all insured commercial Banks' deposits are insured by the FDIC, compared with 45 per cent in 1934.
70. Indeed, this explains the opposition of the savings and loans and the independent bankers to deregulation of rate ceilings. Evidence provided by James of the impact of deposit rate changes on the market value of commercial banks and stock savings and loan associations shows that the existence of ceilings conferred a subsidy on the owners of both retail commercial banks and savings and loans, the savings and loans receiving the largest subsidy. Liberalisation of ceilings resulted in positive abnormal returns for wholesale money centre banks, and concomitant declines in the market value of retail banks. James speculates that additional deregulation, such as inter-state branching, may also have a differential effect on commercial banks. Christopher James, 'An Analysis of Intra-Industry Effects in the Effect of Regulation. The Case of Deposit Ceilings', *Journal on Monetary Economics*, vol. 12, no. 3 (1983), pp. 417-32.
71. According to Rhoades, smaller banks are likely to be able to survive the introduction of inter-state banking since they have traditionally grown faster and performed better financially than banks owned by large organisations, even when located in the same market; and small banks have been able to adapt and use new applications of electronic technology. Rhoades, 'Interstate Banking and Product-Line Deregulation', p. 23.
72. At the end of 1983, the Continental Illinois Bank had $16.6 billion in foreign deposits and $13.4 billion in domestic deposits. Only about $3 billion of this was in amounts of $100,000 or less. Memo. Timothy E. Wirth, Chairman, Subcommittee on Telecommunications, Consumer Protection and Finance to Members of the Committee on Energy and Commerce, 5 October 1984, pp. 8-9.
73. On a number of occasions, the GAO has pointed to important shortcomings in bank examination practices. See e.g. US Comptroller General, Report to the Congress, *The Federal Structure for Examining Financial Institutions Can Be Improved*, General Accounting Office GGD-81-21 (24 April 1981);

US Comptroller General. *Despite Improvements, Bank Supervision Could Be More Effective and Less Burdensome.* General Accounting Office GGD-82-21 (26 February 1983).

74. Stephen A. Rhoades, 'The Effect of Bank Holding Company Acquisitions of Mortgage Bankers on Mortgage Lending Activity', *Journal of Business*, vol. 48, no. 2 (July 1975), pp. 344-8; Samuel H. Talley, 'Banking Holding Company Performance in Consumer Finance and Mortgage Banking', *Magazine of Bank Administration* (July 1976), pp. 42-4; Stephen A. Rhoades and Gregory E. Boczar, 'The Performance of Bank Holding Company Affiliated Companies' *Federal Reserve Board. Staff Economic Studies* no. 90 (1977); Stephen A. Rhoades, 'The Performance of Bank Holding Companies in Equipment Leasing' *Journal of Commercial Bank Lending* (October 1980), pp. 53-61. I would like to thank Dr. Rhoades for drawing these studies to my attention.

75. With the failure and bail-out of the Continental Illinois Bank and the threatened failure and acquisitions of a number of thrift institutions, Congress and the regulatory agencies have been addressing these problems but has not been able to find and adopt an acceptable solution although few commentators are recommending the reimposition of deposit rate ceilings. Indeed, the deposit funds recognised this change when a large number of thrifts have found themselves in difficulty over the last few years, federal regulators have encouraged out-of-state acquisitions as a means of obviating dispersal of insurance funds. This, however, will only remain a temporary solution since geographic barriers are being removed thus removing the attraction of firms like Citicorp taking them over.

76. Just after deposit insurance was introduced in 1934, 45.1 per cent of insured banks' deposits were covered. Since then, the percentage has increased steadily and particularly after 1979 when the limit was raised to $100,000. Currently, about 72 per cent of deposits are insured.

77. This argument is pursued in William Keeton, 'Deposit Insurance and the deregulation of Deposit Rates', *Federal Reserve Bank of Kansas City Economic Review* (April 1984), pp. 38-42. See also US Comptroller General, Report, *An Economic Overview of Bank Solvency Regulation*, General Accounting Office GAO PAD 81-25 (13 February 1981), p. 25.

78. Some of Continental Illinois's deposits appear to have been lost in 1984 because the FDIC had made only a modified payout on deposits over $100,000 in the Penn Square failure. As a result, the FDIC announced that it would underwrite all of the deposits in Continental and the parent bank holding company. This incident illustrates well the point that banks runs are not necessarily an historic phenomenon. On this point, see also US Comptroller General, *An Economic Overview of Bank Solvency Regulation* General Accounting Office, PAD-81-25 (13 February 1981), pp. 29-33. From 1941 to 1964, the largest bank to fail had deposits of only $17 million. During 1965 - 75, however, much larger banks failed with deposits ranging from $93 million to $1.4 billion.

79. These funds are obtained by brokers from investors throughout the country. The broker channels them to the client depository institutions, assigning

ownership for the deposits in separate units up to the insurance limit of
$100,000 to a number of investors. Recently, the chairman of the FDIC
has criticised the growth of brokered deposits in 'problem' banks. See,
for example, *Washington Financial Reports*, vol. 43, no. 13 (1 October 1984).

80. Kane has estimated that in December 1981, the net worth of insured savings
and loans and mutual savings banks was a *deficit* of $100-175 billion. Edward
J. Kane, 'The Role of Government in the Thrift Industry's New Worth
Crisis', in George J. Benston (ed.), *Financial Services. The Changing
Institutions and Government Policy* (Englewood Cliffs, New Jersey: Prentice
Hall, Inc. 1983), pp. 176-7.

81. Data supplied by the Office of Policy and Economic Research, Federal
Home Loan Bank Board. Faced with a strong demand for mortgage funds,
savings and loans were willing to pay slightly higher rates for funds. Despite
the absence of a mandated legal maximum rate (Regulation Q), thrifts
continue to offer a rate premium over commercial banks. *The Kaplan -
Smith Report* (March 1984), pp. 3-5; (August 1984), p. 3.

82. US Comptroller General, Report to Congress, *Net Worth Certificate
Assistance Programs: Their Design, Major Differences, and Early
Implementation* GAO/GGD-85-8 (5 November 1984), p. 9. Generally,
see Andrew S. Carron, *The Plight of the Thrift Institutions* (Washington,
D.C.: The Brookings Institution, 1982); Andrew S. Carron, *The Rescue
of the Thrift Industry* (Washington, D.C.: The Brookings Institution, 1983).
As recently as July 1984, *The Kaplan - Smith Report* was emphasising
the vulnerability of the thrift industry to increased in interest rates,
p. 3.

83. John J. Mingo, 'The Impact of Removal of Deposit Rate Ceilings on Bank
Thrift Viability and on Housing Finance', *Proceedings on the Deregulation
of Depository Institutions*, A Berkeley Business School Colloquium (School
of Business Administration, University of California, Berkeley, (19 March
1981), pp. 1-16; Dwight M. Jaffee 'Housing Finance and Mortgage Market
Policy', and Thomas Mayer, 'Credit Allocation: A Critical View', in
Government Credit Allocation: Where Do We Go From Here? (Institute
of Contemporary Studies San Francisco, 1975), pp. 93-122, 39-92; Citibank
Economics Department, *Credit Allocation. An Exercise in the Futility of
Controls* (Citibank, New York, 1976).

84. E.G. FDIC, *Deposit Insurance in a Changing Environment*; Federal Home
Loan Bank Board, *Agenda for Reform* (23 March 1983); US Comptroller
General, *Net Worth Certificate Assistance Programs*.

85. Deregulation of interest rates has encouraged thrift institutions to turn
increasingly to adjustable rate mortgages (ARMs) as a means of reducing
the interest risk on their asset portfolios. State and Federal regulations have
been liberalised to facilitate this change. Since mid-1983, the numbers of
adjustable rate mortgages has risen sharply. *The Kaplan-Smith Report* (July
1984), p. 1. Before the middle of 1983, however, borrowers had not been
very willing to take on this kind of risk particularly when other lenders
have been willing to offer fixed-rate mortgages. *The Kaplan - Smith Report*
(August 1993), p. 3. Generally, see George G. Kaufman, 'The Role of

Traditional Mortgage Lenders in Future Mortgage Lending: Problems and
Prospects', *Federal Reserve Bank of Chicago. Staff Memoranda*, SM84-4,
p. 7.

86. See for example, Stephen A. Rhoades, *Power, Empire Building, and
Mergers* (Lexington, Massachusetts: Lexington Books, 1983), especially
chs. 11, 12. For a British example of this phenomenon, see Geoff Meeks,
Disappointing Marriage: A Study of the Gains from Mergers (Cambridge:
Cambridge University Press, 1977).

87. The 1983 *Survey of Consumer Finances* shows that only 22 per cent of
families in the medium income group ($20-30,000) use non-local banks
of thrifts, but they do not use money market mutual funds. Similarly, only
about 15 per cent of families with income below $20,000 use non-local
institutions, but not money market funds. Robert B. Avery, Gregory E.
Elliehausen, Glenn B. Canner and Thomas A. Gustafson, 'Survey of
Consumer Finances, 1983', *Federal Reserve Bulletin*, vol. 70, no. 9
(September 1984), pp. 679-92. A survey of small business conducted by
the National Federation of Independent Business showed that about 85 per
cent of loans to operating small businesses came from commercial banks.
Jonathan A. Scott and Williams C. Dunkelberg, *Credit, Banks and Small
Business* (San Mateo, California: National Federation of Independent
Business, May 1983), Table 2, p. 5.

88. Regulation Q ceilings on deposits rates paid by commercial banks existed
before 1966 but were not particularly effective.

89. Crane, Kimball and Gregor, *The Effects of Banking Deregulation* pp. 86-92.

90. Whether these mechanisms for credit allocation are more or less efficient
than some other method is impossible to demonstrate. However, it is
unlikely that inter-state banking would allocate credit more efficiently than
at present. See Stephen A. Rhoades, 'Interstate Banking and Product Line
Deregulation: Implications from Available Evidence', *Loyola Law Review*
(forthcoming), p. 28. Equally, since further deregulation of geographic
banking restrictions may have little effect on where funds flow, there is
no reason not to pursue such a policy.

91. See for example, Wassily Leontief, 'Supply Side May not be On America's
Side', *The New York Times* (5 April 1981) sec. 4, p. E20. In 1979, the mean
net return on investment in Japan was 10.3 per cent; in the US, it was 16.9
per cent.

92. The Federal Reserve has discontinued collecting and publishing data on
term loans (from large banks) because of its limited use. Similarly, no data
are available for loan distribution by geographic region.

93. These processes are discussed in Barry Bluestone and Bennett Harrison,
The Deindustrialization of America (New York: Basic Books, 1982), pp.
82-92, 145.

94. Crane, Kimball and Gregor, *The Effects of Banking Deregulation*, p. 93.

95. E.G. Benston, 'Federal Regulation of Banking', cf. Stephen A. Rhoades,
'Market Share As a Source of Market Power', *Journal of Economics and
Business* (forthcoming). Rhoades argues that market leaders enjoy a degree
of monopoly power inherent in being a leader because consumers perceive

them as better because of their leading position.

96. E.G. US Congress, House Committee on Banking, Finance and Urban Affairs, Subcommittee on Economic Stabilization. Hearings, *Industrial Policy*, 98th Congress, 1st session (June 1983). The establishment of a Capital Markets Commission to evaluate the impact of changes in the credit system on the economy has been proposed by Congressman Tim Wirth (Democrat, Colorado), chairman of the Subcommittee on Telecommunications, Consumer Protection and Finance. See US Congress, House Committee on Energy and Commerce, Subcommittee on Telecommunications, Consumer Protection and Finance Hearings, *Financial Restructuring: The Road Ahead*, 98th Congress 2nd session (April-May 1984). The leading statement of the arguments for industrial policy may be found in Robert B. Reich, *The Next American Frontier* (New York: Times Books, 1983).

97. For example, community redevelopment corporations have been authorised by the OCC through interpretations of the National Banking and Bank Holding Company Acts. Most have been active in making loans on housing and real estate particularly as they can qualify for tax write-offs and urban development action grants from the Department of Housing and Urban Development which normally are not available to banks. Some CDCs, however, have been active in providing venture capital. CDC have not been enthusiastically promoted by the OCC and by December 1984, only 15 had been organised. Some have failed - notably one organised by Bank of America in Oakland. Others, such as the North Carolina National Bank's CDC, have been criticised for investing in luxury housing.

98. Time and space preclude any discussion here of financing of small business by pension funds through venture capital pools, by various institutions through equity participations, or small business access to equity financing. See Richard Zock, 'Small Business Access to Capital Markets Through Pension Funds'; Hans R. Stoll, 'Small Firms' Access to Public Equity Financing'; David J. Brophy, 'Equity Participation Agreements and Commercial Bank Loans to Small Business Firms'; and Harry P. Guenther, 'The Impact of Bank Regulation on Small Business Financing', in Inter-Agency Task Force, *Studies*. On the establishment of business development credit corporations to fill credit gaps in several states, see Paul S. Anderson, 'Business Development Credit Corporations' in Inter-Agency Task Force, *Studies*. On the loan programmes of the Small Business Administration, see Timothy Bates, 'A Review of the Small Business Administration's Major Loan Programs', in Inter-Agency Task Force, *Studies* and Tom Richman, 'Will the Real SBA Please Stand Up?', *Inc.* (February 1984), pp. 85-90.

99. For example, according to the President's Report on *The State of Small Business*, small firms generated all of the net new 984,000 jobs in the US between 1980 and 1982.

100. According to surveys conducted by the National Federation of Independent Business, what small business values most from its bankers, and most often do not receive, are a good relationship with their banks and credit at the right price. Scott and Dunkelberg, *Credit, Banks and Small Business*,

pp. 40-9; William C. Dunkelbert and Jonathan C. Scott, 'Small Business and the Value of Bank-Customer Relationships's, *Journal of Bank Research*, vol. 14, no. 4 (Winter 1984), pp. 248-258.

101. William J. Dennis, 'The Impact of Financial Institution Deregulation on Small Business: A Small Business Perspective', Paper delivered to the Annual Meeting of the American Political Science Association, Washington, D.C. (31 August 1984), p. 11; Staff of the Inter-Agency Task Force on Small Business Finance, 'Responses to the Small Business Administration Federal Register Notice Requesting Small Business Comments on Credit Needs' in Inter-Agency Task Force, *Studies*. Table 8, p. 10.

102. Scott and Dunkelberg, *Credit, Banks and Small Business*. pp. 32-5; Council for Northeast Economic Action, *An Empirical Analysis of Unmet Credit Demand in US Capital Markets*. A Report prepared for the Economic Development Administration, US Department of Commerce (Boston, Mary 1984). This Report was commissioned by the Carter administration and suppressed by the Reagan administration for about two years.

103. Hearings, *Current Trends in the Financial Services Industry*, Testimony of the Independent Bankers' Association.

104. Dennis, 'The Impact of Financial Institution Deregulation on Small Business', p. 13.

105. Dennis, 'The Impact of Financial Institution Deregulation on Small Business', p. 13. It is not possible, however, to assess whether or not explicit charges is advantageous or not.

106. Dennis, 'The Impact of Financial Institution Deregulation on Small Business', p. 15; William C. Dunkelberg and Jonathan C. Scott, 'Bank Structure and Small Business Loan Markets', in Federal Reserve Bank of Chicago, *Proceedings of a Conference on Bank Structure and Competition* (12-14 April, 1982), p. 211. The Inter-Agency Task Force on Small Business Finance also reported that two-thirds of the respondents to its questions believed that size of location of a bank affects its willingness or ability to meet the respondent's credit needs. Of these two-thirds, more than two-fifths preferred dealing with a local bank (with no mention of size), while another two-fifths preferred a small bank and less than one-fifth preferred a large bank. See *Staff*, 'Responses', Table 9, p. 11. Most small business obtains its funds from small and medium-sized banks whereas big business obtain most of its loan funds from large banks. 97 per cent of the commercial loan portfolios at banks with less than $100 million in assets are loans to small business; whereas the money centre banks (with assets over $1 billion) make only 13 per cent of the loans to small business. Peter L. Struck and Lewis Mandell, 'Impact of Financial Deregulation on Small Business: Evidence from April 1980', in Federal Reserve Bank of Chicago, *Proceedings* (1982), p. 182; Hearings *Current Trends in the Financial Services Industry*, Testimony of the Independent Bankers' Association. See also Joel Kotkin, 'The New Small Business Bankers', *Inc.* (May 1984), pp. 112-26.

107. Scott and Dunkelberg, *Credit, Banks and Small Business*, p. 35; Council for Northeast Economic Act, *An Empirical Analysis of Unmet Credit*

Demand pp. 64-7; cf. Staff, 'Responses', p. 5.
108. Struck and Mandell, 'Impact of Financial Deregulation', p. 190; see also Bernard Shull, 'Changes in Commercial Banking Structure', Inter-Agency Task Force on Small Business Finance, *Studies in Small Business Finance* (December 1981, p. 34. The NFIB surveys also showed, however, that once a small business is established and is reasonably successful, bank size becomes less important in small businesses evaluations of their banks.
109. Evidence suggests there has been an increase in concentration and centralisation in those states which permit state-wide branching and where geographic expansion has resulted from bank mergers and bank holding company acquisitions. Although the effect of these changes on the availability of credit to small business is uncertain, it can nevertheless be assumed that since small businesses mainly borrow locally, loan conditions will be improved if funds are available at local unit banks. However, whether optimal loan conditions are more often found in branching or non-branching systems has been the subject of a lively debate in the economics literature. The limited empirical evidence available indicates that although branch banks make more small business loans than unit banks, branch offices of a bank outside the immediate community do not make as much small business credit available as would a unit bank. However, the cost of credit to small businesses does not appear to be affected by expanded branch banking, except that loan rates are higher where banking concentration is higher and higher concentration is associated with branch banking. Thus, if the expansion of branch banking - intra-state or inter-state - or the elimination of existing restrictions on bank holding companies were to lead also to increased concentration, the cost of small business credit would probably increase. For a summary of the economic literature, see Donald T. Savage, 'American Commercial Banking Structure and Small Business Lending', in The Inter-Agency Task Force on Small Business Finance, *Studies of Small Business Finance* (November 1981), pp. 14-20.
110. National banks may invest in small business or venture capital through small business investment companies (SBICs), minority enterprise SBIcs (MESBICs), by establishing special types of trust funds, through equity participation agreements (EPAs), or by creating or investing in a community redevelopment corporation (CDCs). Bank holding companies enjoy even greater freedom to invest in venture capital through SBICs and a section of the Bank Holding Company Act which allows them to hold up to 5 per cent equity share in any other business unrestrained by geographic banking restrictions. These efforts to stimulate small business and community investment reflecting the changed emphasis since the 1970s on private rather than public sector investment. Often banks have offered venture capital investment through these routes after their regular loan officers have rejected loan applications. The classic case concerns the First Chicago Corporation, the holding company of the First Chicago National Bank, whose commercial loan department apparently refused the highly successful Federal Express Company's application for $1 million start-up capital. Subsequently, however, first Chicago's SBIC approved the application. In four years,

Federal Express had made $10 million profit. Pensions funds, insurance companies and securities firms have also increased their participation in small business debt and equity markets. See Irving Leveson, *Capital Markets Serving Small Business: Implications for the Rapid Evolution of the Financial Services Industry.* Prepared for the Small Business Administration (Washington, D.C.: August, 1982).

111. Hearings, *Current Trends in the Financial Services Industry* Testimony of the Independent Bankers' Association.

112. From 1947 to 1974, well over 1 million new private houses were started each year. See *S/L Fact Book*. The percentage of housing units which were owner-occupied rose from 44 per cent in 1940 to 65 per cent in 1976.

113. One economist has calculated the loss to savers (or implicit grant to savings and loans and home mortgages) between 1968 and 1975 at $22 billion. 60 per cent of these losses were on commercial bank accounts, although banks held only 48 per cent of total savings deposits. David H. Pyle, *Interest Rate Ceilings and Net Worth Losses by Savers* Comptroller of the Currency, Division of Research and Analysis. Research Paper 77-3.

114. Measuring the amount of outstanding mortgage debt is not easy because there is no certainty that funds are actually used for the purchase of houses or for education, stocks, consumer durables or other items. A comparison of mortgage debt to new home values over the last 25 years suggests that a good deal of the mortgage credit extended in the late 1970s was not used to purchase houses. See Kaufman, 'The Role of Traditional Mortgage Lenders', p. 8.

115. See e.g. Constance Dunham and Margaret Guerin-Calvert, 'How Quickly Can Thrifts Move Into Commercial Lending', *New England Economic Review* (November - December 1983). Some savings and loans, however, have apparently being quite aggressive in seeking this sort of business.

116. R. Alton Gilbert and A. Steven Holland, 'Has the Deregulation of Deposit Interest Rates Raised Mortgage Rates', *Federal Reserve Bank of St. Louis Review*, vol. 66, Issue 5, (May 1984), pp. 5-15.

117. See the data in Stephen A. Rhoades, 'Are the big banks big enough?', *The Antitrust Bulletin*, vol. 26, no. 2 (Summer 1981), pp. 315-25.

118. Henry Kaufman, 'Financial Institutions in Ferment', *Challenge*, vol. 26, no. 2 (May-June 1983), pp. 20-5.

119. US Congress, Senate Committee on Banking, Housing and Urban Affairs, Hearings, *Failure of Penn Square Bank*, 97th Congress, 2nd session (10 December 1982), pp. 4-6.

120. US Congress, House Committee on Banking Finance and Urban Affairs, Subcommittee on Financial Institutions, Regulation and Insurance. Hearings, *Inquiry into Continental Illinois Corp. and Continental Illinois National Bank*, 98th Congress, 2nd session (18 September 1984).

7 The State, Finance and Industry in Britain
Michael Lisle-Williams

INTRODUCTION

This chapter examines the effects of the state upon post-war British industrial development. Its main concern is to identify how the relationship between the state and the mechanisms of finance has affected industrial investment since 1945. Although quantitative economic data are used throughout this chapter, its main purpose is to explore institutional and organisational factors that shaped the direction and limits of state activity in respect of industrial investment. It is regrettable that much crucial evidence is lacking, but systematic research may be provoked by highlighting and tentatively answering questions to which mainstream economics cannot offer coherent responses.

The inadequacies of existing pluralist, structuralist and instrumentalist explanations of state policies and practices need no rehearsal.[1] While it may be agreed that the contemporary British state is instituted to facilitate the process of private capital accumulation, 'theories' of the capitalist state provide no guidance as to which priorities will be pursued under a given set of conditions.[2] The striking fact about Britain is not the support given by the state to what could be expected to be the principal and general interests of capital, but rather the low and frequently perverse response of the state to threats to the strength of British capitalism. Certainly, a Milibandian would be inclined to believe that the British capitalist class was majestically inept in protecting its collective, long-term interests. However, reasons other than class malaise or incompetence help to explain the peculiar economic role of the post-war British state.

These reasons are brought together in the central argument of this chapter. Briefly and rather baldly, this argument claims that Britain's external financial relations interacted with the institutionalised priorities of the Treasury and the short-term interests of organised labour and the representatives of capital to preclude the choice of means that would enable the state to effect the long-run rejuvenation of manufacturing industry and the promotion of economic growth. Britain's imperial legacy was pervasive and enduring,[3] not only in the high culture of statecraft but in the international conventions and duties which circumscribed state economic activities, and which were enforced by sanctions that could be applied from without by other states and from within by financial institutions organised behind the Bank of England. Yet it is a misapprehension to propose that 'financial capitalism' was hegemonic,[4] particularly in the post-war era. Undoubtedly, the Bank of England continued to press an austere financial orthodoxy upon successive governments after its nationalisation in 1946, and its role as the City's mouthpiece is beyond dispute. However, state economic policies were never formed as straightforward response to the preferences conveyed by the Bank of England on behalf of the banks and financial institutions of the City of London. The priorities of Treasury, the institutional controller of the public purse,[5] were not those of the Bank.

The Treasury was called upon to do the impossible, although this only became widely apparent by the mid-1960s. Operating within the framework of macro-economic demand management, Treasury budgetary preparation and ministerial advice were orientated towards the simultaneous achievement of several objectives: economic growth, full employment, low inflation, strong sterling and elimination of balance of payments deficits. In practice, Treasury's attempts to minimise fluctuations in economic activity translated into a preoccupation with the balance of payments and the exchange rate that undermined the very basis of economic growth, namely capacity and productivity. This is not to say that Treasury or the Department of Industry was unconcerned about the circumstances of manufacturing industry, but that the latter's long-term position was not represented strongly enough in government decision-making to prevent it from being sacrificed to short-term solutions to financial emergencies. Why this should be so is at first puzzling, but some answers are proposed later in the chapter. These answers include the concentration of capital in internationally-oriented British companies; the legacy of family control in industry; the weakness of British industry's peak organisations until the mid-1970s; the absence of clear industrial policy which had the backing of the union movement; and the varied interests and ideologies accommodated within both the Conservative and Labour Parties.

As early as the mid-1950s, Labour and Conservative politicians had begun to acknowledge that the long-term solution to balance of payments deficits lay in a drastic improvement in the quality and quantity of manufactured output,[6] yet neither Party when in government was able to bring about the redirection of investment necessary for a sustained build-up of productive capacity. This was not simply because of a lack of will, but because the state could not secure the necessary wage and employment concessions from the union movement or induce industry to modernise voluntarily or abandon the obligations to protect sterling that were insisted upon by the Bank of England and the US government. Until 1972, when sterling was allowed to float, state initiatives towards manufacturing were well-intentioned but inconsistent, and frequently frustrated by the priority given to short-term and belated adjustments to the balance of payments position. The combination of class, institutional and international politico-financial forces prevented the implementation by the British state of a viable programme of industrial growth before 'catching up' had become impracticable. Since the early 1970s, full employment has disappeared from the political agenda, and reduction of inflation has become the prime objective of economic policy. In a severely weakened, slow growing economy, the divisions within capital have been accentuated as concentration and reorganisation proceed apace, led by Britain's largest multinational companies. Domestic manufacturing capital's representatives have requested state assistance to revitalise industry. The Treasury as well as the Bank of England has an institutional affinity for the Thatcher government's commitment to low inflation, free trade, a strong pound, free international money and capital flows, and a minimalist role for the state in investment and economic direction. Under these conditions, the prospect that British industry might begin recapturing its domestic market, let alone increase its share of world trade, appears remote.

It is not claimed here that Britain's comparatively poor economic performance is attributable either to the events of the 1970s or to a single factor, such as insufficient finance for industry. Neither the drastic reduction of real wages nor the nationalisation of the clearing banks and insurance companies offers a path to sustained industrial revitalisation. The roots of Britain's crisis are much deeper than the purveyors of panaceas have admitted. Some of these roots are disentangled and examined in the sections which follow. Emphasis is given to the changing relations between finance, industry and the state since the Second World War, although a thorough analysis of the 'British disease' would require investigation of developments since the middle of the last century.

FEATURES OF THE POST-WAR POLITICAL ECONOMY

The period since 1945 can be divided in various ways. There have been five changes of government: 1951 (Conservatives replaced Labour), 1964 (Labour victory), 1970 (Conservative victory), 1974 (Labour victory) and 1979 (Conservative victory). During this period, Britain has had eleven general elections and nine prime ministers. The Conservative Party has held office for 24 years and the Labour Party, 17 years.

Although the discontinuity between administrations should not be exaggerated, there have been sharp changes in the principles underlying state economic policies at several points. Labour's abandonment of its commitment to planning and direction[7] and its acceptance of market sovereignty - albeit tamed by Keynesian demand management - by the late 1940s marks one turning-point. A second was anticipated by the Conservatives in 1961 and given strong support by Labour after 1964. Fundamental to it was the establishment of an institutional framework to provide industry with greater guidance and stability. Rules, agreements, mechanisms for tripartite decision-making, organisations for analysing industrial needs and setting priorities - all were elements of a return to planning, in Opie's sense of the term. That is, the change entailed some progress towards the creation of a consistent, plausible, integrated, comprehensive framework for policy.[8] Of course, this was not socialist planning, but capitalist corporatism: Labour's moral critique of capitalism was submerged beneath an attack - both rhetorical and practical - on the inefficiency of British industrial capitalism. In 1970, Heath attempted to provoke British industry to endogenous revitalisation, offering incentives and competitive opportunities. Holmes identifies the nature of this third major change in the principles of economic policy:

Unlike Wilson's 1964 conception of harnessing the 'white heat of the technological revolution' the 'Quiet Revolution' was prepared to confront every aspect of Britain's poor economic record in the hope of shaping a future that would be ... radically different from the past.[9]

The 'Quiet Revolution', with its neo-liberal thrust, was in tatters within two years, in part because of the breakdown of voluntary tri-partism and the imposition of a statutory incomes policy. In the second half of the Heath government's term of office and the term of the Wilson (1974-76) and Callaghan Labour governments, growth and revitalisation of industry were replaced as policy objectives by a strengthening commitment to controlling inflation, coupled with resignation to the inevitability of state-organised rescues of major industrial companies. Left-wing Labour's 'industrial strategy'[10] was set aside in favour of policies to restore business confidence and gain the approval of the financial institutions and, after 1976, the International Monetary Fund.[11] Election of the Thatcher government in May 1979 marked the fifth turning-point in post-war economic strategy. Although one should recognise the gap between neo-conservative philosophy and state practices, the unequivocal priority given to combating inflation and the low value attached to both employment and industrial output levels are distinctive. Urged on by a metamorphosed monetarist Treasury and supported by the financial institutions, the Thatcher Cabinet has undertaken privatisation of profitable components of nationalised industries, emphasised targets for monetary growth, struggled to reduce the Public Sector Requirement (PSBR) and removed obstacles to capital mobility. Triumphant in the 1983 general election, the second Thatcher government may be able to brush aside the demands of domestic manufacturing with as little trouble as it has ignored the TUC, placing its hopes on the eventual reorganisation of British industry by the largest few hundred companies.

Between the early 1950s and the early 1970s, peaks in economic growth occurred approximately every four years, separated by periods of falling and then rising rates of growth. When output was rising most rapidly, as in 1959-60, 1963-4, and 1967-68, unemployment fell and wages tended to increase more rapidly, but imports also grew and deficits were recorded on the balance of payments current account. At these points, governments applied deflationary policies to reduce demand, hold down inflation and turn the balance of payments deficit around to a surplus. As unemployment rose and output fell in response to mild deflation, the government typically brought in an expansionary budget to prevent unemployment growing further. State policies towards industry were enacted within the considerable constraints of these stop-go budgetary measures.[12]

Graham and Beckerman discuss the options available to a government confronted with a balance of payments deficit: 'if there is to be a deficit, it *must* be financed.'[13] This can be done from reserves, government borrowing by international agreement and/or private borrowing. In Britain's case, reliance was placed increasingly on the last two, since, as a reserve currency, sterling assets were illiquid. By the early 1960s, however, deficits had been financed overwhelmingly by acquiring short-term liabilities - 'hot money' - which could be converted into other currencies, creating a run on the pound. Governments had avoided the two means of instantly correcting deficits - floating sterling or suspending convertibility - and had chosen deflation rather than the other options for correcting deficits gradually. The option of devaluation was anathema to the Treasury and the financial institutions; import controls and increased tariffs were ideologically unacceptable to the Conservatives, who also invoked possible retaliation from other countries; and the possibility of lowering domestic production costs through incomes and prices policies, while attractive, depended on an apparently unattainable level of agreement with both organised labour and capital. Although the Wilson government tried to avoid deflation in late 1964 by imposing import tariffs and limiting capital movements, these measures were unsuccessful. Pressure on the exchange rate increased and when devaluation actually occurred in November 1967, it was a belated and badly managed response to a succession of sterling crises which had been overcome temporarily at the expense of domestic output.

Fiscal and monetary tightening in 1968 and 1969 had the anticipated effects of increasing unemployment and eventually bringing about a balance of payments surplus, but these were combined with increasing prices and wages. The government was faced with a new problem: the Phillips curve was dead. Expansionary budgets in 1971 and 1972 sought to reduce unemployment, but the effects were contradictory. Imports took a larger share of the domestic market for manufactured goods, wage and price increases reached double figures, and unemployment dipped slightly before rising rapidly. Although the pound was floated in June 1972 and effectively devalued, the balance of payments position worsened, chiefly because of the international commodity price boom.

Within Britain, rapid expansion of the money supply made possible a speculative boom in property and shares which added to inflation and diverted funds from already low manufacturing investment. A three-fold increase in oil prices in late 1973-early 1974 exacerbated the situation, which was characterised by increasing wage and price inflation, sharply falling output, declining company profits and a burgeoning deficit on balance of payments current account. Manifestations of crisis were widespread - in banking and the Stock Exchange, property, labour relations and unemployment - and culminated in heavy downward pressure on the exchange rate which prompted the Callaghan government to seek assistance in the IMF in December 1976. Major constraints were forcibly and promptly imposed on the state's capacity to respond to organised labour or the representatives of manufacturing.

Since 1977,

the adjustment to the second oil shock, the tight stance of economic policy and the substantial loss of competitiveness have contributed to the deepest recession in the post-war period. The downturn was considerably stronger in the United Kingdom than elsewhere in the OECD area; real GDP declined by about 5 per cent in the three years to mid-1982 compared with a rise of 2 per cent in the OECD area as a whole.

The loss of output and employment in manufacturing has been particularly severe and there has been a considerable contraction of the industrial base.[14]

North Sea oil production has resulted in escape from traditional balance of payments constraints, as the current account has been in large (but declining) surplus since 1980. However, this may be temporary, and misleading as 'in the first eleven months of 1982 the non-oil trade deficit was running at an annual rate of $4.5 billion, compared with an annual average deficit of $1 billion during the 1970s'.[15] Registered unemployment passed 12 per cent in 1982, real wages continued to fall, interest rates remained above 10 per cent, and manufacturing investment receded to less than 1965 level. On the other hand - and this reflects Government priorities - inflation dropped below 10 per cent in 1982 and continued down in 1983, the exchange rate has stabilised, and earnings from financial services and foreign investment have risen markedly since 1979.

While Jessop is quite correct in concluding that the economic policies of the British state 'not only failed to halt the long-term decline in the roles of sterling and Britain in the international system (but) also reinforced the conditions making for continued industrial decline across successive cycles'.[16] It is important to add an observation made by Pollard.[17] Stop-go policies did not merely inhibit industrial investment, although this was important, but each expansionary phase actually enlarged the market for manufactured imports which held up better than the market for domestic manufactures when the 'stop' phase reduced demand. Reduction in investment prompted by the balance of payments deficit meant that domestic industry lacked the capacity to respond rapidly and fully to the subsequent expansionary stimulus, and fared badly against imported manufactures. At the same time, its export competitiveness was impaired by the combination of low capacity, unreliable output, outmoded technology and over-valued sterling. The result was a successive weakening of the real elements of production - employees' skills, organisation, plant and machinery: 'Britain, sacrificing her productive power on the altar of monetary symbols, suffered not only in real welfare, but in the end damaged also the symbols for which it had been sacrificed.'[18]

Britain's poor economic performance (see Appendix 1) has generated diverse attempts to explain it, to make excuses for it, and to allocate blame for it. The purpose of this chapter is to contribute only to the first of these by concentrating on the effect that the British state has had on the financing of industrial investment. Subsequent sections therefore examine whether Britain's low level of industrial investment is attributable to an obvious shortage of finance, or whether other factors are responsible. The role of the state in shaping both the supply of finance and the demand for finance in manufacturing is considered.

FINANCIAL STARVATION OF INDUSTRY?

Numerous 'financial starvation' theses have been advanced on the left and right. From the left, the most basic of these is that the division of the British capitalist class into an industrial and a financial fraction reflects contradictory principal interests. In simpler forms of this thesis, finance has diverted the credit and capital that industry required into overseas investments. From the right emanate arguments that state borrowing has crowded out industrial borrowers, either directly or by inflating interest rates. Not only does the ideological content of these arguments tend to be high, but they invariably lead to recommendations for drastic surgery to be performed on either the financial institutions (from left) or the trade union movement and the welfare state (the right).

The recently released *Report of the Committee to Review the Functioning of Financial Institutions*[19] (known colloquially as the Wilson Report) cast doubt upon the 'financial starvation' thesis, but failed to lay the issue to rest. Indeed, the insertion of two dissenting proposals in the focal chapter (Ch. 20, 'Stimulating Industrial Investment: The Role of the Institutions') indicates that the unionists,[20] and academic economists,[21] were not persuaded that existing arrangements for the supply of investment finance were completely adequate. The unionists and Wilson argued for a new institution, drawing its funds both from the government and the investing institutions, whose primary function would be to provide large volumes of low-cost finance for approved projects. This group emphasised the need for cooperation into existing financial enterprise, promotion and encouragement of investment, and tripartite control. While the proposed facility was to be authorised to diverge from normal market practices, the extent to which it would actually do so remained ambiguous. It was less a step towards the 'Alternative Economic Strategy' than an idealised version of the National Enterprise Board (see below, p. 260) which had been burdened with corporate rescue duties soon after its establishment. The academic economists opposed the Wilson-TUC proposal on the ground that it was unworkable, and suggested instead a semi-autonomous public sector investment bank. This group stressed the skilled appraisal and nurturing of the new industrial projects; the proposed institution would be a nursery for fledgling industries with good long-run prospects. The majority, on the other hand, disputed the efficacy of either proposal. Although they recognised that the two outstanding defects were that (a) 'the real cost of capital is now almost certainly too high relative to prospective profitability'; and (b) 'shortage of demand for finance is a major part of the problem', they thought 'it wrong to exaggerate the contribution which can be made ... by changes in the financial system'.[22] The majority suggested that remedies had to be sought elsewhere: 'in the fields of industrial relations, management education and attitudes towards work'.[23] In the majority view, the supply of industrial finance is not an important factor in Britain's poor economic performance, compared with aspects of class conflict and culture that shape the context of demand. These views do not exhaust the range of analyses of the financial-industrial nexus, but they indicate some of the more clearly developed positions, and the underlying assumptions about legitimate intervention by the state in the market.

The following section surveys the sources of industrial credit and capital in post-war Britain. After a largely descriptive summary of industrial financing, the section reviews five changes in the financial system that have had a profound effect upon the volume and type of external funding available to industry.

SOURCES OF INDUSTRIAL CREDIT AND CAPITAL

Britain's slow and uneven economic growth since the Second World War has been extensively researched and well documented.[24] Main dimensions of that economic performance are summarised in Appendix 1. As a preface to a discussion of industrial financing, however, the specific tendencies in recent manufacturing investment merit close attention, and are described briefly.

In the decade to 1971, total manufacturing investment grew at an average annual rate of 3.3 per cent, although this masks considerable cyclical fluctuation (the stop-go alternation). Investment slumped badly in 1974 and 1975, before rising sharply in 1976 and increasing steadily throughout 1977-79. Investment in the three years 1977-79 rose at an average annual rate of 8 per cent. However, since 1980 there has been a sharp decline in investment, which has contracted at an average rate of 9 per cent per year. By 1982, it was estimated that investment had fallen to the 1965 level,[25] (see Appendix 1 section 2.5).

Fixed Investment

Fixed investment comprises only about 60 per cent of industrial companies total investment requirements, but it is the key to improving capacity, productivity and growth in output. Although investment in plant and machinery

held up much better over the last ten years than total investment, it still experienced a marked deceleration in its trend rate of growth from about 4 per cent in the ten years to 1974 to slightly less than 1 per cent since then. After allowing for accelerated obsolescence and scrapping rates (following the market rise in energy prices and the accompanying shifts in production technologies) net investment in plant and machinery swung even more, turning negative after 1980.[26]

Corresponding to this trend has been a decline of at least 7 per cent in manufacturing industry's net capital stock, indicating shrinkage of productive capacity. Here, then, is the process Pollard identified as characteristic of the stop-go decades, developing into full-blown deindustrialisation.

The 'vicious vortex effect' implied in this process can be summarised. On the one hand, there has been an absolute decline in manufacturing capacity, coupled with a general ageing of plant and machinery. On the other hand, capacity utilisation has fallen even faster, to a relative level below that of the troughs of 1971 and 1976. In other words, while there is an apparently substantial potential for increasing production to meet rising demand, and therefore some justification for industrialists to resist further investment and enlargement of capacity, the quality of existing capacity compares poorly with foreign productive means.[27] Simplifying considerably, the failure to improve the quality of British capital stock consistently and rapidly has resulted in poor competitiveness, loss of markets, poor returns, a further disincentive to invest and increasing relative deterioration in efficiency and quality. British industry has lost ground particularly when demand has expanded, apparently lacking the *appropriate* capacity to meet increased demand on the consumers' terms: 'the October 1982 CBI Survey of Industrial Trends ... indicated further declines in orders and output despite the recovery in consumer demand'.[28]

Other Investment

In addition to the fixed investment discussed above, companies routinely finance the acquisition of other assets - liquid assets, foreign investments, new subsidiaries and trade investment - and works in progress, addition to stocks and credit to customers. On average, these non-fixed investment uses of finance absorb about 40 per cent of industrial and commercial company funds. From 1968 to 1978, spending on liquid assets averaged around 15 per cent, three times higher than the level in the preceding and succeeding periods.[29] This statistic indicates that larger companies bought government stocks and other securities on an unprecedented scale, and became major lenders in their own right. During the mid-to late 1970s there also occurred a running-down of stocks and a decline of works in progress. Together, these point to a reluctance to expand productive capacity and a search for less risky investment with high, short-term returns.

Sources of Finance

Financing British Industry, recently published by the Bank of England,[30] begins with a concise summary of developments since the Second World War:

For much of the 1950s and early 1960s, the financing needs of private industry and trade were readily met within a financial system which was changing only slowly ... By and large, profitability did not place undue constraint on new investment, while companies' requirements for outside finance were met without the appearance of undue pressure, notably through the provision of equity finance and fixed-interest loans for the larger firms by the capital markets, and of overdraft finance for firms of all sizes by the banks. During the late 1960s and 1970s, however, the financial climate became increasingly harsh: companies' profitability was squeezed by accelerating inflation, and their liquidity was subject to intermittent but growing pressures. The long-term capital and equity markets to which companies had previously turned for funds fell into disuse, though the equity market only temporarily, while more novel forms of finance - most notably leasing - rapidly gained in popularity.[31]

This summary alludes to two major changes in industrial financing: (1) internally-generated funds satisfied a decreasing proportion of financial needs; and (2) companies became substantially more dependent on bank finance as raising long-term funds in capital markets grew increasingly unappealing. It makes no judgement about the adequacy of industrial investment levels in the 1950s and 1960s, except to note the apparent lack of supply constraints. However, by the standards of advanced industrial capitalist economies, British investment was indeed low and grew relatively slowly.[32]

Historically, British industrial companies relied overwhelmingly on internal funds for working capital and investment. Levels of taxation, the size and flexibility of depreciation allowances, types of government assistance,and the level of dividend and interest payments have been major determinants of the volume of retained earnings or trading profits. Since the Second World War, internal funds have covered a steadily declining proportion of financial requirements, falling from 100 per cent in 1952 to less than 60 per cent during the 1970s. The shortfall has been funded by a combination of new equity capital, loans, government grants and credits, and overseas investment. W.A. Thomas concludes that:

the general fall in the percentage of funds derived from internal savings may be ascribed to influences on both demand and supply. Falling profitability, together with increased tax burdens, reduced the flow of internal earnings. On the supply side there has been an increased flow of assistance from the public sector in the form of government grants and various types of regional aid.[33]

Company gearing ratios reached an historic high of more than 50 per cent in 1974, receding to around 40 per cent by the late 1970s. Gearing ratios, that is, long-and short-term debt as a percentage of shareholders' equity, are much lower in Britain than in most other OECD economies,[34] the US excepted. The Japanese average, by far the highest, was over 300 per cent throughout the 1970s, while the French ratio was above 150 per cent in 1979.[35] Gearing ratios indicate the relative reliance on bank borrowing as opposed to the capital market: the higher the ratio, the greater the debt. Over the longer run, British industry has exhibited relatively low reliance on bank borrowing and high reliance on equity finance, although small companies have typically depended on bank finance. A high gearing ratio need not indicate a satisfactory relationship between industry and finance: it may well reflect inadequate capital markets and investing institutions and insufficient spreading of risks. One cannot infer that British industry's low gearing ratios are due to the excessive caution of bankers: they may plausibly indicate efficient capital markets and adequate internal funding. However, when they are found in conjunction with indicators or low net fixed investment and slow growth of productivity, they do suggest conservatism on the part of potential borrowers.

Since 1974, larger companies have turned increasingly to bank finance. The increased gearing of the 1970s can be attributed to the combination of declining retained profits, high long-term interest rates and difficult conditions in the primary capital market in 1973-74. Noticeable in the data for gross capital issues, apart from a very low level of activity in 1973 and 1974, is a boom in rights issues and a slump in public issues and placements after 1975. Companies raised extra capital from existing shareholders rather than risk a poor reception from the investing public and institutions under unpropitious conditions. Larger manufacturing companies accounted for around half of equity capital raised after 1975, reducing their short-term debts to banks - at least temporarily.

Thomas,[36] attaches considerable significance to the impact of taxation on investors as a determinant of the type of capital raising undertaken by a company.

The change to corporation tax in 1965 greatly increased the incentive for companies to borrow by way of debt rather than equities. Debt capital was subject to income tax, while dividends were subject to corporation tax *and* income tax, while in 1965 meant a total payment of 64.75 per cent on the stream of dividends.

Between 1963 and 1972, issues of fixed-interest loan capital had exceeded share capital issues, although since 1973 the former have been relatively unimportant. Since 1973, in response to high but unstable interest rates, companies have borrowed heavily from banks and, in the case of subsidiaries of foreign companies, from overseas parent companies.

While new issues raised the equivalent of 0.5 per cent of GDP on average for the years 1973-77, bank borrowing by industrial and commercial companies was around 3 per cent of GDP over the same period. In 1974, loan interest comprised £2424 million, a third of total corporate current expenditure. However, this is somewhat deceptive because, as Thomas points out,

towards the end of 1973 it was observed that, while bank advances continued to be the 'outstanding source of funds' for the company sector, a large part of the accommodation so obtained was channelled back to the banks in the form of interest-bearing deposits. This arose because the prevailing structure of interest rates offered scope for such arbitrage.[37]

The corporate sector was a net lender during the mid-1970s. In a nutshell, large companies were playing the money market, buying certificates of deposit with cheap bank credit.[38]

To summarise, then, three trends stand out in the financing of industrial companies in post-war Britain: (1) an increasing reliance upon external sources of funds; (2) extensive use of rights issues to raise equity capital, except in the critical period of the mid-1970s, and declining use of public issues and bond issues; and (3) heavy borrowing from banks in the period 1971-74 and again after 1977. In 1979, bank borrowing was equal to 50 per cent of retained earnings, compared to 23 per cent in 1978. Undoubtedly, these trends are symptomatic of major changes in the relationship between the industrial and financial sectors, indicating at a minimum a growing interdependence which has reduced the autonomy of individual industrial companies. One dimension of reduced autonomy is that corporate financial performance is subjected to more rigorous scrutiny - and more severe sanctions - than ever before. The structures which make this possible have significantly altered the countenance of the financial system since the 1960s (see *Salient Changes in the Organisation of the Financial System*, below).

A Shortage of Finance?

The Confederation of British Industry,[39] in its 1977 submission to the Wilson Committee, asserted that

the clear conclusion of an overwhelming majority of our members is that it has not been a shortage of external finance that has restricted industrial investment but rather a lack of confidence that industry will be able to earn a sufficient return.[40]

The CBI's two important claims are that (1) supply of finance has not been a constraint; and (2) Britain's level of industrial investment 'compares well' with that of other countries. The latter is preposterous, especially viewed from the mid-1980s, and deserves no further comment. The former, however, merits examination.

Like the financial institutions, the CBI argues that neither more finance nor cheaper finance is needed to raise investments, but a higher and stable real rate of return on capital. Declining profitability and the expectation of continued poor performance are identified as the problems. The CBI solution is to increase profits by controlling wages, reducing taxes, weakening union power and rationalising employment[41] Moreover, the CBI claims, it is unreasonable to expect firms to invest heavily when there is slack capacity. However, as Pollard and others have shown, the recurring problem faced by British industry since the 1950s has been its inability to expand quickly enough to exploit sudden upturns in demand. It seems a little disingenuous to propose that 'if conditions for investment become more favourable - with improving profitability and demand - then investment will be increased without any radical change in the present system of private sector financial institutions'[42] The difficulty with this view is that it ignores the poor track-record of private investment decision-making under reasonably favourable conditions in the past. The CBI refused to admit that a substantial part of Britain's industrial problem has stemmed from the unwillingness of industrialists to invest enough over the long run in the right sorts of productive means, and also denied that the supply or cost of finance were serious issues. Clearly, the CBI was reaffirming the sovereignty of the market: individual decision-makers should be left to act upon their judgements of the desirability of investment in the light of expected profits. The state's role is simply to increase the incentive to invest by enhancing profitability and reducing uncertainty.

The CBI's submission raises the question of who can best judge the need for investment and therefore the adequacy of credit and capital supply. Its own unequivocal answer hinges upon some controvertible assumptions about the mechanisms of supply and demand. Much of what follows is intended to identify the structural and institutional barriers to the operation of the CBI and CLCB 'models' of investment decision-making. In particular, the fervent belief of market enthusiasts that individually rational decisions within a short-term time-frame will aggregate into societally optimal outcomes is challenged.

The next section examines five major changes in the structure of the British financial system that might have significantly altered the volume and forms of finance to which different types and sizes of industrial companies had access.

SALIENT CHANGES IN THE ORGANISATION OF THE FINANCIAL SYSTEM

Investing Institutions and Equity Ownwership

The rapid diminution in the percentage of UK share capital held directly by persons and the corresponding growth in the share-holding of the investing institutions - principally insurance companies and pension funds, but also unit trusts and investment trusts - has been widely noted[43] Its implications for the financing of British industry have yet to be traced accurately, but several issues are under intense discussion. The Governor of the Bank of England has observed that:

The equity capital of the larger British companies, accounting for perhaps three quarters of the output of our private sector industry and commerce, is increasingly owned by the main institutional investors. Given the size of their stake in the equity of British industry, the time has passed when the institutions can avoid closer involvement ... it will be inevitable that they assume a more direct responsibility for the fortunes of companies they partly own[44]

Whether this will mean 'patient commitment', 'remedial action' and even collective action by institutions to produce desirable outcomes for industry as a whole remains to be seen, but is unlikely in the absence of state encouragement to do so.

Investing institution practices to date suggest that industrial investment and reconstruction have not been major goals in themselves. The institutions define their responsibilities in terms of maximising returns to their shareholders, superannuees and policy-holders. Their interests lie in spreading risks and shifting investments, and their asset portfolios reflect this. Evidence collected by the Wilson Committee revealed that the institutions' rate of share turnover much exceeded that of private investors, and had increased significantly during the 1970s[45] The institutions consume financial intelligence voraciously, so the boards of companies in which they have shareholdings are well aware that their performance is closely monitored. In the conditions that have prevailed since 1973, there may well be a serious conflict between investment for long-run benefits and short-term returns. Investing institutions are likely to press for the latter. Company boards are not in a strong position to resist in the present climate, particularly as their corporate finance advisers probably are employed by the merchant bank which manages the funds of at least one of their institutional shareholders (see *Diversification of Merchant Banks* below).

Following the abandonment of exchange controls by the Conservative government in 1979, investing institutions and the larger companies rapidly increased their overseas assets. Taking the investing institutions first, it is improbably that abolition of controls upon international financial mobility will strengthen their commitment to British manufacturing. Secondly, most of the largest 200 UK listed companies are multi-product, multi-national entities whose attachment to domestic industry ought not to be overestimated: removal of exchange controls facilitated the establishment of overseas production sites and the purchase of foreign assets[46]

London as an Offshore Financial Centre

London's establishment as an offshore financial centre in the late 1960s had profound effects upon British banking. Although banks in the UK were leading participants in the explosive growth of international money and capital markets after 1967, the number and identity of these banks altered significantly[47] Numbers increased from around a 100 to over 300 in less than a decade, the vast majority being branches or subsidiaries of foreign-owned banks. By the later 1970s, the domestic deposit and lending activities of the London clearing banks had been dwarfed by international banking operations in the Eurocurrency markets. In 1979, two-thirds of the assets of British-based banks were in foreign currencies, but less than a quarter of the total assets of these banks were held by the clearing banks. Furthermore, the foreign-owned banks had made serious inroads into the clearing banks' domestic business. By 1978, foreign banks had a 9 per cent share of UK Sterling deposits (up from 2 per cent in 1964), a 28 per cent share of market loans to UK residents (up from 7 per cent), and provided 31 per cent of all bank lending to UK manufacturing companies[48] During the early 1970s 'fringe' banks flourished, encroaching further upon the clearing banks' domestic markets and fuelling the speculative boom that ended in the property and financial crashes of 1974[49] The new linkages between the City and a transformed international financial system made traditional modes of supervision and control ineffective, provoking a crisis of regulation that has called forth increased state intervention[50]

Three consequences arose for the supply of industrial finance. The first was the manufacturing companies gained access to a wider and more competitive range of lenders, although the main beneficiaries have been the large companies. A second consequence was that the larger multinational companies became heavily involved in wholesale money markets, as lenders as well as borrowers, acting as financial intermediaries. Thirdly, clearing bank interests diversified to take advantage of new international opportunities, dramatically reducing their dependence on domestic business. Conventional advances to industry mattered less than before the 1960s as a source of clearing bank revenue. Although there is no published evidence of worsening relations between the clearers and smaller industrial customers, the latter's long standing requests for less stringent lending conditions are unlikely to have been heeded[51]

Diversification of Merchant Banks into Fund Management and Corporate Finance[52]

The merchant banks' pre-1930 dominance in capital mobilisation and trade credit was central to the City of London's international reputation.

However, the First World War and the Great Depression destroyed much of their traditional business and they stagnated until the early 1950: they were small family firms with famous names and Victorian partners. During the 1950s, though, the merchant banks experienced a revival of fortunes, based initially on demand by companies for advice on acquisitions and financing - this was the time of the first wave of contested takeovers - and on opportunities to manage the rapidly increasing contractual savings flowing into occupational pension funds and insurance companies. Both activities have been lucrative and expanding sources of income for the merchant banks, but they have had another consequence for the finance-industry nexus: they have increased the interdependence and integration of the big company sector.

A dozen leading merchant banks, including subsidiaries of the clearing banks, simultaneously provide the largest companies with financial and strategic advice, dominate the issuing business, and exercise strong influence over the investments of the financial institutions. Most have directors on the boards of some major companies. They also collect and process economic intelligence. Moreover, they operate within a fraternally competitive sub-culture, an outgrowth of the City's insularity and 'clubbiness': rivalry occurs within a framework of solidarity.

Organisationally, the fund management and corporate advisory functions are independent of each other: in-house rules stress the need to keep customers' trust and therefore prohibit communication. Nevertheless, the merchant banks unavoidably act as clearing houses for intelligence, and as the City's interpersonal network is dense, extensive and efficient in conveying information, their judgements of corporate strengths and weaknesses help to determine the terms on which companies obtain finance. Support from a respected merchant bank is worth a great deal of money.

Merchant banks affect the direction of investment and the form in which industrial companies obtain it. In particular, the merchant banks stand between the large companies and the primary capital market, as issuing houses, and between the companies and the parallel money markets as wholesale bankers. In their role as fund managers and advisers, the merchant banks have some effect on the aggregate supply of finance earmarked for industry, and at the same time influence demand for finance and the strategic decisions of corporate customers. Their coordinated functions entail a concentration of investing power ignored by advocates of the deregulated market.

Merchant banks have also facilitated the reorganisation of production and the sale of redundant assets in many industries, primarily by urging mergers and takeovers. However, this activity need not lead to greater productivity or to increased productive capacity. Nor is it more profitable and innovative companies that typically drive out the inefficient:

> it is large rather than profitable firms which are most likely to survive. The majority of mergers and takeovers do not seem to lead to a more profitable use of assets ... The bulk of the immediate gains appear to be captured by the shareholders of the companies which are taken over, who usually receive a premium on the previous market value of their securities.[53]

As promoters of mergers and acquisitions, merchant banks may well have discouraged expansion of productive capacity in manufacturing.[54]

Building Societies and the Competition for Sterling Deposits

Popular attachment to private home-ownership is reflected in the 16-fold increase in building society assets over the period 1959-78. The building societies' share of domestic sterling deposits was 38 per cent in 1978, compared to the clearing banks' 30 per cent. This share, comprising deposits of £40 billion, had doubled in less than 15 years. Although the main loser in the competition with the building societies has been the savings banks,[55] the clearing banks' share of deposits fell by 7 per cent between 1964 and 1978.

It might be argued that taxation benefits associated with home loans have resulted in a major misallocation of funds. Certainly, the Committee of London Clearing Bankers suggested this, politely.[56] On the other hand, new investment in residential buildings does not comprise a high proportion of GDP by international standards[57] so even if building society deposits had been captured by the clearers, it is improbable that a significant proportion could have been diverted to industrial lending.

Government Securities

The capital markets have always been more important sources of finance in Britain than in France or Germany. Three times as many companies are quoted on the London Stock Exchange as on the Paris Bourse, and seven times as many as in Germany. In Britain, moreover, the capital markets have become increasingly important in funding government debt. Trading in government securities accounted for 78 per cent of turnover by value on the secondary market in 1979.

More than two-thirds of British government securities are held by financial enterprises, including banks. The investing institutions owned 46 per cent of the total in 1978. Government securities ('gilt-edged') have yielded 12-14 per cent since 1973, compared to around 5 per cent for company equities. On the grounds of both risk and return, it has been rational for individual investors to take up gilts rather than equities. The issue of gilts was the main means by which the government financed its growing deficit after 1973. The Wilson Report calculates the 'during the years 1958 to 1967 gilts provided finance equivalent to less that half per cent of GDP. This rose to one per cent in the period 1968 to 1972 and five and a half per cent in 1979'.[58] Between 1973 and 1977, almost 80 per cent by value of new securities issued on the British capital market were gilts. It is this trend that gave some *prima facie* plausibility to the argument that industrial companies had been squeezed out of the capital markets by public sector debt issues.

The collective power of the investing institutions is reflected in the high rate of interest paid by the government on its securities. Caught between the two undesirable options of paying a large ransom in interest or expanding the money supply rapidly, government has consistently chosen the former. It has been argued by monetarists that this course of action has crowded out other borrowers by setting excessively high interest rates, but this is contested by neo-Keynesians, who ascribe high interest rates to investors' preference for liquid assets under conditions of extreme uncertainty. Two quite different interpretations lead to two distinct sets of policy recommendations.

The monetarist position attacks not the power of the financial institutions to demand high rates of return, but the public sector deficit itself. Government expenditure must be cut, allowing economic activity to slow enough to bring interest rates down.

The neo-Keynesian emphasis on the expectations of investors points towards a crucial role for government in reducing uncertainty by policy and intervention. In arguing for a direct connection between expectations and liquidity preference, the neo-Keynesians acknowledge the concentration of power in the financial system:

Because of the extent to which wealth-holders now hold their wealth indirectly via financial intermediaries the community's liquidity preferences - and changes in it - are increasingly determined by the preferences and expectations of the institutions.[59]

The options open to the state are therefore two: either to intervene in the pattern of wealth-holding and reduce the liquidity preference-setting power of the financial institutions, or else to establish a benign, low-uncertainty economic climate in which long-term industrial investment is favoured. The first option involves the usurpation of market sovereignty to a degree probably unacceptable to Keynesians. Yet it is not inconceivable that the union movement might mobilise for greater control of its members' contractual savings, even to the extent of trading off lower returns to pension fund contributors against increased industrial investment. The second option might be implemented with the combination of instruments advocated by members of the Cambridge Economic Policy Group or the National Institute for Economic and Social Research.

INDUSTRIAL FINANCE: SUPPLY AND DEMAND

There is no straightforward answer to the question of whether the supply of finance to industry has been adequate. Clearly, the level of investment in manufacturing has been low by the standards of the industrialised world, but this cannot be understood without reference to the structure of industry, the institutionalised biases of the financial system and the exceptional constraints upon state intervention. The discussion of sources of industrial investment and structural changes in the financial system identified several factors which might have contributed to a smaller, less appropriate and more costly flow of funds to industry than might have been possible under somewhat different conditions. It is not suggested that any one practice in isolation was 'the cause' of low industrial investment: simply to assert that the clearing banks should have lent longer or less cautiously or that the merchant banks should have raised more capital for domestic ventures does not take us very far. It ignores the complex interaction between supply and demand factors. It also ignores what has been central to the development of the financial system, namely, the state-endorsed legitimacy of financial self-regulation and self-governance and the determined refusal by finance's spokesmen to accept responsibility for the wider consequences of their operations.[60]

Successful institutionalisation of the doctrine of financial autonomy arose through the Bank of England, the bankers' bank.[61] Its effects have been manifold, including toleration of gross market 'imperfections' in the name of stability and confidence, but most obvious have been the tentative and ineffectual attempts by Labour governments to harness the financial system to overarching social priorities, among them the development of an efficient, productive manufacturing sector.

Financial spokesmen reject suggestions that the organisation of the financial system may be responsible for Britain's poor economic performance, and stress the determining effect of demand factors. Although recognising some 'gaps and defects' in the financial system, the CLCB has argued that

> lack of finance is not reckoned to have been a primary constraint on investment. Industry would no doubt invest more if finance were extremely cheap and plentiful, but ... the quantity and cost of finance available to industry is determined chiefly by forces outside the control of the financial system itself.[62] The actual amount that [the banks] lend at any one time is determined primarily by their customers. (Manufacturing companies have latterly been borrowing less than half the amounts that the banks have agreed to lend them). The banks believe it would be neither appropriate nor prudent for them to 'force feed' their customers by pressing them to borrow funds which they had not themselves requested, or to lend to customers who would otherwise be turned down on the grounds of creditworthiness.[63]

The view assumes that demand is independent of the financial system's activities, determined by the autonomous perceptions of customers. In the light of the increasing integration of financial institutions and the 'meso-economy' through managed shareholdings, corporate advice and board level interlocks this assumption is highly questionable[64]

The CLCB also overlooks the extent to which the state's capacity to increase demand for industrial finance - directly or indirectly - has been constrained by the power of the financial institutions,[65] to defend their interests. Such defence has been legitimised by an ideology associating the national interest with British creditworthiness abroad, private control of financial institutions, and strong sterling. Its consequence has been that objectives related to the exchange rate, balance of payments, level of inflation and money supply have taken precedence over the quantity and quality of capital stock, manpower and output in manufacturing, and over more general social goals.

The next section considers aspects of industrial organisation which are likely to have affected the level and type of demand for industrial finance. The widespread tendency in more theoretical analyses to treat industry as an undifferentiated entity obscures not only the contrasting circumstances of successful and declining industries, but also the gulf between the largest several hundred companies and the many thousand smaller ones. Multinational, multidivisional, multi-product giants are densely and continuously linked with both domestic and overseas financial institutions, and scarcely resemble the ideal-typical firm of marginalist micro-economics.

Aspects of Industrial Organisation

Inequality of size, market share, access to financial services and political voice characterises the corporate sector. The steps towards the concentration of capital in modern British industry have been well documented, and need not be described here[66] However, several aspects might be considered briefly.

A tradition of agreed mergers which had governed pre-war concentration of capital broke down in the 1950s.[67] This tradition had had the effect of guaranteeing continuity of family control as long as companies remained solvent. It had also encouraged managerial and technical conservatism. The level of fixed investment was susceptible to short-term pressures, including excessive dividend expectations. Moreover, desire to retain family control inhibited economies of scale, research expenditure and installation of capital-intensive production processes. Of course, bankers and financiers already had advisory functions in some sectors of industry, and tended to encourage rationalisation, but the limited reliance of industrial enterprise on external funding meant that it was only in times of near crisis that bankers could insist on reorganisation and innovation.[68] Agreed mergers achieved in failing industries such as iron and textiles might not have been happy unions from the standpoint of the smaller owners, but they were quite distinct from the contested takeovers and lightening raids on shareholdings which proliferated from the late 1950s. The pace of concentration and levels of investment were quite uneven, but it would appear that few older orders of industry were not retarded technically by the preponderance of family control.[69]

The breakdown of the agreed merger tradition was due to several factors, including the willingness of some members of owning families to sell their shares to the highest bidder, the increasing proportion of equities owned by investing institutions, and the attractions of cash and stock-rich, underpriced companies to the 'new breed' of entrepreneur. Merchant banks rapidly adjusted to the violation of the old conventions, and turned corporate acquisitions and defence into a major revenue source. By 1970, most major companies (the largest 1000) retained merchant bank advisers and developed close relationships, as mentioned earlier.

Differences between industries in output and productivity are found in all economies. Recent studies by Prais[70] and Johnson[71] confirm that while British manufacturing output as a whole has grown fitfully and slowly compared to Europe, certain industries have actually stagnated or contracted since the 1950s. These include shipbuilding, metal manufacture, textiles and vehicles. The contribution of these industries to GDP has fallen much faster than that of manufacturing as a whole. Conversely, growth industries have been chemicals, mechanical and instrument engineering, and electronics. However, even in those industries which maintained a steady or growing share of GDP, output growth and productivity stayed below the levels of Britain's main competitors.

Britain not only has a high level of industrial concentration,[72] but its largest companies include a large proportion of internationally-oriented multi-product conglomerates. 'International orientation' refers to three distinct properties which tend to be correlated empirically: (a) dependence on (usually control of) foreign supplies of raw or semi-finished materials: (b) reliance on exports, particularly through well-established markets; and (c) overseas production, through subsidiaries or affiliates. Prais has suggested that large-scale, functionally differentiated multinational corporations may act as financial intermediaries, using profits from one set of operations to invest in others.[73] A separate point is that multinationals are not only major borrowers, but significant lenders and investors. Indeed, one reason for low industrial investment in the 1970s appears to have been that leading companies acted as creditors and rentiers, investing heavily in the money markets and government debt. The multinationals' ability to switch production to sites outside Britain, not only for reasons connected with labour relations but also to be 'close' to foreign markets in which national differences in taste are significant,[74] may be a major disincentive to invest in plant and research and development within Britain. Arguably the interests of companies engaged in production and services outside as well as within Britain are not necessarily best served by the strong development of domestic manufacturing industry.

Relations between finance and industry depend substantially upon both the *size* and the *order* of industrial companies. Relations between the largest several hundred companies and 'finance' are close but diverse. Each large company tends to have one or more merchant bank advisers and stockbrokers, several clearing banks, and special connections with one or two insurance companies. Furthermore, large companies may participate directly or through international banks in the Eurocurrency markets. Some 60 of the largest 150 British industrial and commercial companies have at least one directorship in common with a leading merchant bank; interlocks also exist between the largest companies, clearing banks and insurance companies. In addition to these formal and functional connections, the large companies are linked to the investing institutions through the latter's large and growing share and loan stock holdings. While these relations do not amount to 'finance capital' in Hilferding's sense,[75] they do constitute a structure of interdependence and constraint that tends to be disregarded in conventional economics, but which cannot be ignored in an analysis of demand for finance,[76] and of the uses made of that finance.

Historically, some orders of industry have had closer connections with finance than others. Heavy industry, for example, had board-level representation in two of the major clearing banks from the First World War onwards. Breweries also have been closely associated with both clearing and merchant banks since the nineteenth century. Electrical goods manufacturers were nurtured by Morgan Grenfell and Lazards, two leading merchant banks. Other orders of industry to have formal ties and close working relationships from an early date were textiles, armaments, chemicals and food processing.[77] Close connections took a variety of forms and arose out of various circumstances. The most common circumstances were where (1) heavy fixed investment was integral to the industry, especially where technical innovation was rapid; (2) merger activity was high; (3) cash flow rises occurred sporadically; (4) as in the case of breweries, close ties had existed with local banks which were absorbed into the London banks; (5) interpersonal or interfamilial connections existed among directors of financial and industrial enterprises; and (6) merchant banks prepared private firms for public flotation, stayed on as advisers, and specialised in that industrial order.

Although there is a clustering of industrial and financial enterprises - that is, an uneven density of total links between industrial and financial companies - it is an overstatement to propose, as Aaronovitch[78] did more than 20 years ago, that the British economy was dominated by perhaps a score of finance-centred business empires or compacts. On the other hand, to speak of British industry or manufacturing as an entity is to ignore the differences - and arguably the conflicting interests - between the 'meso-sector' and the small and medium-sized, single-product, regionally confined majority of manufacturing firms.[79] That the latter are seriously disadvantaged in acquiring both credit and capital was recognised by the Macmillan Committee[80] more than half a century ago, and confirmed by the Wilson Committee.[81] Relationships with larger companies also tend to be asymmetrical in terms of dependence, rather than directly competitive.

Capital's representatives explain the demand for industrial finance as the aggregate of individual preferences of industrialists. This appeals to common sense and to an heroic view of the businessman as entrepreneur and decision-maker, but it draws attention away from the effects of concentration, multi-product diversification, oligopoly and industrial-financial interlocks on the pattern of demand. It also obscures the importance of non-market considerations such as the desire to create dynastic control. Unless structural features of the industrial context are understood, the economic instruments available to the state are unlikely to be applied in ways that lead to effective real investment. Certainly, taxation incentives, allowances and subsidies have frequently failed to direct investment in accord with government priorities. More importantly, the conflicting or at least non-convergent interests of the largest internationally active companies and the great number of British domestic manufacturers have not been recognised adequately in state policies.

THE BRITISH STATE AND INDUSTRIAL INVESTMENT

Successive governments have been encouraged by the departments of the state to maximise market freedom, particularly at the micro-economic level. Making rules (e.g. to enhance competition) has been acceptable, but direct intervention has been discouraged. With the exception of the early post-war period, direct intervention in industry has been a response to the failure of indirect methods to achieve the usual objectives of economic policy.

The mild Keynesianism of the post-war Treasury provided an intellectual rationale for the replacement of war-time planning by macro-economic methods of demand management. Direct controls and detailed planning were abandoned in the first post-war years, reflecting unresolved tensions between left and right in the Attlee Labour government over the role of state direction and further nationalisation of industries. Pollard,[82] summarised the government's approach to 'democratic planning' as 'eclectic, varied and changing rapidly in its brief years of office'. The Conservative governments of the 1950s removed import restrictions and constraints on capital issues, and in 1959 restored the external convertibility of sterling. In the long run, the latter act contributed to the weakening of monetary policy instruments by opening the British economy to uncontrolled international money markets centred on Eurocurrency transactions in London itself.

Governments throughout the 1950s used fiscal and monetary instruments to juggle full employment and low inflation, although as indicated earlier, balance of payments constraints preoccupied policy-makers. During the 'stop-go' decade of the 1950s, domestic industrial investment not only failed to receive consistent, institutionalised government support, but was cut back during the 'stop' phases of economic policy.

Nationalisation of industries by the Attlee government was not the sharp end of a revolutionary programme; nor was it a measure explicitly undertaken to enable the rapid rejuvenation of British industry. Five major Acts were passed, bringing the coal, electricity, transport, gas and iron and steel industries into public ownership between 1946 and 1949. In addition, the Bank of England and the airlines became public corporations in 1946. From the outset, the objectives of nationalisation were either confused or unattainable. Pollard identifies the problem succinctly:

the nationalised industries, far from acting as instruments of controlling the rest of industry, were directed increasingly to become its servants, and to suffer the worst buffetings in their long-term investment plans with every change of wind of Government policy, with unfortunate results on their morale and their economic returns alike. Forced increasingly to deny the principle which they were established to promote, the principle of public service, and to justify themselves on the same commercial grounds as privately owned firms, the Board of the nationalised industries have been neither able to maintain consistent financial policies nor give adequate attention to consumers' interest.[83]

Uncertainty and inconsistency were compounded by the sale of the iron and steel firms back to private owners between 1953 and 1957 and their re-nationalisation under Labour in 1967.

The Heath Conservative government moved reluctantly to nationalise the failing Rolls-Royce Company and recapitalise the Upper Clyde shipyards. Labour rescued British Leyland via nationalisation in 1975, and a year later the British National Oil Corporation was established to participate in North Sea oil production and to offer energy policy advice.[84] However, since the Thatcher Conservative government's election in 1979, a privatisation programme has been undertaken, resulting in the transfer of BNOC capital to private interests and the sale of other profitable ventures to investors. Remaining public corporations have experienced unprecedented budgetary stringency, and have been encouraged to 'rationalise' - not an easy aim to achieve if the British Steel Corporation's recent history is a guide.

The contribution of nationalised industries to investment (gross fixed capital formation) in 1976 was 20 per cent - proportionately higher than its contribution to GNP (12 per cent in 1976). Real investment (at constant prices) was greater in the public corporations than in manufacturing during the 1970s, but a much lower proportion came from internal funds. Financing controls on public corporations changed at various points during the post-war period, resulting in different sources of external funding. While borrowing from central government remained the major source of funds (65 per cent) during the late 1970s, overseas loans had risen to around 22 per cent. The main borrowers were the Electricity Council, the Post Office, the British Steel Corporation and the British Gas Corporation. In addition, public corporations have raised funds by issues of fixed-interest debt. The need for investment has varied between industries since the war, with the Post Office and the Electricity Council accounting for more than half of public corporation investment in recent years. Returns on investment and increases in productivity have been variable but generally lower than those in the private sector.[85] In part this has been because in the 1970s, strict price limits applied to the nationalised industries as part of the government's attack on inflation increased their reliance on external funding, and reduced the prospects for improving the performance of these corporations engaged in production.

The absence of a coherent framework of industrial policy contributed to the vicissitudes of the nationalised sector.[86] Although the deleterious effects of stop-go policies gained political recognition by the late 1950s - and led the Conservatives to model the National Economic Development Council and Office on French economic planning structures - a vast gulf remained between good intentions and effective stimulation of national industrial development. NEDC's growth target of 4 per cent annually for the years 1961-66 was not achieved (2.9 per cent was the actual rate), and manufacturing investment increased by a mere 0.2 per cent annually instead of a projected 3.3 per cent. Although the rhetoric of economic growth and industrial productivity occupied a prominent place in the political discourse of the 1960s and 1970s, the organisations and measures employed proved to be quite inadequate for the task. This section surveys the bodies and agencies established to promote industrial growth, evaluates their effects, and identifies the major impediments to success.

The NEDC's parentage is a matter of some dispute, but it was fostered by Macmillan's Conservative government as a positive counter to yet another sterling crisis. The Council was a tripartite body chaired by the Chancellor of the Exchequer, and charged with responsibility for charting the economic future and proposing strategies for growth.[87] NEDC was to be semi-independent of government, an organised voice that might not always be in harmony with Treasury, the traditional repository of economic advice and the architect of stop-go management. Its first report established the growth targets mentioned above, but these were based on a prognosis that depended on questionable assumptions about the possibility of corporatist consensus, the strength of exports, and sterling's role in the international monetary system. By the time of the 1964 election - and Labour's victory - a deflationary response to a severe balance of payments situation had proved NEDC's optimism to have been ill-founded. No respite was in sight either, for 'the years 1964 68 formed one long squeeze, punctuated by several financial crises'.[88]

The incoming Labour government established the Department of Economic Affairs, intending to lessen the Treasury's hold on economic policy formulation. Harold Wilson (who claimed the idea as his own) argued for the 'fundamental distinction between monetary responsibilities on the one hand, which must come under the Treasury, and on the other, the coordinating responsibilities for industry and everything to do with the mobilisation of real resources for productivity and exports'.[89] On Labour's first day in office, there was pressure to devalue sterling. This was resisted by both the Cabinet and the Treasury (for different reasons) for another three years, but it was not an auspicious start for a government intending to break free from the stop-go cycle. Nevertheless, the DEA produced a major document (*The National Plan*) of indicative planning which proposed growth in output of 25 per cent between 1964 and 1970.[90]

Labour's Ministry of Technology was also intended to promote industrial development. According to Wilson, the Ministry of Technology was to undertake two main functions: to increase 'productivity and efficiency, particularly with those industries in urgent need of restructuring or modernisation' and 'to speed the application of new scientific methods to industrial production'.[91] In general, the Ministry of Technology was more successful[92] than the DEA, which was dissolved in October 1969 after failing to displace the Treasury from its dominant position in policy formulation.

Two bodies which provided some isolated support for industrial investment and innovation were the Industrial Reorganisation Corporation and the National Research and Development Corporation. The IRC, which reported to the DEA but was financially separate, was to 'act as a catalyst for industrial restructuring', in fact, supporting some ailing companies while encouraging reform and reorganisation in others. It was strongly interventionist but lacked 'a clear view of conditions for increased efficiency other than the obvious one of economies of scale'.[93] The NRDC operated under the aegis of the Ministry of Technology. Despite obvious successes in preparing inventions for industrial utilisation, it complained to the Wilson Committee that it 'finds itself more limited by opportunity than by resources' and argues 'that there are serious gaps in the provision of financial support for technological innovation in Britain, that the mortality rate of small companies is high and that there is a general lack of encouragement for new technology-based firms'.[94] Labour's desire to forge a new society in the 'white-heat of technology' had been quenched in the confrontation with the emerging symptoms of British industry's underlying defects.

During the 1970s, several public sector and special purpose financing bodies were established in response to industry's worsening position. To describe them as sticking-plaster solutions would be unjust, but they were hardly the basis for a consistent, coherent industrial policy. The Heath government abolished the Ministry of Technology and the IRC, but in 1973 it instructed the Bank of England to form Finance for Industry. FFI is owned jointly by the Bank of England (15 per cent) and the clearing banks, and acts as the holding company for several special finance agencies which had been formed in 1945 (Industrial and Commercial Finance Corporation; Finance Corporation for Industry; and Finance for Shipping). FFI provides funds for investment, through loans, leasing, and various other means. In 1978-79, new investments amounted to £242 million, undoubtedly filling a gap but none the less a mere 2 per cent of gross domestic fixed capital formation by industrial and commercial companies.

The Labour government of 1974-79 established the National Enterprise Board under the Industry Act 1975. It represented the emasculation of a relatively radical proposal to control the 'commanding heights' of the economy through a programme of selective nationalisation. The early proposals for the NEB evolved from a Labour Green Paper of 1972, substantially authored by Stuart Holland, which argued for the need to bring some large industrial, commercial and financial enterprises into public ownership. A powerful NEB would be justified in terms of both equity and efficiency. Selective public ownership was to be combined with extensive planning agreements with manufacturing industry.[95] However, the NEB that emerged from the cocoon of successive Labour Party conferences and White Papers disappointed its original advocates on Labour's National Executive. As instituted, the NEB was to be preoccupied with getting British industry out of its slump rather than with objectives derived from a socialist programme. In practice, while the NEB provided equity capital for manufacturing expansion, much of it was furnished as part of a rescue and resuscitation service, principally for Rolls-Royce and BL (British Leyland). In 1978, half of the NEB's total investment of £1.25 billion was committed to BL.[96] However, the incoming Conservative government cut back the NEB's role substantially by removing its authority to encourage industrial reorganisation, reducing its borrowing capacity, transferring Rolls-Royce from its control, and requiring it to sell its equity holdings.

Eight less colourful and less significant public sector finance bodies operated under the 1974-79 Labour government. Together, their assets comprised about one-quarter of those of the NEB. The most important were the Scottish Development Agency and the Welsh Development Agency, which were intended to promote regional economic development. Direct investments in industry were quite small, however - a total of £11 million in 1979.[97]

Brief mention might be made of the Export Credits Guarantee Department (ECGD), a long-standing insurer of British export credits. Exporters with ECGD insurance obtain advantageous terms of credit from banks, because the latter are guaranteed total repayment: 'finance at a fixed rate of interest is available from banks at levels determined by ECGD in accordance with international agreements; the difference between this fixed rate and an agreed commercial rate of return is made good by payments from ECGD to the banks'.[98] In other words, the banks receive the market rate for riskless lending, while the ECGD recoups its subsidisation of the banks from the exporters' premiums. By 1978/79, the ECGD had commitments of some £25 billion, covering a third of all British exports.

CUMULATIVE CAUSATION: THE STRUCTURE OF PERVERSE EFFECTS

The failure of the British state to correct recurring balance of payments problems during the 1950s meant that its industrial objectives were constantly threatened by strategies to preserve the 'top' currency status of sterling.[99] By 1960 it had become widely apparent that British industrial performance compared poorly with several competitors, but the plans and strategies chosen by the state avoided encroaching on major market principles and in particular, on the autonomy of the financial institutions. Despite good intentions and some minor successes, British industrial policies were frustrated and undermined by the staunch defence of several organised interests - labour, finance and the bureaucracy - as well as by a plethora of cross-cutting minor and sectional interests. Even as support of sterling ceased to be the overriding objective of government policy, full employment and low inflation could no longer be achieved together, and improvements in productivity and output were given lower priority than regulation of prices and incomes. It was assumed that the latter was a prerequisite for the former. State industrial investment was subordinated to corporate rescues and regional aid. A rising balance of payments deficit in the mid 1970s was financed with an IMF loan with deflationary conditions attached which was repaid after a period of government cut-backs. But neither inflation nor unemployment was at a politically or economically acceptable level. Interest rates, too, were high, and long-term prospects were discouraging. Labour unrest, indicative of loss of strategic control by union leadership, further weakened the reliability of industrial production and manufacturing profitability. Labour's 1979 electoral demise was entirely predictable, for the state had failed to create a context that would ensure market-generated industrial revitalisation, yet lacked legitimate means to impose a non-market solution. Since 1979, reduction of inflation and restoration of profitability have taken priority over other objectives. The state may claim some success with the former, but the latter has been confined to companies not dependent on domestic manufacturing. De-industrialisation has been signalled by falling output, reduced investment, multiplication of bankruptcies, ageing of capital stock, and heavy unemployment, unevenly distributed by region and industry.[100] In particular, 'metal manufacture, textiles, shipbuilding and vehicles appear to have sustained losses in real terms',[101] and it is in these older industries that de-industrialisation has been most apparent (see Appendix 1).

Despite the unpromising historical record, belief that something can be done to bring British economic performance up to French or German levels remains widespread. Although critics of economic growth have questioned the desirability of such a goal, most of the literature on British economic performance advocates one or another route to success. There are almost as many proposals as there are permutations of means but these tend to be closely aligned with a small number of models of the economy, state and society. Between liberal and Marxian political economy one might locate various models of the reformist-interventionist state, with differing emphases on the legitimate mix of market and authoritative allocation.

Liberal political economy is clear about the causes of British economic decline: the market has been incapacitated by expansion of the state and the power of organised labour. Sir Keith Joseph's list of culprits is typical:

> We have a demotivating tax system, increasing nationalisation, compressed differentials, low and stagnant productivity, high unemployment, many failing public services, and inexorably growing central government expenditure; an obsession with equality and with pay, price and dividend controls; a unique set of legal privileges and immunities for trade unions.[102]

Several well-known proposals for achieving economic growth derive from liberal political economy. They have in common an injunction not to violate market imperatives and to limit democracy in order to maximise liberty. The Thatcher government has renounced discretionary intervention to achieve particular ends, although the discrepancy between certain of its practices and its ideology is obvious. Nevertheless, it has avoided the formulation of an industrial policy which might insinuate that market freedom was ineffective. Friedman's monetarism was believed to provide the means to overcome inflation, which was essential before removal of the obstacles to market freedom - trade union power, bureaucratic regulation, excessive government spending - could be expected to have the desired effect.

Within liberal political economy, Bacon and Eltis based their influential proposal on the claim that the non-market sector was parasitic upon the market sector, arguing that post-war policy-makers, befuddled by Keynesianism, had been choking the goose that laid the golden eggs.[103] State expansion had been predicated upon an erroneous expectation of market sector growth and had eaten into the 'seed corn' of the British economy. Furthermore, the non-market sector was inefficient. Over-taxed workers responded by demanding higher wages than the market sector could afford, while maintaining excessive manning levels and exhibiting antipathy towards greater productivity. Low profits and high interest rates - due to state borrowing - resulted in declining industrial investment and increased unemployment. Remedies were to be sought in reduced government expenditure, lower taxes, greater competition, and measures to undermine union power.

This perspective identifies some factors which restricted the state's capacity to achieve several economic objectives simultaneously. Yet it ignores the limits imposed by financial interests and by the institutionalisation of liberal political economy itself within the state - reflected in personnel, practices and discourse. It also ignores Britain's long history of low industrial investment, lagging productivity and slow economic growth.[104] Liberal political economic analyses are silent or apologetic about concentration of corporate power, interdependence and capital mobility within modern economies; nor are they convincing in their handling of multinational and multi-sectoral companies. Furthermore, the mechanism which will lead to regeneration of manufacturing in Britain and to recapture of domestic and export markets is left unspecified; statements of faith in the market offer little comfort.

From the other end of the ideological continuum, Aaronovitch and Smith[105] advance a plausible diagnosis of British economic decline. They argue that the British state has refused to facilitate the modernisation of the industrial base; that long-term investment has been hampered by the relationship between industry and finance, which has been preoccupied with its international role; that the international orientation of the British economy weakened its competitiveness against manufactured imports; and that the trade union movement has used its 'substantial defensive power' to pursue sectional interests rather than socialism. Aaronovitch and Smith's analysis resembles the arguments of this chapter in so far as it emphasises the significance of international financial relations and the defensive or constraining power of the union movement for the state's role in modernising the domestic manufacturing base.

However, important differences need to be highlighted. Perhaps the most important of these is that the means available to the state to modernise industry and *maintain* rapid innovation were inadequate. Only in the first few years after the war were the instruments of public ownership, extensive planning and direction of investment and production legitimised, but external financial constraints and internal factionalisation weakened the resolve of the Labour government to use those instruments. Post-1960 attempts by the state to improve manufacturing capital stock were enacted within a strait-jacket of external constraints kept in place by fear of foreign retaliation and an inter-state morality guarded by the Bank of England. Far-reaching forms of intervention were not on the political agenda and were distrusted by public opinion. The means realistically available to the state, that is, those that could be employed without eliciting an immobilising response from labour, finance, the meso-corporate sector, domestic industry or state departments were weak. It must be remembered that until 1970, the British economic environment was characterised by full employment, rising real wages, low inflation, confidence in the British financial system, historically high levels of industrial output and real pre-tax rates of return on equity that were steadily above 10 per cent. During the years when politicians favoured state-promoted industrial regeneration, then, powerful interests had something to lose from the combination of floating exchange, directed investment, forced reorganisation, rationalised manning, import control and income and price regulation measures that might have enabled a rapid and enduring improvement in manufacturing productivity and output. Governments could not expect the major organised interests to concede the losses that such measures would have entailed. As the history of incomes policies shows, agreement of leaders is not enough: they have to deliver their members' ungrudging compliance. After the early 1970s the conflict over employment, real wages, stable prices and profits sharpened, and industrial development disappeared as a direct aim of state policy. The Conservatives' electoral success of 1979 swept away the relics of the previous government's industrial policies: helped by a diminution of union rights, manufacturing industry was to be left to respond to market forces. At the same time, international capital mobility was made easier, enabling larger companies to relocate production sites overseas rather than upgrade their British capacity. In addition, North Sea Oil production has resulted in a large but falling balance of payments surplus and a strengthening exchange rate which has further undercut manufacturing competitiveness.

Under these circumstances, one might ask what opportunities exist for the state to play an effective role in the re-industrialisation of Britain. Undoubtedly, the re-election of the Thatcher government in 1983, strengthened the determination of the 'social marketeers' to allow market forces to reshape the economy.[106] It is improbable that the continuing high level of unemployment will deter the Cabinet from its course, particularly as inflation has fallen and the Tory 'Wets' have been marginalised. While the Bank of England and the Department of Industry under Sir Keith Joseph organised some corporate rescues, 'sink or swim' is more likely to characterise the regime's second term. There is some prospect, however, that the Confederation of British Industry may cause the government increasing embarrassment as it nears the next election: much will depend on the perceived electoral threat from the Labour Party and the attractiveness of the Liberal/Social Democrat Alliance as an alternative government.[107] Motions carried at the CBI Conference in 1983 included calls for greater public capital investment as well as an increase in PSBR. Hostility from manufacturers was exemplified by a chief executive of a Sheffield tool company [who] described the British economy under Mrs. Thatcher as "still being directed by a mixture of Friedmanesque mumbo-jumbo and the tea-caddy accounting of a *hausfrau*".[108] If the Conservative government could be induced by the CBI and the TUC to institute policies designed directly to rebuild manufacturing capacity, it is conceivable that the options would include devaluation, control of wages, fiscal stimulation and import controls. The Cambridge Economic Policy Group advocate the latter two. Godley has argued for a 'high tariff applied uniformly on all imports', but the government would also 'simultaneously cut general taxation by enough to stimulate the economy so much that the total volume of imports is as high as it otherwise would have been'.[109] Eatwell,[110] has gone further to assert that 'the bases of a successful industrial policy are control of demand, control of finance and some direct influence on investment and hence on the evolution of the structure of industry'. Blackaby and others associated with the National Institute of Economic and Social Research have proposed devaluation combined with an incomes policy as appropriate responses to balance of payment difficulties. Deservedly, these strategies are taken seriously by industry and the union movement, but only an extraordinary *volte face* by the Conservative government would enable their implementation.

Finally, it is appropriate to review the 'Alternative Economic Strategy', which actually exists in several versions. Despite the low probability that its recommendations could be implemented before 1988, the mainstream of the political left claims that the AES contains the combination of institutional changes and economic strategies needed to reindustrialise Britain. The AES is premissed upon the capacity of the state to impose a substantive rationality upon the formal rationality of market system. Certain goals, including full and dignified employment, egalitarianism, democracy and prosperity not achieved by the existing organisation of the British economy are to be brought about through extensive state intervention. Substantial nationalisation of the financial and meso-corporate sectors is designed to reduce the impact of short-term market demands and to extend the time-frame relevant to investment decision-making. Nationalisation is to be bolstered by major public spending, exchange regulations and import controls, and by a system of 'democratic planning'. The AES envisages a planned and agreed role within the global economy, not autarchy, but the emphasis is firmly upon the production of real goods and services in Britain. It is hardly necessary to list the hazards that might way-lay the AES,[111] or the social relations on which its implementation would depend. Yet the analysis presented here suggests that anything short of a concerted policy to protect domestic markets, build up real investment, increase productivity and quality, and prevent undesired capital flows will not achieve rapid, sustained growth of manufacturing industry. The structural impediments to an essentially market-led process of industrial regeneration have been discussed: the alternative requires structural changes which would encounter fierce resistance, and which might, under conditions of acute social conflict, lead to sub-optimal outcomes. Nevertheless, because the 'tinkerers' have failed,[112] the British electorate can be expected to face a choice of this sort within the next decade.

ACKNOWLEDGEMENT

I would like to thank Regina Ganter for her assistance. It is a pleasure to acknowledge the support of Griffith University's Research Grants Committee.

NOTES

1. R. Jessop, 'The Capitalist State and the Rule of Capital', *West European Politics*, 6(2) (April 1983), pp. 139-62, examines some of these inadequacies.

2. Ibid., p. 159, acknowledges that 'We appear to have reached an *impasse* in the analysis of the capitalist state and the rule of capital. It seems that the interests of capital in general cannot be identified outside the framework of historically specific accumulation strategies and that there is no state form that can serve as an unambiguously favourable political shell for advancing these interests'.

3. See, for example, A. Gamble, *Britain in Decline: Economic Policy, Political Strategy and the British State* (London: Macmillan, 1981).

4. Cf. R. Jessop, 'The Transformation of the State in Post-War Britain', in R. Scase (ed.), *The State in Western Europe*, (New York: St. Martin's Press, 1980), pp. 23-93.

5. S. Brittan's analysis of the Treasury is outstanding if dated: *Steering the Economy* (Harmondsworth: Penguin, 1971, rev. edn).

6. See N. Harris, *Competition and the Corporate Society: British Conservatives, The State and Industry 1945-1964* (London: Methuen, 1972) for a lucid account of the divisions over industrial policy and the economic role of the state within the 'party of the ruling class'.

7. Despite the rhetoric of planning and public ownership, the Labour government of 1945 - 51 by no means succeeded in imposing a 'bureaucratic mode of resource allocation' upon British society. See A. Cawson and P. Saunders, 'Corporatism, Competitive Politics and Class Struggle', in R. King (ed.), *Capital and Politics* (London: Routledge/Kegan Paul, 1983), pp. 8-27. The advice of Labour's economists (and their opponents) is

268   *State, Finance & Industry*

reviewed in T. Hutchison, *Economics and Economic Policy in Britain,
1946-1966* (London: George Allen/Unwin, 1968), pp. 15-87.

8. R. Opie, 'Economic Planning and Growth', in W. Beckerman (ed.), *The
Labour Government's Economic Record: 1964-1970* (London: Duckworth,
1972), p. 160.

9. M. Holmes, *Political Pressure and Economic Policy: British Government,
1970-1974* (London: Butterworth, 1982), p. 12.

10. S. Holland, *The Socialist Challenge* (London: Quartet, 1975) contains the
best scholarly argument for the left's 'Alternative Economic Strategy' by
one of its main instigators. D. Currie and R. Smith (eds.). *Socialist
Economic Review* (London: Merlin Press, 1981) carries the debate much
further.

11. See T. Forester, 'Neutralising the Industrial Strategy', in K. Coates (ed.),
What Went Wrong? (London: Spokesman, 1979), pp. 74-94.

12. See J.C.R. Dow, *The Management of the British Economy, 19455-60*
(Cambridge: Cambridge University Press 1964), esp. Part 1 (Historical
Narrative); and F.T.Blackaby (ed.), *British Economic Policy, 1960-74*
(Cambridge: Cambridge University Press, 1978), esp. Ch. 2 (Narrative,
1960 - 74, by Blackaby).

13. A. Graham and W. Beckerman, 'Economic Performance and the Foreign
Balance?', in Beckerman' (ed.), *op. cit.* pp. 11-27. In this concise piece,
two economic advisers to the 1964 - 70 Labour government analyse the
balance of payments constraint and conclude that 'The unwillingness of
the Labour Government to recognise that the exchange rate should be the
means to other ends and not an end in itself was Labour's real mistake'
(p. 27).

14. OECD Economic Surveys, *United Kingdom* (February 1983), p. 7.

15. Ibid., p. 18.

16. Jessop, *op. cit.*(1980), p. 31.

17. S. Pollard, *The Wasting of the British Economy* (London: Croom Helm,
1982).

18. Ibid., p. 73.

19. Committee to Review the Functioning of Financial Institutions, *Final Report*
(London: HMSO, 1980) (Cmnd. 7937). Sir Harold Wilson, Labour ex-
Prime Minister (1964 - 70, 1974 - 76), was appointed by his successor to
chair an 18-person committee whose manifest brief was to examine several
aspects of the financial system, including regulatory mechanisms and the
financing of industry. Its latent brief, however, has been recognised as being
to spike the guns of Labour's left-wing advocates of nationalisation of leading
financial institutions. Whatever its eventual functions, the Wilson Committee
produced a vast amount of information about the financial system, which
has been drawn upon extensively here.

20. Lord Allen, Clive Jenkins, Leif Mills and Len Murray.

21. Actually, two economists (Joan Mitchell, Andrew Graham) *The Times*
financial editor (Hugh Stephenson) and a prominent accountant (Sir Kenneth
Cork).

22. Wilson Report *op. cit.*, p. 268.

23. Ibid.

24. See e.g. W. Beckerman (ed.). *Slow Growth in Britain: Causes and Consequences* (Oxford: Clarendon Press, 1979); F.T.Blackaby (ed.), *De-Industrialisation* (London: Heinemann/NIESR, 1978).
25. Data taken from OECD, *op. cit.*, pp. 44-5.
26. Ibid., p. 44.
27. An indication of this is Britain's low productivity (GDP per man hour) in manufacturing and coupled with this, the very slow rate of productivity growth. See e.g. P. Johnson, 'The Changing Structure of British Industry', in P. Johnson (ed.), *The Structure of British Industry* (London: Granada, 1980), Ch. 1. A. Maddison's attempts to make valid cross-national comparisons are noteworthy. See e.g. 'The Long Run Dynamics of Productivity Growth', in Beckerman (1979), *op. cit.*, pp. 194-212.
28. OECD, *op. cit.*, p. 37.
29. Wilson Report *op. cit.*, Table 34, p. 133.
30. Financing British Industry, *Bank of England Quarterly Bulletin* 20(3), (September 1980), pp. 319-23.
31. Ibid., p. 319.
32. See e.g. Pollard, *op. cit.* p. 25. Net manufacturing investment as a percentage of GNP was little more than half the German and Italian levels through the 1950s.
33. W.A. Thomas, *The Finance of British Industry, 1918-1976* (London: Methuen, 1978), p. 332.
34. However, accounting practices differ so markedly that valid comparisons are not easily made. See e.g. the defence of the clearing banks in Britain's Financial System and Economic Performance, *Barclays Review* (May 1982), pp. 28-34.
35. Wilson Report, *op. cit.*, pp. 151-5.
36. Thomas, *op. cit.*, pp. 154-5.
37. Ibid., p. 327.
38. *BEQB*, (1980), *op. cit.*, p. 322.
39. See W. Grant and D. March, *The CBI* (London: Hodder/Stroughton, 1977).
40. Committee to Review the Functioning of Financial Institutions, *Evidence on the Financing of Industry and Trade*, vol. 2 (London: HMSO, 1977), p. 1.
41. Ibid., p. 5.
42. Ibid., p. 11.
43. See the Wilson Report, *op. cit.*, Chs. 4, 19; see also R. Minns, *Pension Funds and British Capitalism* (London: Heinemann, 1980).
44. Lecture by the Governor, 'Reflections on the Role of the Institutions in Financing Industry', *Bank of England Quarterly Bulletin*, 21(1) (March 1981), p. 83.
45. Wilson Report, *op. cit.*, Appendix 7.
46. Direct investment and portfolio investment abroad 'surged' ahead after the abolition of exchange controls. (OECD, *op. cit.*, (1983), pp. 18-20.
47. See e.g. D. Channon, *British Banking Strategy and the International Challenge*, (London: Macmillan, 1977), and articles in *The Banker* and *Euromoney*.
48. Wilson Report, *op. cit.*, p. 69.

49. See M. Reid 'The Secondary Banking Crisis - Five Years on', *Banker* (December 1978), pp. 21-32; also M. Lisle-Williams, 'The Banking Crisis of 1973-75' (Oxford University, unpublished, M.Phil thesis, 1980).

50. Statutory regulation has been extended to the banking system and to Lloyd's of London. New bodies and codes have been established to regulate mergers and acquisitions and other capital market activity. See e.g. Sir A. Johnson, *The City Take-Over Code* (Oxford: Clarendon Press, 1980).

51. Refer to Wilson Committee, *Research Report No.3: Studies of Small Firms' Financing* (1977); *The Financing of Small Firms*, Interim Report, (1979); and G. Bannock, 'The Clearing Banks and Small Firms', *Lloyds Bank Review*, 142 (October 1981), pp. 15-25.

52. See M. Lisle-Williams, *Changing Social Organisation and Market Conduct in the English Merchant Banking Sector* (Oxford University, unpublished, D. Phil thesis, 1982); also *idem*, 'Controllers and Coordinators of Capital', *Social Science Information*, 1984(1).

53. Wilson Report, *op. cit.*, p. 190.

54. However, they have established subsidiaries to purchase capital goods which are leased to companies.

55. The savings banks have traditionally attracted small-scale deposits from working-class savers. There is a government-owned and controlled National Savings Bank and a sector of unincorporated Trustee Savings Banks. See Wilson Report, Appendix 3 (II, III).

56. Committee of London Clearing Bankers, *The London Clearing Banks* (London: Blades, 1978) (the published submission to the Wilson Committee), p. 190.

57. Wilson Report, *op. cit.*, Table 10.19, p. 602.

58. Ibid., p. 63.

59. Ibid., p. 169.

60. This has been characteristic since Victorian times. See S. Checkland, 'The Mind of the City', *Oxford Economic Papers* (1957), 9, pp. 251-78.

61. R.S. Sayers, *The Bank of England, 1891-1944* (Cambridge: Cambridge University Press, 1976), is a sympathetic, detailed analysis of policies and personalities.

62. Committee of London Clearing Bankers, *op. cit.*, p. 97.

63. Ibid., pp. 215-16.

64. Cf. Holland, *op. cit.*; J. Scott, *Corporations, Classes and Capitalism* (London: Hutchinson, 1979); P. Stanworth and A. Giddens, 'The Modern Corporate Economy: Interlocking Directorships, 1906-70', *Sociological Review* (1975), 23(1); M. Lisle-Williams, 1982, *op. cit.*

65. Here I must part company with M. Moran ('Power, Policy and the City of London, in R. King (ed.) *op. cit.*, Ch. 3) who claims that changes in the financial system mean that 'The City is no more likely to exhibit a continuing capacity for collective action than is the dispersed and incoherent collection of interests ... common in other sectors of business'. This seems to ignore the dense functional and interpersonal ties between the clearing banks, merchant banks, insurance companies, pension funds and large stockbrokers, and the substantial convergences of specific interests.

66. Refer to L. Hannah, *The Rise of the Corporate Economy* (London: Methuen, 1976); S.J. Prais, *The Evolution of Giant Firms in Great Britain* (Cambridge: Cambridge University Press, 1976).
67. See Johnston, *op. cit.*
68. See the discussion in Hannah, *op. cit.*, Ch. 5; and also A. Francis, 'Families, Firms and Finance Capital', *Sociology*, 14(1) (February 1980).
69. Ibid.
70. S.J. Prais, *Productivity and Industrial Structure* (Cambridge: Cambridge University Press, 1981).
71. Johnson, *op. cit.*
72. See L. Hannah and J. Kay, *Concentration in Modern Industry* (London: Macmillan 1977); S. Aaronovitch and M. Sawyer, *Big Business* (London: Macmillan, 1975).
73. *op. cit.* (1976).
74. F. Fishwick, *Multinational Companies and Economic Concentration in Europe* (London: Gower, 1982), p. 25.
75. H. Overbeek in 'Finance Capital and the Crisis in Britain', *Capital and Class*, II (1980) argues that they do, but this seems to come from a misunderstanding in his evidence.
76. Cf. Scott *op. cit.*, for a useful discussion.
77. P.L. Cottrell, *Industrial Finance, 1830-1914* (London: Methuen, 1980), Ch. 7 reveals some surprisingly close relations between banks and industry, as well as antecedents to contemporary debates about industrial investment.
78. S. Aaronovitch, *The Ruling Class* (London: Lawrence/Wishart, 1961).
79. Holland, *op. cit.*, Ch. 2.
80. Committee on Finance and Industry, *Report* (London: HMSO 1931) (Cmnd. 3897).
81. See the oral evidence of Treasury and Department of Industry Officials, Wilson Committee, *Evidence on the Financing of Industry and Trade*, vol. 1 (London: HMSO 1977).
82. S. Pollard. *The Development of the British Economy, 1914-1967* (London: Edward Arnold, 2nd edn. 1969), p. 373.
83. Ibid., p. 391.
84. See C. Robinson and C. Rowland, 'North Sea Oil and Gas', in Johnson, *op. cit.*, Ch. 2.
85. Refer to Thomas, *op. cit.*, Ch. 10; and also S. Lumby, 'New Ways of Financing Nationalised Industries', *Lloyds Bank Review* (July 1981), pp. 34-44.
86. See K. Jones, 'Policy Towards the Nationalised Industries', in F.T. Blackaby *British Economic Policy, op. cit.*, Ch. 11.
87. See P. Meadows, 'Planning', ibid., Ch. 9.
88. Pollard, *op. cit.* (1969), p. 481.
89. H. Wilson, *The Labour Government, 1964 - 70* (Harmondsworth: Penguin 1971), p. 26.
90. See Opie, *op. cit.*, A. Graham 'Industrial Policy', in Beckerman (ed.), *op. cit.* (1972), Ch. 5.
91. Wilson, *op. cit.*, p. 30.

272 State, Finance & Industry

92. See Graham, *op. cit.* p. 215, for an indication of the importance of the Industrial Expansion Act 1968, which enlarged Min. Tech's powers: 'this act was virtually the only time during the whole period of the Government when it was explicitly stated in relation to the private sector that the justification for the intervention was 'because of a divergence between national and private costs and benefits'. It is this divergence which is ignored in the submissions of capital's representatives to the Wilson Committee.
93. D. Stout, 'Medium-Term Policies', in D. Morris (ed.), *The Economic System in the U.K.* (Oxford: Oxford University Press, 1979), p. 487. See also P. Mottershead, 'Industrial Policy', in Blackaby (ed.), *op. cit.*, (1978), Ch. 10.
94. G.F. Ray, 'Comment on Technical Innovation', in Blackaby (ed.). *op. cit.*, p. 76.
95. Wilson Report, *op. cit.*, Appendix 2 (XII).
96. See A. Budd, *The Politics of Economic Planning* (Manchester: Manchester University Press, 1978), and D. Marsh and G. Locksley, 'Capital in Britain', *West European Politics* 6(2) (April 1983), pp. 50-3.
97. Wilson Report, *op. cit.*, Appendix 2 (XIII).
98. Ibid., p. 484.
99. See 'Analysis' in F. Longstreth, 'The City, Industry and the State', in C. Crouch (ed.), *State and Economy in Contemporary Capitalism* (London: Croom Helm, 1979), which builds on the work of S. Strange, *Sterling and British Policy* (Oxford: Oxford University Press, 1971).
100. See A. Thirlwall, 'Deindustrialisation in the United Kingdom', *Lloyds Bank Review*, 144 (April 1982, pp. 22-37 for a breakdown of unemployment by industrial orders and an argument for export-led recovery.
101. 'The Profitability of UK Industrial Sectors', *Bank of England Quarterly Bulletin* 19(4) (September 1979), p. 398.
102. Sir Keith Joseph, *Solving the Union Problem is the Key to Britain's Recovery* (London: Centre for Policy Studies, 1979), p. 5.
103. R. Bacon and W. Eltis, *Britain's Economic Problem: Too Few Producers* (London: Macmillan, 2nd edn., 1978).
104. See A. Maddison, 'The Long-Run Dynamics of Productivity Growth', in Beckerman (ed.), *op. cit.*, (1979).
105. S. Aaronovitch and R. Smith, *The Political Economy of British Capitalism* (London: McGraw-Hill, 1981), see esp. pp. 366-7.
106. C. Pratten, 'Mrs. Thatcher's Economic Experiment', *Lloyds Bank Review*, 143 (January 1982), pp. 36-51 presents a clear summary of the Conservative government's ideology and policies.
107. See W. Grant, 'Representing Capital', in King (ed.), *op. cit.*, Ch. 4.
108. *The Australian*, 9 November 1983, p. 12.
109. W. Godley, 'Britain's Chronic Recession: Can Anything Be Done?', in Beckerman (ed.), *op. cit.* (1979) p. 231.
110. J. Eatwell, *Whatever Happened to Britain?* (London: Duckworth BBC, 1982), p. 159.
111. Cf. A. Glyn and J. Harrison, *The British Economic Disaster* (London: Pluto Press, 1981); S. Aaronovitch, *The Road from Thatcherism: the Alternative Economic Strategy* (London: Lawrence/Wishart, 1981);

and Bacon and Eltis, *op. cit.*, Ch. 3.
112. 'Those who seek to manage economies or advise on their management are either tinkerers or structuralists', Bacon and Eltis, ibid., p. 1.

APPENDIX 1: INDICATORS OF ECONOMIC PERFORMANCE

1. OECD Comparisons

1.1 *Comparisons of GDP*

	GDP at market prices (US $billion, 1980)	GDP per capita (US $, 1980)
United States	2,587	11,360
Japan	1,040	8,910
Germany	819	13,310
France	652	12,140
United Kingdom	523	9,340
Italy	394	6,910
Canada	253	10,580
Spain	211	5,650
Netherlands	168	11,850
Australia	140	9,580
Sweden	123	14,760
Belgium	116	11,820
Switzerland	101	15,920

Source: *OECD Observer*, March 1982, 115.

1.2 *Growth of real GDP*

	Average 1971 to 1981 (% p.a.)
United States	2.8
Japan	4.8
Germany	2.5
France	3.1
United Kingdom	1.4
Italy	2.9
Canada	3.7
OECD average (24 countries)	3.0

1.3 *Gross fixed capital formation as % of GDP*

	1961	1965	1969	1973	1977	1981
United States	17.4	18.8	18.2	19.1	18.3	17.9
Japan	32.6	29.9	34.5	36.4	30.5	31.0
Germany	25.2	26.1	23.3	23.9	20.3	22.0
France	21.2	23.3	23.4	23.8	22.3	21.2
United Kingdom	17.3	18.3	18.5	19.5	17.9	15.9
Italy	23.2	19.3	21.0	20.8	19.6	20.3
Canada	20.9	23.5	21.4	22.4	22.7	23.7
OECD average (24 countries)	20.2	21.3	21.4	23.2	21.5	21.2

1.4 *Unemployment rates (% of total labour force)*

	1967	1970	1973	1976	1979	1982
United States	3.7	4.8	4.8	7.5	5.7	9.5
Japan	1.3	1.1	1.3	2.0	2.1	2.4
Germany	1.3	0.8	0.8	3.7	3.2	6.1
France	1.9	2.4	2.6	4.4	5.9	8.0
United Kingdom	3.3	3.1	3.2	6.0	5.6	12.5
Italy	5.3	5.3	6.2	6.6	7.5	8.9
Canada	3.8	5.6	5.5	7.1	7.4	10.9
Average of the 'major seven'	2.8	3.8	3.4	5.5	5.0	7.9

1.5 *Inflation (annual rates of consumer price change %)*

	1967	1970	1973	1976	1979	1982
United States	2.8	5.7	7.6	5.3	12.3	5.2
Japan	4.4	6.7	14.7	9.6	4.3	2.6
Germany	1.1	3.8	7.1	4.1	5.1	5.0
France	2.9	5.3	8.0	9.8	11.1	10.3
United Kingdom	1.9	7.3	9.8	14.3	17.2	7.1
Italy	4.0	5.0	11.7	19.2	16.3	16.7
Canada	4.1	2.6	8.7	6.2	9.2	10.2
OECD average (24 countries)	3.1	5.6	9.1	8.4	8.8	7.1

1.6 *Total outlays of government as % of GDP*

	1961	1965	1969	1973	1977	1981
United States	29.0	27.9	30.9	31.3	33.3	35.4
Japan	17.4	20.0	19.3	22.3	29.1	34.0
Germany	33.8	36.7	28.8	41.7	48.1	49.3
France	35.7	38.4	39.6	38.5	44.2	48.9
United Kingdom	33.4	36.4	41.5	41.1	44.1	47.3
Italy	29.4	34.3	34.2	37.8	42.5	50.8
Canada	30.0	30.1	33.5	36.0	40.6	41.4
OECD average (24 countries)	29.3	29.9	32.2	33.3	37.8	40.9

1.7   *Average annual real rates of return* in manufacturing industry*

	1955–59	1960–62	1963–67	1968–71	1972–75	1976–79
United States	28	27	36	26	21	22
Japan	n/a	n/a	n/a	n/a	18	15
Germany	38	29	21	22	16	17
United Kingdom	17	15	14	11	8	6

* 'Net pre-tax operating surplus after adjustment for stock appreciation and the consumption of fixed assets, as a percentage of the net capital stock of fixed assets at current replacement cost'.
Source: *Barclays Review*, May 1982, p. 29.
Note: This may underestimate returns on *aged* stock.

1.8   *Manufacturing investment* (gross fixed capital formation per head of employed labour force in manufacturing industry, 1960–1975, $US)

	1960	1965	1970	1974	1975
United States	—	1675	2145	2785	2947
Japan	492	460	1317	2141	1768
Germany	—	—	—	1707	—
France	—	905	1439	2288	2682
United Kingdom	334	460	604	920	1006
Italy	332	367	751	1469	—

Source: C. Brown and T. Sheriff, Table 10.9, in W. Blackaby (ed.), *De-industrialisation* (London: Heinemann, 1978), p. 247.

1.9   *Productivity* (Gross value added per man-hour in manufacturing, 1955–74) UK 1970 = 100; semi-log scale.

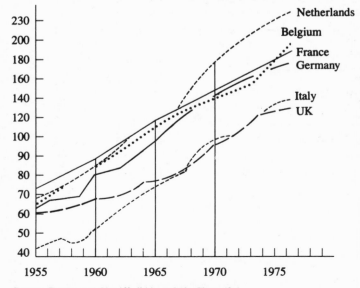

Source: Brown and Sheriff, ibid., p.249, Chart 10.4.

1.10 *Productivity growth* (annual average compound growth rates of GDP per man-hour, 1870–1976

	1870–1913	1913–1950	1950–1960	1960–70	1970–1976
United States	2.1	2.5	2.4	2.5	1.8
Japan	1.8	1.4	5.8	10.1	6.1
Germany	1.9	1.2	6.8	5.4	4.7
France	1.8	1.7	4.4	5.3	5.0
United Kingdom	1.1	1.5	2.3	3.3	2.8
Italy	1.2	1.8	4.3	4.3	5.0
Canada	2.0	2.3	3.1	3.1	2.3

Source: A. Maddison, in W. Beckerman (ed.), *Slow Growth in Britain* (1979), p.195.

1.11 *Productivity Growth*: *Industry* (annual average compund growth rates of output per person employed in industry, 1950–76)

	%
United States	2.8
Japan	8.1
Germany	5.4
France	4.8
United Kingdom	2.6
Italy	4.3
Sweden	3.9

Source: Maddison, ibid., p. 208.

APPENDIX 2: TREND DATA FOR THE UK

2.1 *Indices of GDP, manufacturing production and employment in manufacturing (1975 = 100)*

	GDP	Manufacturing production	Manufacturing employment
1972	96.0	100.0	103.9
1973	102.8	108.4	104.4
1974	101.1	106.6	104.7
1975	100.0	100.0	100.0
1976	102.6	101.4	96.9
1977	105.3	103.0	97.2
1978	108.7	104.0	96.7
1979	110.6	104.3	95.3
1980	108.0	95.4	90.0
1981	105.4	89.4	80.7
1982	106.0	89.0	76.4

Source: OECD *Economic survey: UK* (February 1983), Table D, p. 67.

2.2 *Industrial Composition of Output*

Shares%   Shares%

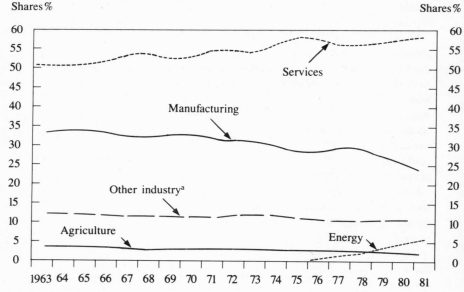

Note: a. Excluding oil. *Sources: National Income and Expenditure*, (CSO, 1982 edn.). OECD Survey: UK (February 1983), Diagram 11, p. 41.

2.3 *Indices of Industrial Production*

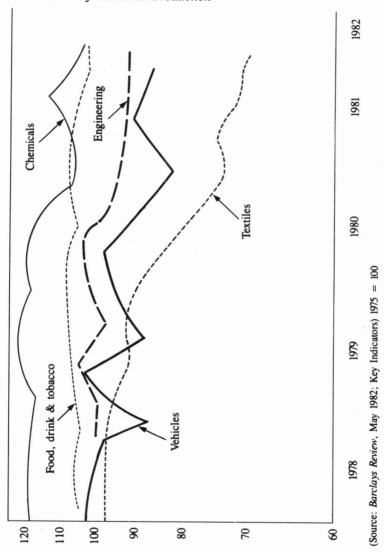

(Source: *Barclays Review*, May 1982; Key Indicators) 1975 = 100

2.4 *Fixed Invesment* (at 1975 prices as a % of GDP)

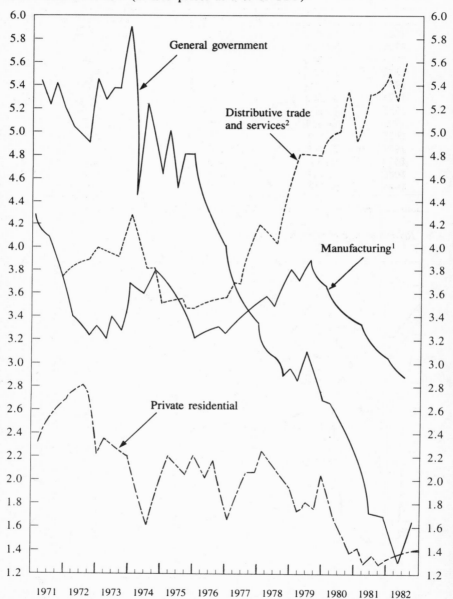

General government

Distributive trade
and services[2]

Manufacturing[1]

Private residential

1971 1972 1973 1974 1975 1976 1977 1978 1979 1980 1981 1982

1. Including leasing. 2. Excluding leasing. (Source: *OECD Survey: U.K.*, Feb. 1983, Diagram 1, p. 9)

2.5   *Gross domestic fixed capital formation* (£ million at 1975 prices)

	Total	Public Corporations	Manufacturing
1969	18,954	3,201	3,877
1970	19,460	3,316	4,178
1971	19,743	3,334	3,896
1972	19,823	2,932	3,370
1973	21,195	3,135	3,440
1974	20,562	3,566	3,782
1975	20,408	3,920	3,522
1976	20,640	4.045	3,326
1977	20,139	3,702	3,476
1978	20,845	3,473	3,769
1979	21,039	3,439	3,969
1980	20,443	3,464	3,573
1981	18,774	3,167	2,938

Source: OECD Economic survey: UK (February 1983), Table B, p. 65

2.6   *Real Rates of Return in Industry*

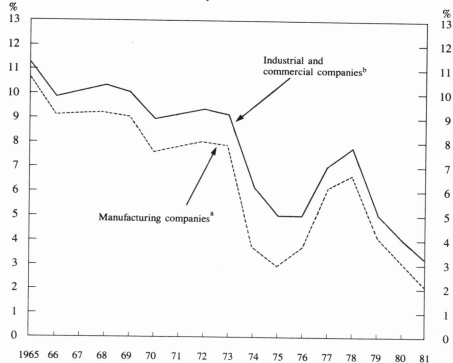

Notes:
a. Gross operating surplus on UK operations (i.e. before tax and interest payments) less capital consumption, at current replacement cost.
b. Excluding North Sea exploration and productive activities.
Source: *British Business*. 17 September 1982.

Index